# LIFE-WORLD EXPERIENCE

# Current Continental Research
## is co-published by
# The Center for Advanced Research
# in Phenomenology
## and
# University Press of America, Inc.

CURRENT CONTINENTAL RESEARCH 210

Rolf von Eckartsberg

# LIFE-WORLD EXPERIENCE

## Existential-Phenomenological Research Approaches in Psychology

1986

Center for Advanced Research in Phenomenology
& University Press of America, Washington, D.C.

Copyright © 1986 by

The Center for Advanced Research in Phenomenology, Inc.

University Press of America,® Inc.

4720 Boston Way
Lanham, MD 20706

3 Henrietta Street
London WC2E 8LU England

**Library of Congress Cataloging in Publication Data**
Life-world experience.

   (Current continental research ; 210)
   Bibliography: p.
   Includes indexes.
   1. Phenomenological psychology—Research—Addresses,
essays, lectures.    2. Existential psychology—Research—
Addresses, essays, lectures.    I.Von Eckartsberg, Rolf,
1932-    . II. Series.
BF204.5.L55    1986        150.19'2        86-1625
ISBN 0-8191-5290-0 (alk. paper)
ISBN 0-8191-5291-9 (pbk. : alk. paper)

All University Press of America books are produced on acid-free
paper which exceeds the minimum standards set by the National
Historical Publications and Records Commission.

CONTENTS

V

CONTENTS

CONCLUDING REFLECTIONS AND
                    IMPLICATIONS FOR THERAPY

# LIST OF TABLES

# ACKNOWLEDGMENTS

I would like to thank publishers and authors in this book for their permission to reprint and quote from previously published materials. Mr. Dowds, Duquesne University Press, Pittsburgh, Pa. **Duquesne studies in phenomenological psychology** (Vols. I-IV) (A. Giorgi: An application of phenomenological method in psychology; C. Fischer: Toward the structure of privacy; P. Richer: Alterations in the reality character of perception and the concept of sensation; R. Fessler: Phenomenology and the "talking cure"; F. Buckley: Toward a phenomenology of at-homeness; B. Jager: Theorizing, journeying, dwelling). Humanities Press International, Inc. Atlantic Highlands, N. J. **Journal of phenomenological psychology** (W. Fischer: On the phenomenological mode of researching being anxious; R. van Eckartsberg: Experiential psychology: A descriptive protocol and reflection). University of Texas Press, Austin, Texas: R. Romanyshyn: **Psychological Life: From science to metaphor.** A van Kaam: **Existential foundations of psychology.** P. Colaizzi: **Reflection and research in psychology.** E. Keen: **A Primer in phenomenological psychology.** J. de Rivera: **Conceptual encounter.** E. Susskind & D. Klein (Eds.) **Community research.** (R. von Eckartsberg: The process of reconciliation). C. Kracklauer: **The drug problem problem,** Dissertation, Duquesne University.

I wish to thank my research assistants who have helped me on this project: Jerrald Meyers, Kevin Smith, Michael de Maria, Carl Bonner, and David Jones. I wish also to express my appreciation to my colleagues at Duquesne University and to our students who have made this journey into phenomenological research methods in psychology such an exciting adventure. A special note of thanks to Lester Embree, Chairman of the Editorial Board of Current Continental Research for his encouragement, advice, and continuous support to bring this project to its completion.

# INTRODUCTION

Reflective analysis of life-world experience has been the focus of interest of philosophical phenomenology (Spiegelberg, 1960). Inspired by this work psychologists and psychiatrists have begun to build a phenomenologically oriented approach to their disciplines (May, et al. 1958; Spiegelberg, 1983). While much of this effort has been oriented toward clinical psychology and psychiatry, some of it is concerned with developing empirical and hermeneutical methods for doing phenomenological research on psychological phenomena. These research approaches are intended to study the meanings of human experiences in situations, as they spontaneously occur in the course of daily life. The emphasis is on the study of lived experience, on how we read, enact, and understand our life-involvements.

In this book I will present the evolution and creative proliferation of ways of doing such research on human experience and action as it has emerged from the collaborative efforts of phenomenologically oriented psychologists. This collective project, in which I have been involved as an active participant for twenty years, has been to rigorously develop and articulate a new paradigm: Existential-Phenomenological Psychology. To this end we have built up a body of human science methods, researches, and theoretical statements which, we feel, do better justice to human experience than those psychologies which still restrict themselves to the paradigm of the natural sciences. According to Kuhn (1962), paradigm shifts involve a radical questioning and reworking of the basic presuppositions of a discipline. In our case, the advance of philosophical understanding during the last century has been a motivating force by virtue of which a new vision of human nature has emerged.

Whether a particular psychological paradigm recognizes it or not, its basic understanding of human nature, its philosophical anthropology, influences the whole conglomerate of problems, facts, and rules which governs its research. Giorgi (1970) has used the term "approach" to denote the way a science's basic presuppositions are intimately interrelated with the content it takes up and the methods it evolves. Thus it follows that the new philosphical anthropology worked out by the existential and phenomenological philosophers of our century calls for new methods for the psychologists who hope to revise their field in the light of these new insights.

1

Foremost among these insights has been the effort to reject the notion that humans are merely objects of biology whose every thought, feeling, and action could then be said to be determined by a complex network of causes. This conception of human nature, borrowed from the natural sciences and ultimately from those philosophers who first extended the notion of causality to human being, is the implicit assumption of much of traditional psychology. These natural science psychologies have been unable to account for human freedom and the meaningfulness of human experience. Instead they resort to quantitative, mechanistic, and computer-models of human nature which, at best, record various regularities of behavior and make predictions, while, at worst, do violence to our forms of self-understanding.

Existential-phenomenological psychology attempts to account for the fullness of human life by reconceiving psychology on properly human grounds. The model of the natural sciences, appropriate as it is for such fields as physics or chemistry, is nevertheless of limited usefulness when it comes to the study of the meaningful character of lived experience. Thus it has been suggested (Strasser, 1963; Giorgi, 1970) that for psychology to fulfill its promise this natural science model should be set aside in favor of a truly **human science** one. The human science approach recognizes that our privileged access to meanings is not numbers but rather perception, cognition, and language. Insofar as everyday human activity can be shown to be continuously informed and shaped by how we understand others and ourselves and by the meanings of the situations we find ourselves in, this is a most significant point. It indicates that the way for psychology to comprehend human behavior and experience as it is actually lived in everyday social settings is to begin by soliciting descriptive accounts of our actual experiences in such settings.

Thus, rather than hastily trying to quantify or abstract from everyday experience in the style of the natural sciences, we begin by more carefully attending to our actual living of it. This is the starting point for existential-phenomenological psychology - the arena of everyday life action and experience (experiaction) - for which Husserl (1913/1962) has given us the metaphor of "life-world". The life world is the place of interaction between persons and their perceptual environments and the world of experienced horizons within which we meaningfully dwell together. It is the world as we find it, prior to any explicit theoretical conceptions.

Of course the world of experiaction does not stand still waiting for us to study it. Like time itself, life is forever streaming on and changing. Fortunately, by way of articulation and reflection we can preserve our experiaction as narrative, as "life-text", and even submit it to rigorous and systematic investigation. While we live more than we can say, we can express more than we usually do if we make the effort, and nothing prevents us from describing our experiaction more carefully. With our ability to observe, remember, report, and reflect on both our own and on other's experience and action, we have a rich source of materials from which to build a truly human science psychology.

In the realization of this project, we acknowledge a heavy debt to the existential-phenomenological philosophers who have formulated the foundational insights for our psychology. These seminal thinkers have tackled many of the persistent and thorny problems which have always haunted psychology, such as that of free will vs. determinism, the mind-body problem, the nature of perception, language, action and so on. Since in many instances we have taken up their thought and adopted some of their methods to the field of psychological research, a brief outline of the most vital contributions of existential-phenomenological philosophers follows.

## § 1.--EXISTENTIAL-PHENOMENOLOGICAL PHILOSOPHY

Existential-phenomenology, as it has developed over the decades, has been primarily a philosophical endeavor. Numerous works, notably Spiegelberg's **The Phenomenological Movement** (1960), and Luijpen's **Existential-Phenomenology** (1963), have traced its rich historical development, focusing upon such key figures as Husserl, Scheler, Jaspers, Marcel, Heidegger, Sartre, Merleau-Ponty, Ricoeur, among others. Curiously, the exact origin of the hyphenated term: Existential-phenomenology is uncertain, as most of the philosphers mentioned either identified themselves as existentialists or as phenomenologists. Although bringing both groups together under a single heading could possibly obscure some of their differences, we feel that the complementary movement of their thought, as discussed here by Luipen (1963), is a good justification for speaking of existential-phenomenology.

The primitive fact itself of the new movement, of the new style of thinking, was reflected upon and expressed after Kierkegaard's existentialism and Husserl's phenomenology had, as it were, fused together in the work of Heidegger. At present it is realized that the new style of thinking uses as its primitive fact, its fundamental intuition, its all-embracing moment of intelligibility, the idea of existence or, what may be considered synonymous with it, the idea of intentionality. (p.36)

As the originator of philosophical phenomenology, Husserl articulated the central insight that **consciousness is intentional**, i.e. that human consciousness is always and essentially oriented towards a world of emergent meaning. Consciousness is always "of something". He argued that experiences were constituted by consciousness and thus could be rigorously and systematically studied on the basis of their appearances to consciousness, - i.e. their phenomenal nature - when an appropriate method of reflection - i.e. phenomenology - had been worked out. Besides the explication of experiences, which Husserl considered to be a psychological project, it would also be possible to reflect upon and articulate the most essential structures of consciousness - i.e. phenomena - such as intentionality, temporality, spatiality, corporeality, perception, cognition, intersubjectivity, and so on, as he in fact did in **Ideas** (1913/1962), and other later works. As philosophy, phenomenology had thus become the reflective study and explication of the operative and thematic structures of consciousness, i.e. primarily a philosophical method of explicating the meaning of the phenomena of consciousness.

Husserl's methodology was to begin with the "phenomenological reduction", or "epoche", which involved the attempt to put all of one's assumptions about the matter being studied into abeyance, to "bracket" them. As Giorgi (1981) has pointed out, to procede without this step when reflecting upon personal experience leaves one open to the "psychologist fallacy", namely the likelihood that one's judgments about such experiences will be biased by various preconceptions, wishes, desires, motives, values and the like. It was just this bias of one's uncritical "natural attitude" that Husserl wished to free himself from, in order to view a given topic from as presuppositionless a position as possible. Only when the bracketing or suspending of such preconceptions had been achieved was the natural attitude said to give way to a more disciplined "phenomenological attitude" from which one could grasp essential structures as they themselves appear. As Giorgi (1981) describes this process:

> Bracketing means that one puts out of mind all that one knows about a phenomenon or event in order to describe precisely how one experiences it. . . . Husserl introduced the idea of the phenomenological reduction, which after bracketing of knowledge about things means that one is present to all that one experiences in terms of the

meanings that they hold out tor consciousness rather than as simple existents. (p. 82)

The assumption of the phenomenological attitude thus implies that we describe something not in terms of what we already know or presume to know about it, but rather that we describe that which presents itself to our awareness exactly as it presents itself. This movement is crisply formulated in the phenomenological imperative: "Back to the things themselves!"

In the above dictum the "things" toward which the phenomenological gaze struggles are no longer "objects" as such (in the sense of naive realism), but rather their meanings, as given perceptually through a multiplicity of perspectival views and contexts. Along with other presuppositions, the phenomenologist puts his or her "existential belief out of action"; the belief that objects exist in and of themselves, apart from a consciousness which perceives them. After suspending this belief, what remains is the phenomenon, the "pure appearance" which presents itself to consciousness. For example, when I eat an apple, I effectively destroy it as a physical object, and yet it remains as a phenomenon. Its various perspectival views, i.e. its redness, its juiciness, its roundedness, and so on, can remain as a matter of contemplation for me, as what Husserl identified technically as "noema".

Whether or not it is possible to put into abeyance all of one's presuppositons about an apple (or any other item of reflection) is put into question by some existential-phenomenologists, among them, Merleau-Ponty. According to him, a totally presuppositionless vantage point cannot be secured, because as we put one presupposition out of action, we uncover beneath it, more hidden ones. He believed that our vital interests and existential involvement with people and things in the world were of a fundamental character, and would not allow themselves to be entirely undercut. Nevertheless, he considered the aim of the movement of the phenomenological reduction to be an extremely fruitful one, for by uncovering our presuppositons and interrogating them, we can clearly advance our understanding of the phenomenon under consideration.

The questions which guide research of philosophical phenomenology would be: What is the essence of this phenomenon? What are the conditions of possibility for the constitution of meaning by human consciousness? Because phenomenology had to do with the intuiting of essences, Husserl sometimes called it an "eidetic science." Like any science, it aimed to provide lasting and objective-universal knowledge, to separate the arbitrary and accidental from the necessary and the permanent, i.e. the essential. To accomplish this, Husserl (1913/1962) augmented the process of phenomenological bracketing with a procedure he called "free imaginative variation." With this method the noematic object was to be varied in imagination by altering its constituents in order to test the limits within which it retained its identity, so as to discover its variants. Applying this to our earlier example of the apple, one would begin by modifying its various aspects in our imagination, so as to engender a manifold of imaginary apples. Although some will be red, like the one which was eaten, others would be green, and even a purple apple could be imagined. That we don't find purple apples in actual experience is irrelevant at this stage, for what we want to discover is the essential structure and the essential constituents of an apple, and to do so we need to consider the possible alongside the actual. Already we can see that redness does not belong essentially to apples, although a skin which may be various colors does.

In principle, with a sufficiently thoroughgoing and deep-reaching imaginary variation, it should be possible to delimit the essence of phenomena such as our apple, or of any other sort. Eventually those aspects of the phenomenon which could be and could not be eliminated without altering its basic structure would become evident. As Gurwitsch (1964) writes:

> By means of the process of free variation, these structures prove invariant by determining limits within which free variation must operate in order to yield possible examples of the class under discussion. These invariants define the essence or eidos of this class, either a regional or a subordinate eidos. They specify the necessary conditons to which every specimen of the class must conform to be a possible specimen of this class. (p. 192)

In the main effort of his work, Husserl employed the phenomenological reduction and free imaginary variation for strictly philosophical pursuits. Nevertheless, he believed these procedures could be applied to other tasks, and he delimited some relevant domains of inquiry. Of the greatest concern to us are the distinctions he provided between phenomenology and psychology, which were conceived in terms of three separate and necessary domains of investigation. As summarized by Spiegelberg (1960) these are:

**Pure Phenomenology** is the study of the essential structures of consciousness comprising its ego-subject, its acts, and its contents

- hence not limited to psychological phenomena - carried out with complete suspension of existential beliefs.

**Phenomenological Psychology** is the study of the fundamental types of psychological phenomena in their subjective aspects only, regardless of their embeddedness in the objective context of a psychological organism.

**Empirical Psychology** is the descriptive and genetic study of the psychical entities in all their aspects as part and parcel of the psychophysical organism; as such it forms a mere part of the study of man, i.e. of anthropology. (p. 152)

We will see later in our presentation of the empirical phenomenological methodologies developed at Duquesne University and elsewhere that these distinctions have continued to play a contributing role, although unlike Husserl's reliance upon various forms of disciplined reflection on consciousness in general, the empirical phenomenological researchers have turned to the analysis of concrete descriptions of lived experience, gathered from the psychologist's most valuable data-resource: other people.

Before we turn to the ways in which existential-phenomenological psychologists have created empirical and hermeneutical research methods, we want to review some of the results of the work of existential-phenomenological philosophical reflection which are relevant. From a methodological point of view the work of philosophers is non-empirical. They do not design experiments nor do they engage in systematic data-gathering methods or data-analysis in a scientific sense. What philosophers do engage in is careful and systematic reflection and interpretation of human experience. What they reflect upon is life-experience in general as it is mediated by the accumulated tradition of philosophy itself. The accumulated biographical and historical stock of knowledge of the philosopher is the context of reference and source of examples and illustrations for philosophical work.

Phenomenology has been considered to be primarily a contribution of method applied to the phenomena of human consciousness. Existentialism, on the other hand, has been characterized as an effort to specify the essential and perennial themes of human existence in its broadest sense, as finite, embodied, mooded, in time, situated, threatened by death, capable of language, symbolism and reflection, striving for meanings and values

and choices, self-fulfilling and self-transcending, as involving and com-
miting itself to relationships, accountable and capable of responsibility.
Existential-phenomenology thus means the application of the phenomenological method to the perennial problems of human existence.

Others have said that existential-phenomenology broadens the base of
understanding of our discipline beyond acts of thematic consciousness by
recognizing the importance of pre-reflective bodily components in the
constitution of meaning (Merleau-Ponty), or by emphasizing the existential
choices a person makes about his or her life-situation, the "existential
project" (Sartre), or by focusing on the totality of personal existence as
being-in-the-world (**Dasein** (Heidegger) including our dwelling in social
relations and historical circumstances. There is still another opinion
(Frings, 1965) which sees the unfolding of the phenomenological movement
and the foundation of contemporary European philosophy to rest on the
threefold foundation of phenomenology (Husserl), of philosopical anthropology (Scheler), and of the ontology of Dasein (Heidegger). Thus there is
much internal development within the phenomenological movement as we shall
see.

## §2.--PHENOMENOLOGY: HUSSERL, SCHUTZ, AND SCHELER

(a) **Edmund Husserl:** The phenomenological approach centers on the
experienced fact that the world appears to us through our stream of consciousness as a configuration of meaning. Acts of consciousness, i.e.
perceiving, willing, thinking, remembering, anticipating, etc. are our
modalities of self-world relationship. They give us access to our world
and that of others, by reflecting on the **content** (i.e. its meaning or "the
what") which we thus encounter and also by reflecting on the **process,**
(i.e. "the how"). Husserl, the founder of phenomenology, hoped to clarify
in a descriptive/reflective manner the foundation and constitution of
knowledge in human consciousness. Phenomenology became the study of human
meanings as constituted by the stream of consciousness. Consciousness
itself is understood as being **intentional.** It is as always **directed toward**
something. As phenomenologists are fond of saying: Consciousness is always
consciousness of something. Consciousness recognizes and creates meanings
which subsequently inhere in the world as experienced.

With Husserl from 1900 on, we enter an era in philosophy and psychology which recognizes the participation of the subject in the creation of
meaning. The subject's role is acknowledged even in physics through
Heisenberg's uncertainty principle. In both physics and psychology, the

"objectivity of reality" assumption collapses under the realization that the observer as well as the actor is existentially and epistemologically implicated in the creation of meaning. There is no "really real" world of independent objective facts. Rather, the world comes into being for us as meanings which we constitute and as political realities for which we fight. Husserl's fundamental contribution was to call our attention to the study of the meaning constituting power of the acts of consciousness. He developed systematic reflection as a research method. In working out some of the implications and strategies of this new reflective philosophical methodology, Husserl (1913/1962) discovered the complexities of the **horizonal nature** of consciousness. That is, our field of awareness always extends beyond the factually given to that which is implied, remembered, anticipated, generalized, etc. Husserl focused mainly on the **temporal horizons** of "inner time consciousness" i.e. on the way people experience their embeddedness in the stream of time: past, present, and future. He explored how these horizons cooperate in creating the temporal meaning of the here and now. He also developed the notion of "inner and outer horizons" - what we might call **cognitive horizons** - which refer to contexts of knowledge playing on the here and now. Such horizons contextualize experience in terms of consensually available cognitive frameworks of perceived meaning. Husserl is the master of the articulation of the "mind space" within the larger sphere of the unified field of a person's consciousness and existence, "the psychocosm" (von Eckartsberg, 1981a).

In his late work, Husserl (1954/1970) developed his idea of the "life world," the world of taken-for-granted everyday activities and common sense meanings. Because we are embedded within the socially constituted meanings of our common sense world, we are explicitly aware neither of the taken-for-granted nature of this reality nor how we constitute it. Yet this unacknowledged realm of the life world is the basis of all scientific activity. Scientific constructs are built on indubitable but taken-for-granted common activities and associated constructs of common sense. The life world is the unexamined foundation and matrix of scientific activity, and phenomenology makes these common sense constructs and phenomena its object of investigation.

(b) **Alfred Schutz:** Whereas Husserl was concerned with how we construct our reality in general, Schutz (1962, 1964, 1966) focused more specifically on our construction of **social reality.** He took up the challenge of Husserl's phenomenology and related it to sociology and social psychology. He was primarily concerned with articulating the common sense structures of consciousness, which he called **typifications** of conscious-

ness, by means of which individuals comprehend the nature of social reality and are enabled to act in everyday life.

**Temporal typifications** articulate our experienced life world in terms
of the "world within reach" (here and now), the "world within restorable
reach" (the past), and the "world within attainable reach" (the future). A
related set of temporal constructs concerns our social partners in life as
"contemporaries," "predecessors," and "successors" in terms of which our
biographical stock of knowledge is organized. For Schutz, the experienced
scheme of temporality itself is formed from the interplay of lived time,
social calendar time, and cosmic time which regulates the natural rhythms
of days and seasons.

Schutz devoted much effort to an articulation of the biographical
stock of knowledge organized in terms of what he called **hierarchical
orders of typifications** (schemes of interpretations, recipes for action,
or role conceptions) and in terms of schemes or orders of relevance which
both express the interests and motivations of individuals and groups and
thematize the world in a relativistic manner. His work opened up within
phenomenology the phenomena of encounter, social interaction, and the
reflective articulation of intersubjectivity. His important and fertile
studies of the social structures of the life-world have been extended and
deepened by the work of Peter Berger (Berger and Luckmann, 1966) on the
social construction of reality and problems of modernity (Berger, Berger,
and Kellner, 1973) and by the work of Maurice Natanson (1970) on the
structure of the "journeying self" engaged in self-other-world typifications. The work of phenomenology has become increasingly recognized and
important for mainstream sociology.

(c) **Max Scheler:** While the main concern of Husserl and Schutz was to
articulate the purely rational structures of human being, Scheler (1961)
was preoccupied with the phenomenological description and analysis of the
non-rational essences in experience with invariant structures in emotional
life. Scheler was the phenomenologist of values, feelings, social senti-
ments and love. He forged a philosophical anthropology guided by the basic
notion of personhood as a spiritual reality, by the belief in the essentially social nature of human existence, by the absoluteness of values and
the eternal in human nature. His concern was to determine the place of
human being in the cosmos. His starting point was the irreducibility of
the person as "ens amans," as a loving being and as the ethical being, and
his method was phenomenological which he developed in an originary way.

Scheler explored the phenomena involved in the immediate apperception
and emotional cognition of values - value-ception: value-awareness and

value-perception - which he considered to be prior and hence foundational for all other acts of cognition. Scheler was a passionate proponent of the primacy of the emotional and vital sphere. He worked out an influential phenomenology of ethics which articulated an objective hierarchy of values ranging from sensible to vital values - both values of life - and then to spiritual values and the value of holiness - both values of the person. Scheler made important contributions to the phenomenology of religion. He brilliantly described the key interhuman phenomena of love and hate, and the variety and forms of sympathy (1954a). He provided us with the exemplary study of the phenomenon of resentment (1954b) (ressentiment) and he made important contributions to the sociology of knowledge distinguishing three types of knowledge: knowledge of **control**, as in the aspirations of science and technology, knowledge of **essences**, as in the aspirations of philosophy, metaphysics and phenomenology, and knowledge of **salvation** as in the religious quest for spiritual fulfillment. Scheler's philosophical anthropology has been called "ethical personalism" within a christocentric spiritual tradition emphasising the multidimensional nature of human existence as bodily/vital, egoic/mental, and personal/spiritual. The highest good must be personal. Scheler emphasized love and the study of the "ordo amoris" - the configuration of love - as the core of the person and as the foundation for social relationships and societal forms. Scheler's work has great originality and masterful phenomenological subtlety. It is fertile and offers many challenges and invitations for corroborative psychological work. (Frings, 1965)

## §3.--THE EMERGENCE OF EXISTENTIAL PHENOMENOLOGY: HEIDEGGER, SARTRE, AND MERLEAU-PONTY

The pure phenomenology of Husserl was later enriched by the "existentialist movement" in the tradition of Kierkegaard and Nietzsche. Expanded into **existential**-phenomenology, associated primarily with Heidegger, Sartre, and Merleau-Ponty, it recognized the importance of preconscious lived experience, i.e. the phenomenon of the "lived body." It emphasized that being in the world involves more than human consciousness and encompasses the total embodied human response to a perceived situation. Such insights led **existential**-phenomenologists to focus their research on **human situated experience.** Intentionality became redefined as a dialogal, relational dynamic of self-other interaction. **Existence** refers to the concrete, biographical, and embodied life of **named persons** who are characterized by uniqueness and irreplaceability. Existential-phenomenology studies existence in terms of the person's involvement in a situation within a world. It aims in its ultimate objective at "the awakening to a special way of life, usually called authentic existence." (Spiegelberg, 1983, p. 255)

(a) **Martin Heidegger:** The main contribution of Heidegger (1927/1967, 1971) lies in his radical questioning of the traditional Cartesian subject-object distinction, which leads to a dualistic universe and the dichotomy of subjective consciousness versus objective matter. With the subject-object split as an operative life world assumption, there is always a gap and separation to be bridged between the two ontological realms of matter and consciousness, leading to unresolvable epistemological difficulties. But if we conceive of our existence completely in relational and field theoretical terms as a field of openness into which things and the world appear and reveal themselves in a dynamic way (Dasein as being-in-the-world) then we can avoid this problem. Persons are not selves separated from their world which is presumed to exist completely independently of them. Rather, they are personal involvements in a complex totality network of interdependent ongoing relationships which demand response and participation.

Heidegger advanced the thesis that the world comes into existence for us in and through our participation. He worked out the essential structures of being-in-the-world as grounded in **care,** i.e. in concernful presence and openness to the world and others. He developed the general approach of phenomenology into an interpretative understanding of Dasein's total being. He called this approach the **hermeneutics of existence,** i.e. the interpretative characterization of existence in the world.

Heidegger's work issues a call for action, personal movement, authentic participation, and a change in one's way of thinking from the calculative to the meditative mode. The movement depends on one's resoluteness to face basic existential contingencies, primarily the anxiety over one's own death. It requires one to acknowledge one's self as an illuminator and creator of one's world. Heidegger also talked about ultimate horizons and concerns. He postulated qualitative transformations in authentic moments and movements of personal existence. By doing so, he brought in a transpersonal context and went beyond a strictly rational world view. His attitude and concrete examples of existential-hermeneutic work (Heidegger, 1971) place him in kinship with the tradition of Zen (von Eckartsberg, 1981a).

(b) **Jean-Paul Sartre:** Sartre (1943/1953, 1963) contributed greatly to the "existentialization" of phenomenology through his challenge that "existence precedes essence." According to Sartre, the person is the totality of his or her life choices, for which he or she is fully responsible. His idea of the **fundamental project** of a person's life refers to the way each person chooses him or herself. This project can be disclosed by **existential psychoanalysis,** Sartre's method of personalistic reflection which was applied in his famous book length case studies.

The concept of fundamental project is of great potential value to clinical and personality psychology. It refers to the unique configuration of meaningful existential choices, i.e. the total web of existential moves a person makes. The project is the inner principle of coherence that we can perceive and articulate in our own and other's lives.

The study of individuals entails gaining an understanding of how they go about the actualization of possibilities, their "not yet." Sartre emphasized the fact that one is always moving beyond oneself towards something else. He worked out what he called a "progressive-regressive" dialectical method which is said to be able to betray the "secret of the self," namely the implicit purpose for which one strives. Sartre's method aims at **comprehension,** a mode of understanding wherein one lives the existence of the other in intuitive and empathic behaviors. To comprehend the action of another we enter the original situatedness of that person biographically in terms of the operative historical and cultural conditions (regressive move); we seek to understand the purpose or goal choice that governs the direction of the action taken (progressive move) by means of which the person surpasses the givens in the direction of his or her possibles.

(c) **Maurice Merleau-Ponty:** Merleau-Ponty (1945/1962, 1964/1968) widened the meaning of intentionality to include preverbal thought (thinking that exists in action) or the pre-personal dimension of bodily intentions and meaning. He maintained that the acting body always already understands its situation as well as its own possibilities quite before we pay any explicit attention to it. For Merleau-Ponty intentionality, no longer merely a matter of cognitive consciousness, includes the life of embodied existence and interactive communication which precedes and is the foundation for explicit and thematic consciousness.

In the most global terms, Merleau-Ponty speaks of the mystery that I am part of the world and that the world is an extension of my body. Body and world mutually imply each other and are of the same nature. They stand in a relationship that he characterizes as "j'en suis" (I belong to it). This is the primordial ground of all of our awareness, a kind of prolongation of our body which Merleau-Ponty in his later writing expresses metaphorically as **the flesh of the world.** The subject-object dichotomy of traditional thinking is overcome by Merleau-Ponty. We are always in the midst of the world and have no vantage point outside of it. We can never achieve total clarity even in our reflective and critical orientation because we cannot fully penetrate the darkness of our primordial awareness in which meaning is always already constituted. We cannot attend the birth of meaning in our life. Bodily existence itself is a giver of meanings. Our body has the power of expression; it gives rise to meaning.

Our body gives us our power of motiliy, the "I can" or "I am able to." This happens on a pre-reflective level, on the level of **operative intentionality,** of **practognosie.** By virtue of our embodiment we find ourselves always already situated and capable of meaningful interaction.

Merleau-Ponty has contributed greatly to our understanding of the person as a participant in and creator of meaning even as a creature **condemned to meaning.** He also makes us aware of the limits of our power of reflection and of the fact that we find ourselves in a situation of essential ambiguity, of "chiaroscuro," not being fully able to penetrate the sources and origins of our meaning making. This ambiguity is grounded in our bodily participation in being and on the paradox that we are ourselves constituted by the very being we become aware of. Merleau-Ponty rejects both materialism and idealism, i.e. the reduction of man's world to an idea. He establishes his own position of existential-phenomenology, which is the middle ground centering on one's embodied subjectivity, and focusing on the **primacy of perception.**

## §4.--FROM INTENTIONALITY TO RELATIONSHIP-BUILDING AND DWELLING

We have surveyed how Husserl's original inspiration of phenomenology has undergone significant development and change through the work of his successors. If we focus on the key phenomenolgoical notion of **intentionality** we can gain a measure of the development that has taken place in our thinking.

Originally intentionality was metaphorized as an "intentional arrow" symbolizing the one-directional act of ego-cogito-cogitatum, an ego directing its attention toward an object revealing its sense or meaning. Reflecting on intentionality revealed to Husserl the existence of horizons or halos extending from the perceptual or cognitive object linking them to their relevant contexts of interpretation and familiarity, **cognitively,** i.e. in terms of outer horizons, **perceptually,** i.e. in terms of the horizons engendered by bodily movement, and **temporally,** i.e. in terms of inner time-consciousness. The early phenomenological work of Husserl focused on **cognitive meanings,** primarily. In his later work Husserl expanded the notion of intentionality to include **operative intentionality,** i.e. the intentionality of spontaneous and competent autotelic body-movement. We could metaphorize this as "auto-pilot intentionality." Merleau-Ponty takes up and elaborates this idea in the context of his notion of the lived-body, the "body subject" (le corps propre) and motility. By means of our bodily insertion into reality, we are always already vitally responsive to the demands of our situation on our body. Our body moves in terms of pre-reflective intelligence and lived involvement which exceeds our conscious awareness and control. Operative intentionality establishes and utilizes secret bonds of correspondence and interdependency: reciprocal involvement. In this way of thinking the "intentional arrow" has become a two-way street of interaction, interexperience and co-constitution.

For Scheler the primordial human act is one of **value-ception.** He emphasizes the emotional and trans-rational nature of our relating to the world and to one another and he concentrates on loving and hating, i.e. value-laden acts by means of which we construct our lives. For Sartre the notion of intentionality is linked up with existential choices and radical freedom to make commitments and to choose our future. Sartre's key notion in this context is the **existential project,** characterizing the way a person chooses his or her long-range life commitments and life direction in and through all particular acts of involvement.

In Heidegger's hyphenated notion of **being-in-the-world,** which radicalizes the subject-object notion and bridges the subject-object split, Dasein's basic ontological structure is characterized as **care,** concernful presence, world-openness. The priority of the subject, or person, or ego, yields to the unitary and coequal relationship of mutual implication or "relational totality": caring-being-in-the-world. In his later work Heidegger develops this notion into **dwelling** by which he means our caring, sparing, spatializing and temporalizing presencing and eventing of being, what we might call: **culture-building.** Revealed by a new epistemological attitude, by meditative, responsive, "thanking thinking" (von Eckartsberg, 1981a) dwelling is concerned with our authentic presence to our situations, our things, our people. Heidegger ushers in a normative dimension: our concern with the authentic and good life in deep relationship to the ground of Being.

In my reading, the concept of intentionality in the phenomenological tradition seems to continue to evolve. We can discern a spectrum that

ranges from intentionality in the original Husserlian sense to relation-
ship-cultivation and culture-building or dwelling in the sense of the
later Heidegger. As we widen the context of understanding of the contributing dimensions in the constitution of meaning to include the role of
our self-moving body, our essential intersubjectivity, and our embeddedness in language and culture, the meaning of intentionality changes from
an emphasis on mostly cognitive understanding to one of existential engagement in the creation of a way of life (dwelling). Heidegger's understanding of dwelling is kin to the understanding and praxis of Zen and
Taoism.

Thus, over time, our understanding of intentionality undergoes a
shift in emphasis or focus, from **consciousness** to **culture-building** acts,
from value-free phenomenological reflective analysis operating under the
self-imposed disciplines of several steps of bracketing (epoches) to
passionate value-engagement and existential commitment. We move from the
primacy of knowing to the primacy of life praxis, to **enactment.**

## § 5. --THE EXISTENTIAL-PHENOMENOLOGICAL APPROACH IN PSYCHOLOGY

The Existential-phenomenological approach to psychology proceeds on the
assumption, as we all do in everyday life, that identically named experience refers basically to the same reality in various subjects.

> This basic identity of experience is an axiom in psychology. . .
> This axiom seems to be confirmed by daily experience. . . If we
> collect descriptions (of a named, i.e., linguistically specified
> experience) then we have to assume that others are focusing their
> attention on basically the same kind of experience, that we are when
> we describe our experience. This statement is founded on the sup-
> postion that experience, with all its phenomena, is basically the
> same in various subjects. (Van Kaam, 1966, p. 312)

In other words, we have to rely on the supposition that people in a
shared cultural and linguistic community, name and identify their experience in a consistent and shared manner. Our shared everyday vocabulary, including both ordinary language and those psychological terms which
have filtered down from professional psychology, constitutes our access to
experience, which is always to some extent already linguistically organized. Van Kaam refers to this basic identity of experience as an

"axiom" underlying all of psychology. While we do not think it to be an axiom, at least it is a fruitful working hypothesis to be checked by empirical analysis. It gives us a starting point in working toward linguistic consensus and the establishment of communication communities.

The interrelationship of language and experience is a difficult psychological conundrum. How is it that we can say what we experience and yet always live more than we can say, so that we could always say more than we in fact do? How can we evaluate the adequacy or inadequacy of our expression in terms of its doing justice to the full lived quality of the experience described?

How are thought and life interrelated so that they can be characterized as interdependent, as in need of each other, as complementing each other, as inter-penetrant? Living informs expression (language and thinking), and in turn, thinking-language-expression reciprocally informs and gives a recognizable shaped awareness to living. Meaning, experience as meaningful, seems to be the fruit of this dialogue between inchoate living and articulate expression. Whereas living is unique and particular, i.e., **existential**, thinking tends toward generalization, toward the universal, the essential, the **phenomenological.**

Our life takes place within this tension, "in between" these levels of participation. This tension and interdependence between life and thought is expressed in the very name of our approach as existential-phenomenological and constitutes what we might call the **existential-phenomenological paradox.** In The Journeying Self, Natanson (1970) writes about this:

> If Phenomenology depicts the typical, Existentialism shows the unique; if Phenomenology deals with essence, Existentialism handles concreteness; if Phenomenology is interested in the structure of consciousness, Existentialism is concerned with the reality of the individual. It would seem these philosophies represent divergent standpoints rather than complementary approaches to human reality. That they are congenial, indeed intimately inter-sustaining and supporting views of man is the methodological thesis on which we have proceeded. What appears to be a paradox is a methaphysical duality which affects all philosophizing as it does the reality which all philosophizing is about. In classical and traditional terms the duality has been called the Universal and the Particular, or Thought and Life. The question is how the truth of the world in general is

related to the truth of individual experience and how a theoretical system can understand the immediacy of the person. (p. 66)

We can express this formulation in terms of a diagram which places life and though in dialectical opposition. It bespeaks the same tension as that between **existentialism,** focusing on the problems and themes of life itself, of existence, and **phenomenology,** which focuses on the explication of the intentional structures of consciousness in general.

This tension is inherent in the very organization of language, which can move on either or both levels simultaneously, with descriptive specificity and uniqueness as well as in the mode of universalizing conceptualization and judgement. Language can encompass and inter-relate both levels through mixed, multi-leveled discourse, and by means of such expressive tools as **metaphors, symbols,** (Murray, 1975), and **Proper Names** (Rosenstock-Huessy, 1970). Each of these latter three linguistic structures constitute a special class of "concrete universals" (Natanson, 1970), useful in aesthetic, religious, moral and legal discourse.

Let us indicate the mystery of the interdependence of these two extreme levels of existence, this mystery of the intertwining and co-penetration by the ancient Chinese symbol of Yin-Yang, which visually dramatizes and represents the living reality of this mutuality, of "one within the other." (See Figure 1)

=====================================================================

PHENOMENOLOGY
STRUCTURE  OF  CONSCIOUSNESS
THOUGHT

LIFE
REALITY  OF  THE  INDIVIDUAL
EXISTENTIALISM

With some justification we can say that the mystery of existential-phenomenology is concealed in the **hyphen** itself. It indicates the difficult expressive problem of languaging the simultaneity and interpenetration of both living and thinking of spontaneous enactment and reflective explication.

The systematization and "proceduralizing" of the movement from implicit to explicit by existential-phenomenological Psychology is essentially a formalization of an everyday activity and general human ability: to reflect on experience. First we report and describe - narratization - and then we think further about something in order to conceptualize it. We keep asking: what does it mean, what does it say, what is concealed in it, what becomes revealed through dwelling with it patiently, what secret lies hidden therein? This is the **reflective attitude**, i.e. openness and listening to Being in all its particular manifestations. This is the basic descriptive-reflective approach utilized by existential-phenomenologists. It is a skill anyone can acquire for himself and integrate into his living as a meaning-enhancing depth dimension of self-development.

How to invite and initiate newcomers into it can be a serious pedagogical problem! It can be entered into if we begin gently with the first linguistic step of expression and description of the experienced flow of living, expressing a particular experience which we specify and identify by giving an account of it, by trying to bring it to as full and accurate an articulation as possible. We create a life-text. From there we move toward the reflective study of this description, focusing on the essential meaning-constituents contained therein, the "experience moments" (van Kaam), the "meaning-units" (Giorgi), the "themes and scenes" (W. Fischer) or the "psychological plot" (von Eckartsberg) which can be inductively synthesized into an essential, structurally integrated description of the universally valid meaning of the phenomenon under consideration. This involves a dynamic dialogue between two levels of description: the everyday level of **narrative language** and the more general and condensing achievement of reflective analysis, i.e. **structural conceptual language,** existential-phenomenologists refer to this general process of meaning-articulation as **explication.**

By explication, implicit awareness of a complex phenomenon becomes explicit, formulated knowledge of its components." (van Kaam, 1966, p. 305)

By means of explication we are to discover what the necessary and sufficient conditions and constituents of the type of event under study are, i.e. what the structure of the phenomenon under investigation is. Explication, as any form of interpretive reading or hermeneutics, is a **qualitative research procedure** in that it wishes to arrive at an understanding and circumscription of **what** the phenomenon essentially is as a lived human meaning (structure), and **how** it is lived by individuals in their everyday existential lived contexts (style).

The existential-phenomenological approach in psychology tries to be **empirical** in the sense of basing itself on factual data which are collected for the purpose of examination and explication.

> Our research is empirical in that shareable, replicable observed events or personal reports are its data. Moreover, we remain true to each of the individual subject's ways of embodying the general structure that we discover through examination of specific, situated instances. (Giorgi, Fischer, C., Murray, E., 1975b, p. XI)

In another formulation:

> By empirical we refer to a) our reflection upon actual events and to b) our making available to colleagues the data and steps of analysis that led to our findings so that they might see for themselves whether and how they could come to similar findings." (Fischer, C. & Wertz, 1979, p. 136)

In contrast to existential-phenomenological philosophers who tend not to specify the "data-base" upon which their reflections are founded, the existential-phenomenological psychology researchers presented here are very explicit about the research-design of their investigation and the methodological steps of data-analysis and explication. In the tradition of experimental psychology they are guided by strict considerations of verifiability and replicability. But in contrast to the traditional **quantitative** approach in psychological research, which uses statistical analysis of sets of data collected in terms of a strict hypothesis-testing research design, the existential-phenomenological approach in psychology does **qualitative** research, i.e. meaning analysis and explication of descriptions of life world experiences. Qualitative research is a form of content-analysis covering a spectrum of approaches ranging from what has been called **empirical-phenomenological** psychology to **hermeneutical-phenomenolo-**

**gical** psychology - depending on the "data source" which underlies the reflective-hermeneutic work.

Empirical-phenomenological psychology has long been aware of this hermeneutical activity as intrinsic to research. The question remains, then, how does a hermeneutical-phenomenological psychology in the strict sense differ from the standard empirical-phenomenological research conducted at Duquesne University for the past twenty years? The essential differences would seem to relate to the grounds (data base) upon which the interpretations are based and the procedures for arriving at these interpretations. Up to now, empirical-phenomenological psychology proceeded by collecting protocols descriptive of the subjects' experience (e.g. learning, envy, anxiety, etc.), and then systematically and rigorously interrogating these descriptions step by step to arrive at the structure of the experience. Hermeneutical psychology suggests another data source and a different method of analysis. (Giorgi, A., Knowles, R., Smith, D., 1979, p. 179)

Hermeneutical-phenomenological psychology focuses on the works of great literature, on myths, autobiography, and works of art including film, theatre, and television, and thus widens the data-base and the understanding of the meaning of life-texts to include fictional and creative accounts as acceptable data for reflective-interpretative activity. (Palmer, 1969; Ihde, 1971; Gadamer, 1975; Polkinghorne, 1983) In terms of the work of explication, the interpretative activities of hermeneutical-phenomenological psychology are as yet less well defined and more idiosyncratic than those of empirical-phenomenological psychology although the attempt is always made to be as explicit as possible about the steps of the movement from concrete experience and description to universalizing conceptualization so that the reader can verify and replicate the process for him or herself (Wertz, 1984).

The **data-source** for existential-phenomenological psychological studies can vary from the collection of many protocols of described experience to the utilization of a single account of one subject. The data may also come from audio and videotapes and from speak aloud protocols (Haustoos, 1985) or from thinking out loud (Klinger, 1978).

The focus of the investigation can be directed at arriving at the **general structure** of a phenomenon in terms of a synchronic formulation of essential constituents or at a **process structure** of a phenomenon which delineates the diachronic unfolding of the phenomenon in terms of essential stages aligned sequentially. (Ricoeur, 1979)

Several empirical and hermeneutical models for the explication of phenomena using the existential-phenomenological approach have been described in the literature. In 1966 van Kaam led the way with the publication of **Existential Foundations of Psychology,** a wide-ranging work which emerged out of his doctoral studies and the research methodology developed for his 1958 dissertation. In 1970 another seminal work appeared, Giorgi's **Psychology as a Human Science.** In the same year Duquesne also began publication of its **Journal of Phenomenological Psychology,** which presents the ongoing struggle for rigorous methodology. Notable among the publications which followed would be the four volumes of **Duquesne Studies in Phenomenological Psychology** (1971, 1975, 1979, 1983), the most complete and detailed record of the work of the Duquesne group. Colaizzi's book on methods: **Reflection and Research in Psychology** (1973); Keen: **A Primer in Phenomenological Psychology** (1975); more recently, the collection of essays edited by Valle and King: **Existential-Phenomenological Alternatives for Psychology** (1979); de Rivera: **Conceptual Encounters** (1981); Romanyshyn: **Psychological Life** (1982). The most recent publications on empirical existential-phenomenological research are: Aanstoos, C. (Ed.) **Exploring the Lived World: Readings in Phenomenological Psychology** (1984) and Giorgi, A. (Ed.) **Phenomenology and Psychological Research** (1985).

This review of research on the analysis of life-world experience will select and present some prototypical examples to illustrate the range and diversity of the spectrum of human science methods as it has evolved in the work of the Duquesne group and other phenomenologically oriented psychologists. For a full and exhaustive representation of the accumulated research we refer to the original publications and the works cited above.

Our aim is to present the concrete ways in which this research and these kinds of qualitative analyses are made so that the reader gets a working familiarity with the design and methods of such work and with the types of language used to present the realities of such investigations. We hope that this presentation and illustration of the ways of doing anaysis of life-world experience from a phenomenological perspective will encourage and enable the reader to engage in his or her own research endeavors into the meaning configurations of human experiences.

In the organization of this book we will use the following outline:

## Part I.  Empirical Existential-Phenomenological Studies

We will first concentrate on the empirical existential-phenomenological branch of research in terms of a **structural** orientation which aims to reveal the essential general meaning structure of a given phenomenon in answer to the implicit research guiding question: **What is it, essentially?** We will present the work of van Kaam (1966), Colaizzi (1973), Giorgi (1975), W. Fischer, (1974), C. Fischer (1971).

We will then present some work that focuses primarily on the articulation of the **process** of human experience which answers to the question: **How does it happen?** We will present as a sample of such research the work of von Eckartsberg (1979).

Thirdly we will present some research work that uses concrete descriptions of experience as data to critically examine and **validate phenomenological constructs** using focussed experiential research (Richer, 1979) or to illustrate the usefulness of phenomenological constructs in understanding everyday events in terms of their phenomenological constitution. (Keen, 1975)

## Part II.  Hermeneutical-Phenomenological Studies

We will then focus on researches which investigate human experience as it becomes expressed in spontaneous productions of speech, of writing or of art work. These researches use the hermeneutic approach. It emphasizes the understanding or model or pardigm that human actions and interactions can be conceived of as **texts** (Ricoeur, 1971) in need of interpretation.

The "data-base" on which hermeneutic work is based is conceived more broadly than in empirical protocol studies. The steps of explication and the questions that are addressed to the text also vary more widely in the hermeneutic approach and are less clear and operationalized.

We have organized our selection of representative hermeneutical-phenomenological work around a) **actual life-text** studies, (von Eckartsberg, 19    ; Fessler, 1983; Kracklauer, 1973; de Rivera, 1981) in which situated speaking was recorded, transcribed, and then reflectively and interpretationally amplified and articulated in terms of inherent hidden meanings. b) Studies of **recollections and literary texts** (Buckley, 1971; Halling, 1979; Jaeger, 1975; Romanyshyn, 1982), in which the data are recall, literary texts, and historical materials.

There may be other ways of organizing these diverse researches of analysis of life-world experience, and there are types and areas of research that are not included in this presentation. We are discussing "work in progress" and the examples offered should be understood as discoveries and formulations along the way, rather than iron-clad, Procrustean schemes of data-analysis. The personality, style, and world view of the interpreter enters into the hermeneutical work. The continuous questioning and examination of implicit assumptions is itself part of the hermeneutical enterprise which makes it sometimes difficult to specify the methodological "steps" involved in doing hermeneutical research. There is an unanalyzable, idosyncratic component operative in interpretative work which is associated with an original vision of human reality held by the researcher.

Wertz (1984) in reviewing the "procedures in phenomenological research" has identified another type of approach which he calls **comprehensive theoretical research:**

> This approach was developed in dissertation research (e.g., Greiner, 1964) under the direction of van Kaam and is also to some extent exemplified by the excellent work of W. Fischer (1970) on anxiety and Barton (1974) on psychotherapy. The crucial context for this research is a fragmented, confused field of psychology containing unresolved disagreements regarding the phenomenon of interest. (p. 2)

Other examples of this approach are found in the work of Giorgi (1970) on "Psychology as a Human Science," of von Eckartsberg (1971) on "experiential social psychology," of Knowles, on basic trust and phenomenology of Human Development (1985), of Smith (1975, 1979) on Freud's metapsychology and on psychotherapy, of Fischer, C. and Fischer W. (1984) on psychotherapy, of Murray (1975, 1985) on metaphor and imagination, of Churchill (1984) on psychodiagnostic seeing, of C. Fischer (1984) on personalized assessment, of Romanyshyn (1982) on the metaphorical nature of psychological life, of Bilotta (1981) on sexuality and spiritual development, of Kraft (1978) on psychopathology, of Rosenberg (1979) on the film experience, of Maes (1984) on listening and psychotherapy, and of Barton (1974) on psychotherapy.

PART I


CONDUCTING EMPIRICAL

EXISTENTIAL - PHENOMENOLOGICAL

RESEARCH

# A.

# EMPHASIS ON GENERAL STRUCTURE:

## WHAT IS IT?

Empirical existential-phenomenological studies focus on the analysis of protocol data provided by research subjects in response to a question posed by the researcher which pinpoints and guides their recall and reflection. There is a clear cut general progression in the various genres of this type of research. We go first from unarticulated living (experiaction) to a protocol or account. We create a "life-text" which renders the experiaction in narrative language, as story. This is our data. Secondly, we move from the protocol to explication and interpretation. Finally, we engage in the process of the communication of findings.

**Step 1: The Problem and Question Formulation - The Phenomenon.** The researcher delineates a focus of investigation. One formulates a question, a "hypothesis." One has to name the phenomenon, i.e. the process in which one is interested in such a way that it is understandable to others. This is easy if the researcher names conventional and universally recognizable phenomena. It is difficult if the researcher studies phenomena that he or she has discovered and that have as yet no consensual meaning.

**Step 2: The Data Generating Situation - The Protocol Life Text.** In the empirical existential-phenomenological approach, researchers start with descriptive narratives provided by subjects who are viewed as co-researchers. The co-researcher reports on his or her own experience in writing. We query the person in his or her experiaction and engage in dialogue, or we combine the two, asking for a written description first and then engaging in an "elaborative dialogue" (von Eckartsberg, 1971).

**Step 3: The Data Analysis - Explication and Interpretation.** Once collected, the data are read and scrutinized so as to reveal their "psycho-logic," i.e. their structure, meaning configuration, principle of coherence, and the circumstances of their occurrence and clustering. In the traditional quantitative and measurement oriented approach, this step involves categorization and statistical treatment of group data organized in terms of sums, averages, percents, and measures of dispersion and convergence. In the qualitative existential-phenomenological approach emphasis is on the study of configurations of meaning in the life text involving both the structure of meaning and how it is created. This **expli-**

**cation** brings out implicit meanings by means of systematic reflection. Reflection is the return in consciousness to scrutinize a particular event via its record in memory or as a life text. As we reflect, we are guided by questions like: "In what way is this description revelatory of the phenomenon I am interested in?"

In order for the life text to reveal itself, we must approach it with an explicit concern expressed as a specific question. We call this the **explication guiding question** because it gives focus as we question the text about its meaning.

The explication guiding questions for the disclosure of **situated and general structures** are: How is what I am reading revelatory of the meaning of the phenomenon in this situation? This question yields the **situated structure** of the phenomenon. What does the text and/or the situated structure tell me about the phenomenon in its generality and universality? What is its meaning essence? This more universalizing question yields the **essential general structure** of the phenomenon.

Wertz (1984) discusses the problems of phenomenological sensemaking or explication in conducting empirical existential-phenomenological research under the heading of a) the general stance of the researcher, b) the active operations of empirical reflection on the individual example of the phenomenon, and c) the operations used to achieve generality of understanding.

As far as the stance is concerned what is important is:

1. Empathic presence to the described situation;
2. Slowing down and patiently dwelling;
3. Magnification, amplification of details;
4. Turning from objects to immanent meanings;
5. Suspending belief and employing intense interest.

With regard to the use of active cognitive operations what is involved is:

1. Recognition and utilization of an "existential baseline";
2. Distinguishing constituents;
3. Reflection on judgment of relevance;
4. Grasping implicit meanings;
5. Relating constituents;
6. Imaginative variation;

7. Conceptually guided interrogation;
8. Psychological languaging.

As to the explication and articulation of the phenomenological findings as universal insights into and constituents of the phenomenon, Wertz (1984) considers the following features to be essential:

1. **Finding general insights in individual reflections.** Since general features of the phenomenon are included in individual cases, the researcher may interrogate a single individual structure and find immanent generality.
2. **Comparing previously analyzed individuals.** In comparing individual psychological structures of her phenomenon, the researcher discards divergences and retains convergences in her considerations of generality.
3. **Generation and imaginative variation of new instances.** In order to extend general insights beyond the previously analyzed individuals, the researcher personally recollects and fancies new examples and counter-examples of the phenomenon to more incisively delineate the essential constituents and boundaries of her specific level of generality.
4. **Explicit formulation of generality.** The researcher formulates her general knowledge of the phenomenon in a language which describes the specified diversity of instances included in the general class under consideration, whether it be a specific group, general type, or universality. (p. 24)

**Step 4: The Presentation of Results - The Formulation.** One's research findings must be presented in public form for sharing and criticism. These formulations present what we have called the "essential constituents" or the structure of a phenomenon, articulating what "it really is" as a human meaning.

Two different kinds of communication networks are involved in the presentation of results: the participants in the research themselves and fellow researchers. The "subjects" get a "debriefing" about the experiment in everyday language; while the "fellow experts" in the researcher community, who share the professional relevancy structure and interest in the phenomenon, are communicated to in their shared expert language or professional idioms.

We will present five examples of empirical existential-phenomenological research in this part in order to show, in detail, how this research
is done and what variety exists within this approach. What are the specific steps of "data-processing," of steps of reflection, involved? How do
we arrive at universal structural characterizations of the phenomenon?
What kinds of results can we expect to encounter?

In line with the intentions of this book to present an overview of
the **spectrum** of qualitative methods for the analysis of life-world experience and to identify some of the major **research genres** we have condensed and summarized the research work. For a full appreciation of the
differentiatedness and subtlety of this kind of research the reader must
turn to tyhe original publications referred to in the text.

### § 1.--ON FEELING REALLY UNDERSTOOD: A. VAN KAAM.

Van Kaam (**Existential Foundations of Psychology,** 1966) is the founder and
originator of the existential-phenomenological empirical psychological
approach at Duquesne University. He characterized "empirical phenomenology" as a "return to the existential data." About phenomenological results in general, van Kaam says: "Research performed in this way is pre-
empirical, pre-experimental, and pre-statistical; it is experiential and
qualitative" (p. 295). In Chapter ten of his 1966 book: "Application of
the Phenomenological Method," he reports on his Ph.D. research at Western
Reserve University in 1958. Doing his dissertation at that time within a
traditional quantitative research-oriented psychology department and
within a Rogerian Client-Centered clincial orientation van Kaam chose to
develop his methodology as a variant of **content analysis,** a traditional
quantifiable research methodology. However, being also interested in the
qualitative and meaning-oriented philosophical approach of existential-
phenomenolgoy, he chose to do his research **both** quantitatively **and** qualitatively using a large sample of subjects in his procedure. Let us look at
the steps in his research procedure:

(1) **The Problem and Question Formulation: The Phenomenon.** Van Kaam
(1966) took his topic and focus of investigation from within a clinical
psychology context - research in psychotheraphy - and the specific frame
of reference of a Rogerian Client-Centered approach. Van Kaam reports:

I have selected one relatively simple concrete phenomenon that
appears in psychotherapy. The patient at times "feels really under

stood" by the therapist. What is the fundamental structure and meaning of this experience of feeling understood? (p. 298)

In order to shed light on this problem, Van Kaam needed to collect "data." Studying experiences, he needed descriptions of experiences, narrative descriptions. His first task, therefore, was to devise a research situation by means of which he could obtain such "data." He chose to formulate a specific question to be answered in writing by a large number of subjects, that he hoped would elicit responses (descriptions as "data") which he could then study as to their meaning-organizaton. Van Kaam thus devised the following instructions:

Describe how you feel when you feel that you are really being understood by somebody.
a. Recall some situation or situations when you felt you were being understood by somebody; for instance, by mother, father, clergyman, wife, husband, girl friend, boy friend, teacher, etc.
b. Try to describe how you felt in that situation (not the situation itself).
c. Try to describe your feelings just as they were.
d. Please do not stop until you feel that you have described your feelings as completely as possible. (pp. 320-321)

(2) **The Data Generating Situation: Collecting Descriptions.** Several criteria had to be met: Van Kaam knew that he wanted verbal descriptions of experiences in response to a fairly delineated and directed question. In other words, he wanted descriptive narratives. To obtain them he gave instructions so as to sharpen the focus of the descriptions - the phenomenon of being really understood by somebody. In terms of the writing of a response Van Kaam had to rely on the "natural story-telling ability" of his subjects (Von Eckartsberg, 1979). This is a taken for granted expressive power that existential-phenomenological psychologists have to rely on. We have to rely on the everyday meaning-making skill of everybody, to be able to express one's experience in words, in the form of a story. As Crites (**The Narrative Quality of Experience,** 1971) claims: the very organization of human experience seems to be given to us in awareness as narrative.

In terms of the justification for using the procedure of written descriptions, Van Kaam states the following:

1. Feeling understood is a relatively common human experience.
2. Common human experience is basically identical.
3. This basically identical human experience is expressed under the same label. (p. 310)

In terms of selecting subjects - the choice of the sample - Van Kaam reports on the following considerations that went into his strategy.

As we have said, the subjects who write down their prescientific explications ought not to be specialists in psychology. Nevertheless, their difficult task requires certain abilities and the fulfillment of certain conditions. The chief ones are:

a. The ability to express themselves with relative ease in the English language.

b. The ability to sense and to express inner feelings and emotions without shame and inhibition.

c. The ability to sense and to express the organic experiences that accompany these experiences.

d. The experience of situations in which the subject felt really understood, preferably at a relatively recent date.

e. A spontaneous interest in his experience on the part of the subject.

f. An atmosphere in which the subject can find the necessary relaxation to enable him to put sufficient time and orderly thought into writing out carefully what was going on within him. (p. 317)

To meet these criteria he selected a group of 365 subjects who were high school seniors and college students, in the Chicago area. He reports that his total sample contained:

150 Female High School Seniors
95 Male High School Seniors
60 Female College Students
60 Male College Students
_____
Total    365 Subjects    (p. 320)

Van Kaam invited the students as a whole school class to participate in the research. They were given anonymity for their descriptions.

In every school concerned, a class hour was set apart for this task. During this hour, the subjects were free to spend as much time as they wished on this project. (p.320)

Van Kaam reports having obtained satisfactory "elaborated descriptions" representing: "A wide variety of situations and personalities with corresponding variety in description." (p.319)

(3) **The Data Study Procedure: Explication.** Having obtained the "data," as narrative descriptions of experiences, the next task was to "work" with these data, to "analyze," i.e. to "study" and "process" these data so as to lead to Results, Findings, Conclusions. Van Kaam calls the procedure he uses: **Explication,** a term taken from existential-phenomenology. This "Scientific Phase of Explication" includes the following steps: "listing and preliminary grouping, reduction, elimination, hypothetical identification, application, and final identification" (p. 314).

Following standard praxis in content analysis procedures Van Kaam divided his total sample into subgroups beginning with N-80 in order to arrive at results which could then be checked by fellow researchers and tested for inter-judge reliability. The preliminary results were then tried out on the remaining samples in order to achieve further validation of the analysis. This multiple-sample procedure and concomitant inter-judge-reliability-check necessitates the complication of the steps called "hypothetical identification" and "application" in Van Kaam's procedure. These intermediary steps have not been used by later existential-phenomenological researchers who typically work with very small samples or even individual case studies, and who have given up the process of obtaining inter-judge reliability measurements relying instead on full presentation of all steps of the explication and on an appeal to immediate intuition on the part of the reader's immediate personal experience for a sort of "existential validation," testing any statement or proposition against the personal stock of experience which serves as the ultimate criterion of evaluation.

Van Kaam distinguishes six **Steps of Explication:**

3a) Listing and preliminary grouping:

The first operation of the scientist is to classify his data into categories. These categories must be the result of what the subjects themselves are explicating. Therefore, the scientist makes his initial categories from empirical data, in this case, a sufficiently large random sample of cases taken from the total pool of descriptions. (pp. 314-315)

The descriptions of experiences constitute a "collection of empirical material." They are stories which have to be prepared for scientific scrutiny. This is done by creating a **listing** of expressions culled from the subject's reports. The judges find and identify relevant descriptive expressions found in the sample and list them. Each listing articulates an identifiable **moment** of the experience. "The actual listing regarding each description must be agreed upon by expert judges."

To insure the validity of this procedure, he must strive for intersubjective concurrence with other experts concerning the agreement of these initial selections with the data taken from the random sample. After this, the researcher analyzes every descriptive expression found in the samples and lists them. When necessary, the initial lists and groups are supplemented by others in order to encompass every basically different statement made by the subjects. Finally, in order to be recognized as objectively valid, the actual listing must be agreed upon by expert judges. (p. 315)

The final listing presents a review of the various moments of the feeling of being understood as described by various subjects. It also presents the percentages of these various elements in this particular population, a possible clue to the predominant features of the phenomenon. (p. 315)

"Devising Categories for Classification" is a synthetic act on the part of the researcher, validated by independent co-researchers, but not further elaborated or specified in Van Kaam's report. The transformation from description to listing by the researcher also implies a change in focus from the emphasis of the **experience of each subject** as a coherent account to an emphasis on the **research phenomenon itself,** the topic: Feeling really understood. The data in the form of personal stories, i.e. narratives, give way to experience moments and to meaning clusters. The personal story becomes a general listing of expressions as universal meanings. The personal context of meaning is transcended.

**3b) Reduction:** The second step in the explication process is now undertaken and again tested for inter-judge reliability.

Now that the elements are laid out for him in a quantitative and qualitative fashion, the researcher can proceed with the second operation of the scientific explication. He reduces the concrete, vague, intricate, and overlapping expressions of the subjects to more precisely descriptive terms.

To a certain extent, this operation of reduction was already active in the initial listing and preliminary grouping.

By comparing the different elements and the different descriptions in which they are used, the researcher attempts to determine those elements that might probably be said to be constituents of the experience of feeling understood. (p. 315)

The reduction operation is a complicated and interpretative step because it involves a linguistic translation. From the subject's own words, Van Kaam, as the researcher, moved to his own formulation, to "more precisely descriptive terms." He gives the following examples of this:

When, for example, a subject writes, 'I feel a hundred pounds less heavy,' or 'a load is off my chest,' the psychologist may reduce this statement to 'a feeling of relief.' (p. 315)

We shall encounter this problem of linguistic transformation - typically from the subject's own words, i.e. first person singular, to the researcher's more technical and third person singular language - again later, because it lies at the heart of the existential-phenomenological process of explication.

**3c) Elimination:** The third step concerns a process of checking and elimination of non-relevant elements.

By means of the same operation, he now attempts to eliminate those elements that probably are not inherent in the feeling of being understood as such, but rather are complexes which include being understood in a particular situation, or which represent a blending of the feeling of being understood with other phenomena that most often accompany it. (p. 316)

Steps a, b, and c result in what Van Kaam calls Hypothetical Identification.

### 3d) Hypothetical Identification:

The operations of classification, reduction, and element-elimination result in the first hypothetical identification and description of the feeling of being understood. The identification is called hypothetical because it was hardly possible to take into account at once all the details of all the descriptions during the element-elimination. (p. 316)

This is referred to by Van Kaam as a hypothetical "formula."

**3e) Application:** We now enter a new phase "Application," which itself may have several steps within it. The work in this step consists in:

The application of the hypothetical description to randomly selected cases of the sample. This tentative application may possibly result in a number of cases of feeling understood that do not correspond to the hypothetical formula. It may be that the formula contains something more than the necessary and sufficient constituents of feeling understood. In this case, the formula must be revised in order to correspond with the evidence of the cases used in the application. (p. 316)

In other words, from the larger "data pool of description" (N=365!) new samples are progressively drawn so as to check the "hypothetical identification formulas" against new evidence. This is continued until a satisfactory level of redundancy is achieved. This then gives rise to Final Identification.

### 3f) Final Identification:

When the operations described have been carried out successfully, the formerly hypothetical identification of the phenomenon of feeling understood may be considered to be a valid identification and description. (p. 316)

The aim of the process of explication has been clearly stated by Van Kaam. It is to answer the question: "What are the necessary and sufficient constituents of this feeling? (p.301) This question is to be answered by the "Final Identification" which turns out to be a "synthetic description of the experience" bringing together, in a cluster, all constituents synthesized by the researcher into one description. On the way to this formulation Van Kaam reports on his findings.

(4) **Presentation of Results: The Formulation.** From step 3a) Van Kaam reports he arrived at a total of 157 different expressions listed under 16 different headings (p. 323). However, Van Kaam does not present the tables in the 1966 publication, but refers us to his unpublished dissertation.

From the second step (3b): Reduction, to which he now refers as the "Phenomenological Explication of the Data" (p. 323) he reports that:

In the operation of further "Reduction," each one of the 157 expressions had to be tested on two dimensions:

1) Does this concrete, colorful formulation by the subject contain a moment of experience that might be a necessary and sufficient constituent of the experience of really feeling understood?

2) If so, it is possible to abstract this moment of experience and to label the abstraction briefly and precisely without violating the formulation presented by the subject?

Next, all expressions discovered in this way, as either direct or indirect representatives of a common relevant moment of experience, were brought together in a cluster. This was labeled with the more abstract formula expressing the moment common to all.

The reduction resulted in nine probably necessary and sufficient constituents, each of them heading a certain number of expressions in which they were originally contained, and each of these expressions accompanied by the percentage of descriptions in which it was present.

The constituents which were identified in this way as being together necessary and sufficient for the experience under study had to be synthesized into one description which then identified the total experience of really feeling understood. (p. 324)

The **Results** of this work of explication are then presented by Van Kaam both as a Table and as a "Synthetic Description" with an amplification of each of the terms used in the description quoted here in full, so as to allow us to inspect the procedure close up. In this way, we arrived

at the necessary constituents of the experience under study, with the
following general operational definition: A necessary constituent of a
certain experience is a moment of the experience which, while explicitly
or implicitly expresssed in the significant majority of explications by a
random sample of subjects, is also compatible with those descriptions
which do not express it. Nine constituents were finally identified as
being together necessary and sufficient for the experience of "really
feeling understood." These are condensed in the following table.

===========================================================================

Table 1: Constituents of the Experience of "Really Feeling Understood"
Finally Identified, with Percentages of 365 Subjects Expressing Each
Constituent, Explicitly or Implicitly.

| Constituents of the Experience of "Really Feeling Understood" | Percentages Expressing the Constituents |
|---|---|
| 1) Perceiving signs of understanding from a person | 87 |
| 2) Perceiving that a person co-experiences what things mean to subject | 91 |
| 3) Perceiving that the person accepts the subject | 86 |
| 4) Feeling satisfaction | 99 |
| 5) Feeling initially relief | 93 |
| 6) Feeling initially relief from experiental loneliness | 89 |
| 7) Feeling safe in the relationship with the person understanding | 91 |
| 8) Feeling safe experiental communion with the person understanding | 86 |
| 9) Feeling safe experiental communion with that which the person understanding is perceived to represent | 64 |

===========================================================================

The synthetic description of the experience of really feeling understood, containing these constituents, is given below, followed by a justification and explanation of each phrase of the description.

The experience of / "really / feeling understood" / is a perceptual-emotional Gestalt: / A subject, perceiving / that a person / co-experiences / what things mean to the subject / and accepts him, / feels, initially, relief from experiental loneliness, / and, gradually, safe experiental communion / with that person / and with that which the subject perceives this person to represent.

**The experience of:** The term "experience" is preferred to "feeling" because the data show that this phenomenon, commonly called feeling, contains perceptual moments too.

**really:** The adverb "really" added to "feeling understood" emphasizes the distinction between object and subjective understanding. The latter includes the "what it means to me" element and the emotional involvement of the subject.

**feeling understood:** This popular expression is maintained because it is used by most people when they express this experience spontaneously.

**is a perceptual-emotional Gestalt:** The data compel us to distinguish between perceptions and feelings (emotions), the former being predominantly object-directed, the latter subject-directed. But the perceptions and emotions are interwoven in experience; the term "Gestalt" implies that the distinction we make between perceptual and emotional moments does not correspond to a separation in reality.

**A subject, perceiving:** The perceptual moment is mentioned first because of its priority in the explications obtained. The feeling of really being understood presupposes the perception of understanding as it is evidenced by various behavioral signs of understanding.

**that a person:** The subject perceives that a "person," a fellow human being, understands him in a personal way. The understanding person is not experienced only as an official, a teacher, an adult or so on, but as being-a-person.

**co-experiences:** The understanding person shares at an emotional level the experiences of the subject understood. The prefix "co-" represents the awareness of the subject that the person understanding still remains another.

**what things mean to the subject:** The subject perceives that the person understanding experiences the events, situations, and behavior

affecting the subject in the way in which they affect him, and not as
they might affect others.

**and accepts him:** Even while sharing experiences of the subject
which the person understanding does not accept personally, he manifests exclusively and consistently genuine interest, care, and basic
trust toward the subject, whether or not the subject intends to
change his views, feelings, or behavior.

**feels, initially, relief from experiental loneliness:** The initial feeling of relief is the joyous feeling that experiental loneliness, a disagreeable perceptual-emotional Gestalt, is receding to the
degree that real understanding is experienced. The adjective "experiental" specifies that it is not primarily a physical loneliness, but
a being-alone in certain psychological experiences.

**and, gradually, safe experiental communion:** This expresses that
the subject gradually experiences that the self is in the relieved,
joyful condition of sharing its experience with the person understanding. "Safe" emphasizes that the subject does not feel threatened
by the experience of sharing himself.

**with that person:** The deep personal relationship between the
subject and the person understanding is prevalent not only in the
perceptual, but also, and still more fundamentally, in the emotional
area. Therefore our synthetic description not only opens, but also
closes with a reference to this person-to-person relationship.

**and with that which the subject perceives this person to repre-
sent:** When the person understanding typifies for the subject a certain segment of mankind, or perhaps all humans, or all beings, i.e.
humanity and nature, or the all-pervading source of being, God, then
the subject will experience communion with all those beings which are
exemplified for him by the person understanding, and do this to the
degree that this person is perceived as their representative.
(pp. 324-327)

If we compare the existential-phenomenological work of Van Kaam with
a more traditonal approach in psychological content-analysis work, for
instance McClelland's work on the Need for Achievement (McClelland, **The
Achievement Motive**, 1953; Brown, **Social Psychology**, 1965), we can note
several similarities and several crucial differences. What is identical in
the two ways of proceeding is the shared starting point: the collection of
data as descriptive stories in response to a task given by the researcher.

McClelland uses adapted pictures of the Thematic Apperception Test (TAT) and asks several leading questions which are to be answered. Van Kaam uses many subjects, "large sample," similar to the traditional measurement oriented approach. The more subjects, the more confident the traditional researcher feels about the validity of his data and the generalizability of his findings.

Another identical commitment is the use of independent judges to establish inter-judge reliability and thus achieve a degree of objectivity and measure of consistency in the tradition of the empirical scientific discipline.

What is crucially different however, and a consequence of the existential-phenomenological orientation which is suspicious of attempts to bring in and in a sense "impose" a pre-conceived theoretical scheme on the data, although in any linguistic approach this can never be fully prevented, is the insistence by Van Kaam to let the **"experience moments"** of the phenomenon reveal themselves from the description, as much as possible. Husserl gave us the injunction: **"Back to the things themselves!"** and existential-phenomenologists generally are convinced and work on the assumption that the data, i.e. narrative descriptions, reveal their own thematic meaning-organization if we, as researchers, remain open to their guidance and speaking, their disclosure, when we attend to them.

Empirical existential-phenomenologists, therefore, reject the praxis of using coding manuals which allow a categorization and subsequent quantification of the data, the development of a measure which can then be applied in the typical traditional psychological research campaign of correlational proliferation to all other established psychological measuring tools.

Content analysis in the existential-phenomenological approach becomes a procedure of **qualitative analysis**, of "hermeneutics," i.e. the study of implicit meanings that are to be explicated by verbal means and illuminated from within by virtue of their inherent experienced "psycho-logic" (meaning). Existential-phenomenologists shy away from the obvious impositions of explicit theoretical schemes in order to "interpret" the data because this procedure often covers up more than it reveals and in its most extreme development leads to the shortcoming of being a self-fulfilling prophecy, incapable of discovering anything new and not already contained within its conceptual definitional framework.

Traditionalists might object and say that they all go through an "inductive phase" of data study beginning with description or pilot data in order to construct their coding manual. In this sense, they can indeed be said to all go through the inaugural existential-phenomenological step: **to let human experience speak!** But that very initial inductive step, at the origin of all research, is all that traditional and existential-phenomenologists have in common. Very early, then, in the research work, in the study process, there is a decisive parting of the ways, toward **numbers** and **quantification** on the part of **traditionalists** who conceive of psychology in the model of a "natural science," and toward **meanings** by **existential-phenomenological** researchers who understand psychology to be a "human science."

We might add that psychological measures, scores, also are human meanings. They are fixed meanings, tied to operational definitions and specific acts using measuring instruments -test performance- . In that context and as predictive and correlational possibilities measurement has value. But the meaning of the psychological dimensions studied and how this meaning is lived in actual personal experience is a task that precedes any form of measurement, to which traditional psychology does ot address itself and which has become the focus and subject matter of exis-tential-phenomenology.

In this sense Van Kaam's study sheds light on the general experienced meaning of the lived process of "being really understood" as perceived moments in a person to person relationship. As Van Kaam himself suggests, one could, upon this clarified basis, develop all kinds of measurements.

### §2.--ON THE PHENOMENA OF LEARNING: P. COLAIZZI

Working under the direction of, and in collaboration with Giorgi, Paul Colaizzi produced a master's thesis (1966) and Ph.D. disseration (1968) devoted to an empirical phenomenological investigation of learning as experienced from the perspective of the learner. In 1973, Colaizzi inte-grated this work in terms of a number of distinctions he made regarding the methodological and epistemological issues involved in doing existen-tial-phenomenological research, and published an interesting book en-titled: **Reflection and Research in Psychology: A Phenomenological Study of Learning.** Before its publication many of the concrete issues involved in doing empirical existential-phenomenological research were only implicitly recognized and often overlooked. For instance, in reviewing Van Kaam's work (1958), Colaizzi (1973) observed that properly speaking, it was indeed **empirical** and even **phenomenal,** but not yet fully **phenomenological,** because it did not penetrate into the implicit horizons of the descriptions gathered, and stopped short of developing a complete **structural** explication of its phenomenon.

In Colaizzi's terms what Van Kaam's studies produced were **fundamental descriptions** (FD's) rather than **fundamental structures** (FS's). Each is a kind of research finding belonging to its own epistemological level, such that investigations at the phenomenal level yield FD's whereas those at the phenomenological one yield an FS. This distinction of "levels of subject matter" is an important but difficult one. The phenomenal level is that at which subjects live through and describe their experience; it involves what happens explicitly for them. Keeping in accordance with Husserl's dictum "back to the things themselves," a reflection on the implicit and structural dimensions of subject's descriptions shifts the researcher from the phenomenal level (that of **the experience of the phenomenon**), to the phenomenological level, where the focus is on **the phenomenon that was experienced**, the "what" that is being researched. In his book, Colaizzi (1973) further sharpens this distinction:

> The structure of an experiential phenomenon need not coincide with a description of that same phenomenon as it is experienced by a subject, because the former is largely implicit and the latter is of a more explicit nature. After all, just as the description of a particular essence is not identical to the essence of a particular description, the FS and the FD of a single experiential phenomenon are not identical. (p. 32)

When a researcher focuses on the phenomenon **as it was experienced** and culls out the essence of that description, he has a fundamental description (an FD) ; in order to arrive at a fundamental structure (an FS), he must interrogate the implicit dimensions of his data, focusing on the essential elements which **constitute the phenomenon** through their internal relations with another.

According to Colaizzi, the fundamental structure of a phenomenon may be accessed via two different types of reflections: 1) **Individual Phenomenological Reflection** (IPR) in which the researcher uses only his or her personal experiences as "data," amplified through "free imaginative variations," and 2) **Empirical Phenomenological Reflection** (EPR) in which the researcher performs his systematic reflections upon a body of descriptive protocols which have been collected from subjects. As will be recalled, the phenomenological philosophers (who did not "trouble" themselves with the descriptions of subjects) preferred individual reflections, believing this would be sufficient to uncover the essence of phenomena. Whereas the more empirically minded phenomenological psychologists had been skeptical of the completeness of such an approach and thus eliminated self-reflection, Colaizzi reintroduced it into empirical research, considering it a necessary first step which would reveal the researcher's own pre-comprehension of the phenomenon. This would be of help to other researchers who might wish to follow up on one's work, as well as providing a starting point for the reflections upon subject's protocols.

In his book on learning, Colaizzi organized all his various distinctions, and arrived at an order in which he felt empirical phenomenological research logically ought to procede, namely:

1) Discovering an FS by Individual Phenomenological Reflection,
2) Obtaining an FD by the method of Phenomenal Study,
3) Obtaining an FD via Empirical Phenomenological Reflection,
4) Discovering an FS via Empirical Phenomenological Reflection.

The following is a summary version of how Colaizzi applied these steps in his work on learning. Since in many instances the detail of his findings are too extensive to reproduce, the interested reader is referred to the 1973 book. What is included below is for illustrative purposes only, and is not meant to do justice to the phenomenon of learning itself.

**1) Discovering an FS of Learning by the Method of IPR.** Colaizzi began his research by setting himself a learning task - to learn the content of Spengler's book: **The Decline of the West.** Reflecting on his experience of this task (which is the method of Individual Phenomenological Reflection), and performing the appropriate imaginary variations, Colaizzi was able to articulate the following fundamental structure (FS), as a preface to his empirical investigations: "Learning is. . . that activity whereby the learner extracts from material his learned content, which is a meaning-idea of which he had no previous knowledge and which he posits as true" (p. 59).

**2) Obtaining an FD of Learning by the Method of Phenomenal Study.** In this phase, Colaizzi set about to collect descriptive data on learning from subjects who had been given an actual learning task. Working in a laboratory setting, Colaizzi used tasks which were both traditional to learning experiments (e.g. memorizing nonsense syllables; solving problems) and non-traditional (e.g. disassembling and reassembling a gun; learning to walk on crutches). The data gathering was organized such that each of 50 subjects would fill out a questionnaire after having satisfactorily completed one task. Criteria (such as memorizing all ten non-sense syllables, or correctly assembling the gun within two minutes), were employed with each task. Since there were ten tasks in all, Colaizzi distributed his subjects so as to receive 5 descriptions for each task.

The questionnaires employed consisted of various open-ended items inquiring about the "changes that occurred" during the course of doing the activity. In order not to prejudice the subjects' responses, the word "learning" was never mentioned. Instead, the questions centered around requests for detailed descriptions of any changes that did occur, asking the subject to distinguish between changes that occurred in himself and those which occurred in the activity, wherever this distinction was possible. Moreover, to account for the constituting role played by the experimental stiuation (i.e. "demand characteristics"), subjects were also asked to describe fully what they believed the purpose of the investigation and the questionnaire itself to be.

With his data gathered, Colaizzi began the reflective work of interrogating the subjects' descriptions, with the aim of deriving a fundamental description (FD). The general process by which Colaizzi accomplished this was organized in terms of the following explication guiding questions:

1) Each statement and expression contained in the original protocols was considered with respect to its significance for the fundamental description of the phenomenon in question (i.e. learning): those that were relevant were retained and those that were clearly irrelevant were discarded.

2) All relevant statements were then classified into naturally forming categories and all repetitive statements were eliminated.

3) The remaining relevant statements were then translated from the raw form in which they were presented in the original protocols to clear and succinct expressions or components.

4) Finally, the components were arranged into a series of statements which was accepted as the FD of the phenomenon of learning obtained by the method of Phenomenal Study (PS).

The fundamental description yielded in this segment of Colaizzi's research is given on p. 71 of his 1973 book. Excerpting from that articulation, we find learning involves:

> An increase of intellectual knowledge, or of bodily or intellectual skill in a task activity, or the discovery of an efficient though possibly slow method for executing the task activity, which is

manifested in. . . cognitive changes and/or performance changes, these changes being affected by the methods employed which methods themselves change, and are accompanied by affective components that are interrelated with the cognitive and performance changes, by personal components, by bodily components, by temporal components, and by situation components, and there is an awareness of all the changes and of all their accompanying components. (p. 71)

Colaizzi then went on to elaborate these changes, detailing cognitive, performance, affective, personal, bodily, temporal, and situational components, as well as the awareness the subjects experienced of all the changes taken as a whole.

**3) Obtaining a FD via Empirical-Phenomenological Reflection.** It soon became apparent to Colaizzi that different emphases could be given to the fundamental description of a phenomenon, or, put differently, he realized that a phenomenon never has just one FD that captures it completely. For him, FD's could always be brought towards either of two ideal limits, one aiming at an **extensiveness of detail,** the other at an **intensiveness of substance.** Applying the method of Empirical Phenomenological Reflection (EPR) to the questionnaire data gathered from the learning tasks described above, Colaizzi sought to generate these two different types of FD's, via the following phases:

1) The first step was simply the realization that the search for an **extensive** FD involved sacrificing substance for the sake of including as much detail as possible from the relevant source statements, whereas opting for a **substantial** FD necessitated sacrificing detail in order to achieve as substantially intensive a description as possible. Colaizzi's recognition was of the importance of "both poles of the continuum," and the need to present not one, but two FD's of learning.

2) Having made the above procedural decision, Colaizzi next reflectively interpreted every relevant statement from the questionnaires to determine the meaning that it expressed, and each unique, i.e. non-repetitive meaning-expression was listed.

3) Next, each meaning-expression was interrogated with respect to its significance for every other meaning-expression, thus resulting in interrelated clusters of meaning-expressions.

4) Next, the recognition that the clusters of meaning-expression exhibited an interdependency demanded that they be synthesized into a

single theme, constituted equally by each of them, which was thus accepted as the **extensive** FD of learning obtained by the method of EPR.

5) Abstracting all specifics from the interrelated clusters of meaning-expressions obtained in phase 3 above, resulted in the **substantial FD** of learning obtained by the method of EPR. (pp. 75-77)

The interested reader may locate Colaizzi's FD's of learning on pp. 81-82 of his 1973 book. The extensive FD seems to focus most upon the general progression from inept to efficient participation in the learning activity (i.e. the task begins as awkward, error-ridden, and forced, etc. and progresses to automatic, easy and errorless, etc., whereas the subject's body loses its initial focus as an uncomfortable, aching burden, and eventually blends effortlessly into the performance), whereas the substantial FD uses a more psychological terminology to discuss participation in a learning activity as no longer an isolated event, but instead as "the nexus of a temporally extended stiuation that is constituted by emotional, mental and physical relations to previous and subsequent activities." (pp. 81-82)

4) **Discovering the Fundamental Structure (FS) by the Method of Empirical Phenomenological Reflection (EPR).** This last step in the procedure of examining the phenomenon of learning entailed reflecting upon the fundamental description (FD) of learning obtained by the preceding operation in order to reflectively explicitate its implicit structure. This structure, as a **fundamental structure** (FS), was obtained by the method of Empirical Phenomenological Reflection (EPR) focussing on the data provided by the **extensive fundamental description** because of the richness and amount of empirical data it contained.

Regarding the explication-guiding question for the FS via EPR:

This involved a dialogue constituted on the one hand by each of the themes, and on the other, the reflective interpretation of them in terms of what they express as fundamental for learning. (1973, p. 83).

**Execution and results of the method of Empirical Phenomenological Reflection directed to the discovery of the Fundamental Structure of learning.** In general, the themes extracted from the extensive FD are related to one another as fiullows. That to which learning participation is directed is first the total situation and then the content of the learning situation inasmuch as this content, initially unknown, becomes known and this participation is manifested in improved performance, the methods employed by the learner to execute this participation are determined by whatever motivational factors are present, and these motives in turn are determined by the learner's acceptance of and attitudes towards the content as it is integrated in what is viewed by the learner as the total learning situation, inclusive of its temporal references and emotional qualities.

However, even if it is acknowledged that the above themes as they are related to one another are indispensable conditions for participation in a learning activity, it must be realized that they are indispensible only because and to the extent that they directly refer to learning participation which itself is prereflective. For example, the progression of performance from aching and awkward, etc., is not itself learning, but is the manifestation of successful participation in learning activity. Thus the manifestation by performance of this participation does not in itself define learning since learning is constituted by participation as well as by performance. Moreover, since this participation is disrupted by the learner's awareness of it, and yet since it does nevertheless proceed, then learning participation occurs at a prereflective level. Likewise to his presence to the content of the learning situation, the learner's movement from involvement in the total learning situation, expresses that the former is but a necessary prerequisite for the latter, learning participation proper.

Accordingly, although learning participation is impossible without these conditions, they are not intrinsic aspects of the participation itself: they are the necessary conditions for participatio but are not themselves participation. In order, then, to capture that which sufficiently distinguishes and identifies learning, these conditions must be set aside in order to focus on actual participation in learning.

Regarding this participation, it is essentially the learner's relation to the content of the learning situation. The relation of the learner to the content defines the very existence of the learning participation. That is, learning participation is directed to the content, specifically, the content as it is constantly given to the learner in new perspectives, these perspectives being co-constituted by the learner as opposed to being restricted to the physical characteristics of the content and of the learning situation. This co-

constitution is determined by what the content means to the learner, whether it is personally, functionally, or emotionally relevant or insignificant. Furthermore, since the perspectives thusly determined in turn determine the motivation of and methods employed by the learner to co-constitute further perspectives of the content, learning participation thus expresses the circular process between the development of perspectives of the content and the learner's co-constituting of these perspectives.

If, then, organization of the content is defined as "the learner's co-constituting of new perspectives of the content, regardless of whether the nature of the content is physical, cognitive or bodily, by a process of disclosing its references to and contexts within which it can be harmoniously integrated," then the FS of learning discovered by the method of EPR may be formulated as follows: the prereflective organizing of a to-be-learned content whereby that content is apprehended by the learner from a new perspective. (1973, pp. 84-85)

Collaizzi presents the variety of research options and operations in terms of a schematic representation. Each operation is valid in its own right and yields a particular set of results so that the fruit of the labor is a pluralistic characterization of essential dimensions and facets of the phenomena which are interdependent and mutually enriching. All of the results together shed light on the meaning of the phenomenon of learning as experienced by the subject from the actor point of view.

**Schematic presentation of operations.** At this point, the function of the four operations may be rendered more clearly by depicting them schematicallyt; thus a schematization of the relationships among (a) the various methods; (b) their corresponding procedures; (c) types of subject matter with a typical finding concerning the nature of the learned-content that were established in this investigation is provided in Table 2 (p. 85)

==

**Table 2.** Methods, Procedures and Types of Subject Matter involved in Research in Phenomenological Psychology

| Method | Procedure | Subject Matter |
|---|---|---|
| IPR | Individual reflection without empirical data | Perspectival FS; leaned-content as, e.g., an affirmed meaning-idea |
| PS | Analysis of empircal data without recourse to re-course to reflection | Organization of empirical data, but no definitive results; learned-content as e.g., network of facts |
| EPR | Reflection on organized, explicitly empirical data | Multiple FD's; e.g., personal involvement in learned content |
| EPR | Reflection on implicit dimensions of organized empirical data | Perspectival FS; learned content as e.g., co-constantly emerging pre-reflective meanings |
| Combined IPR and EPR | Individual reflection without empirical data **and** reflection on implicit dimensions of organized empirical data | Comprehensive FS; learned-content as, e.g., an affirmed meaning-idea **and** co-constituted, constantly emerging pre-reflective meanings (1973, pp. 85-86) |

========================================================================

In this complex study of the issues, levels, and strategies of existential-phenomenological research procedures regarding the phenomena of learning Colaizzi clarifies two important issues: the **plurality-individual difference** and the **empirical-reflective** difference. We can approach the study of any experience by drawing on our **individual stock of knowledge and personal experience** which includes all that we know including our socially mediated theoretical knowledge and our power of imagining human possibilities on the basis of this knowledge. We can also utilize **other people's reports** and descriptions or answers to a questionnaire to gather experiential protocols or data from a **plurality of subjects** to be reflectively analyzed. In some sense we are always dealing with a combination of these two in that personal experience is always social and also in that event the study and interpretation of others' experience occurs within the the at least implicit context of the researcher's own precomprehension and understanding. Similarly, although the empirical-reflective difference can be established as an ideal postulate, it can never be sustained in a completely successful manner because empirical-factual reporting already implies some reflective-organizing and even the most universal and abstract of formulations appears within horizons of concrete-factual-empirical references in the mutually interpenetrating dialectic of living and thinking. It is instructive to keep these conceptual distinctions in mind when formulating a phenomenologically based qualitative research-strategy. What is the source of our data? Is it one's own experience or the reports of a plurality of subjects? What is the level of analysis? Are we talking about empirical summary-descriptions or the results of content analysis (the phenomenal level of fundamental descriptions) of the phenomenological level of structural analysis which articulates the minimally necessary constituents and defining characteristics of a phenomenon: the fundamental structure, as articulated by the reflective work of the phenomenological researcher.

In the provocative comparative discussion of the results in the last part of his book, Colaizzi presents a detailed and sophisticated argument both for the distinctiveness of each of the operational steps of the method and for the interdependency and complementarity of the results. The difference between the findings regarding the **fundamental description** (FD) and the **fundamental structure** (FS) is see to arise from a difference in focus on two layers of existence: **reflective** and **pre-reflective** life. Whereas the FD is a description of the subject matter in its reflective dimension which is thematically present to the subject's experience and can thus be directly reported upon request, as an appearance, the FS represents a structural elucidation of the pre-reflective dimensions which cannot be directly accessed by the subjects but which can be revealed to and elucidated by the reflective explication of the investigator by an act of interpretive reading.

Colaizzi's statements regarding the issue of the relationship between reflective and pre-reflective dimensions of human experience raise some important methodological issues. Can one never be present and privy to the pre-reflective dimensions of one's experience? Is it necessary to artuculate the pre-reflective dimensions after the fact, in the manner of the theory of the retrospective constitution of meaning (Schutz, 1962)? Does the pre-reflective have to be articulated in phenomenological-conceptual terms as fundamental structures? Can there be an experiential alternative to reflective phenomenological work in the direction of an "increasing effort of attention" or of an "intensification of consciousness" a la Thevanaz (1962)? Even if a new structural meaning dimension is discovered reflectively and retrospectively, does not this insight become a permanent prospective horizon of meaning that enriches the experience of the subject's thematic field (Gurwitsch, 1965) irrevocably?

Regarding the differences between the fundamental structure (FS) via the method of Individual Phenomenological Reflection (IPR) articualted as ". . . that activity whereby the learner extracts from material his learned content, which is a meaning-idea of which he had no previous knowledge and which he posits as true" (1973, p. 100), and the Fundamental Structure (FS) via the method of empirical phenomenological reflection (EPR) articulated as: ". . . the pre-reflective organization of a to-be-learned-content is apprehended by the learner from a new perspective which disclose different aspects of the total phenomenon of experienced learning. (1973, p. 100)

We will see in the following sections how the issues formulated by Colaizzi were selectively emphasized and elaborated by others who subscribed to a basically **empirical-reflective strategy.** They all collect "data" and they all "analyze" the data reflectively although there is much variation with regard to the particular steps taken in the actual research procedures. In this development some of the rigorous distinctions worked out by Colaizzi between FD and FS and between IPR and EPR, between a phenomenal and a phenomenological study were given up or transformed. Giorgi (1975), for instance, worked out a series of steps of analysis which progress from "raw data," i.e. descriptions of experiences, to an articulation of constitutive **meaning units** characteristic of a particular protocol description, to a formulation of the **situated structure** of a the phenomenon, i.e. the reflective articulation of the meaning-configuration for each subject and, finally, the **general structure,** i.e. the reflective-universal characterization of the phenomena across all subjects. In Colaizzi's terminology this involves working out the fundamental structure

(FS) by means of the method of empirical phenomenological reflection (EPR) and utilizing the distinction between **individual experience** expressed by the **situated structure** and that of the "**plurality of subjects**" expressed by the **general structure.**

Compared to Colaizzi, Giorgi's research progression aims at a more clear-cut focus of results in that all the operations are designed to ultimately cull out **the** essential, general structure, i.e. a characterization of what "it" (for example: learning) essentially is, an aim that Colaizzi consideres unattainable when he says:

> According to Heidegger, when man discovers any phenomenon he simultaneously co-discovers the world. What is meant by this is that there is nothing that is wholly isolated unto itself, but rather it is always related to an infinite horizon or an unlimited system of references. Each insight into something is accompanied by new areas of opacity concerning it. Expressed otherwise, man's knowledge is essentially finite. Yet the fact that man cannot possess infinite knowledge of something, or that he cannot even possess all his potential knowledge of something immediately does not imply that his knowledge is "absolutely relative." It means only that what he knows is always and necessarily contingent, constantly in tension, awaiting further though never completed fulfillment. Accordingly, he must accept the idea of "absolutely absolute" knowledge as a chimera and satisfy himself with "relatively absolute" knowledge. In terms of a criterion for having articulated fully the fundamental structure of a phenomenon, this means that **the** fundamental structure is an absurdity. All that an investigator can hope to accomplish is to articulate how a phenomenon fundamentally is revealed to him from his finite perspective and submit this articulation to other concerned investigators who then reject it, modify it, complement it or temporarily accept it, and so on. Thus the endeavors of an individual investigator stimulates a dialogue between his results, a community of scholars and reality. There is no higher court of appeals for establishing a criterion for a fundamental structure than this dialogue. The reason for this is that a fundamental structure is an expression of an aspect of man as a transcendent being; and as a transcendent aspect, that which is expressed by the fundamental structure can never be fully captured by the laws which define, i.e., which definitely establish criteria for, a natural event. In the meantime, during the unending dialectical development and evaluation

of the fundamental structure, it can be measured against the cri-
terior of its fruitfulness. For example, does it accurately and
intelligibly reveal the phenomenon under investigation from within
the perspective of the current comprehension of it? Does it eliminate
confusions generated by the prevalent established system of knowledge
concerning it? (1973, pp. 98-99)

In this way of speaking Colaizzi expresses and anticipates the attitude of
a hermeneutical-phenomenological and of a dialogal approach - to be discussed later in this book - which is forever cognizant of the relativity
of its own perspective and of its role as a contributing voice to an
ongoing and ever changing dialogue. The fundamental structure of the
meaning of a phenomenon is the expression of a moment in the researcher's
vision and understanding based on tacitly accepted presuppositions and
situational circumstances. It is part of the hermeneutical work to critically examine, acknowledge and discuss these operative assumptions. Colaizzi's work gives us a sophisticated and differentiated vocabulary and
conceptual distinctions which can help us in defining these terms, tasks,
and difficulties of a qualitative human science research approach.

In his later work on phenomenological research and the phenomenology
of reading and existentially significant learning (1978) Colaizzi moves
into a dialogal-existential position. The emphasis is placed on the dialogue between the co-researchers in which the relevant contexts of operative presuppositions and the disclosure of existential contexts are explicated, revealing how they shape the person's understanding. For Colaizzi
phenomenological human research becomes: "existential therapy."

> Genuinely human research, into any phenomenon whatsoever, by
> seriously including the trusting dialogal approach, passes beyond
> research in its limited sense and occasions existential insight. This
> is nothing other than therapy. All human research, particularly
> psychological research, is a mode of existential therapy.
> Viewed as a mode of existential therapy, it can be understood
> why the phenomenologist has for so long maintained that human re-
> search into any particular phenomenon should shed light on the to-
> tality of the human situation, since it is clear that existential
> therapy should draw in the totality of the human person, e.g., his
> perceptions and cognitions, emotions and attitudes, history and pre-
> dispositions, aspirations and experiences, and patterns, styles, and
> contents of behavior. (1978, pp. 69-70)

Colaizzi argues that all research, including natural science research, should be human research:

>All research should be initiated by, engaged in with, and directed toward the clearing of **existential significance.**
>(1978, p. 70)

The co-researchers by uncovering their presuppositions have to discover and articulate the humanly significant context in which they conduct their investigation. "They must be able to make explicit the existential significance of their research," and take full responsibility of its self- and world-transformative consequences.

### §3.--ON THE LEARNING EXPERIENCE: A. GIORGI.

Giorgi (1975a) has developed another form of existential-phenomenological empirical research which has been very influential at Duquesne. However, Giorgi cautions us that there are many ways in which one can develop an empirical existential-phenomenological psychology. He states:

>In light of our introductory comments, it should not have to be emphasized that the method we are using as a demonstration is neither exclusive nor exhaustive and it should not be considered paradigmatic for all phenomenologically based research. It should be taken for what it is, one example of the application of phenomenology to psychology with some limited but valid generalizations of the value of phenomenology for methodological issues. (p. 83)

Being a theoretical and experimental psychologist with a traditional experimental psychology background, Giorgi has focused primarily on the topics of experimental psychology: perception and learning, and he is trying to reformulate these problems from an existential-phenomenological perspective leading to the articulation of "psychology as a human science" (Giorgi, 1970), and to develop an alternative human scientific and qualitative approach to psychological research. Giorgi has done much path-finding and programmatic work to bring this about.

In a series of theoretical and critical papers on the relationship of phenomenology and experimental psychology (1965, 1966, 1967), Giorgi pointed out the need for a new qualitative, human-scientific research methodology in psychology. In close but critical dialogue with the tradition

Giorgi argued that a rigorous phenomenological science of human experienced meanings is possible but that it has to develop its own methodology which involves the creation and collection of "unprejudiced verbal descriptions" as data, and the explicitation of meanings from the protocol in order to arrive at the formulation of the essence of the phenomenon under study. Giorgi explicitly accepts and affirms the goals of philosophical phenomenology to be an eidetic science of essences as valid for psychology also, and he proposes to apply this approach and method to the content area of psychological phenomena. Giorgi's own effort centered on the phenomenon of learning. He published an early example of the phenomenological approach to the problem of meaning and serial learning (1967) in which he demonstrated "the usefulness of applying a phenomenological interpretation to an empirical study" (p. 98) adding a qualitative dimension - experiential reports and their analysis - to the traditional focus on behavioral acts. Thus, in this early paper Giorgi argued for the complementarity and mutual enrichment of the two approaches, using traditional methods and content areas but complementing them with experiential data and the perspective and meaning of the subject, i.e. adding a "phenomenological corrective." Comparing the two approaches Giorgi summarized the two realms of the natural and human sciences in a table (See Table 3).

The "new vision for research in the human sciences" is based on a dialectic of the approach, i.e. the fundamental viewpoint toward man and the world that the scientist brings with him and which provides the foundation - the **method** and the **content** of the phenomenon that is being studied. Giorgi argued that the method is always developed in dialogue with the content or the phenomenon under study. (1970)

As compared to Van Kaam and Colaizzi with whom he is in dialogue, Giorgi, by 1975, as compared with his earlier work on learning (1967) has moved the focus of the content area of existential-phenomenological research psychology into life-worldly situations. The phenomenon is studied in the world and as part of the unfolding existence of the individual and the research is moved away from the contrivances of the individual and the research is moved away from the contrivances of the experimental psychology laboratory design which is an abstraction and artificial construal of real world experience. We can study the phenomena when and where they occur in the person's experience, and we can access this experience legitimately and scientifically in and through a retrospective, narrative account, an experiential protocol, a story, which constitutes our data.

==

Table 3

Factors Important for Research in the Natural Sciences and
Suggested Correctives for Parallel Paradigm for
Research in Human Sciences

| Realm of Natural Sciences | Realm of Human Sciences |
| --- | --- |
| Experimentation | Experimentation and Other Forms of Research Activity |
| Quantity | Quality |
| Measurement | Meaning |
| Analysis | Explication |
| Determined Reactions | Intentional Responses |
| Identical Repetition | Essential Phenomenon Known Only Through Manifestations |
| Independent Observer | Participant Observer |

========================================================================

We can say that empirical existential-phenomenological psychologists study life in and through texts, as "life-texts." What to do with these texts; how to read them, how to study, analyze, and amplify them, and how to disclose other, latent meanings within them? These hermeneutical questions and issues come into play when one does this kind of empirical phenomenological psychology. How does one get **results** from stories? It is the contribution of the work of the Duquesne group to have developed and published detailed and documented, step by step procedures for doing explication of meaning-essences called: **structures,** from reports, thus "operationalizing" hermeneutic activity whose aim is to enrich and deepen the meaning which is given by disciplined dialogue with the text. Whereas

hermeneutic studies usually address artistic and cultural products, we
have ventured to create the life-texts to be studied in the framework of
psychological research.

In two publications: (1) "Convergence and Divergence of Methods in
Psychology," 1975b and (2) "An Application of Phenomenological Method in
Psychology," 1975a, Giorgi reports on his empirical methodology. In the
second paper (1975b) he outlines his Data-Study and Explication-Procedure
as follows:

The Procedure for qualitative analysis is as follows:

1) The researcher reads the entire description straight through
to get a sense of the whole. A phenomenological interpretation of
this process would be that the researcher is present to the situation
being described by the subject by means of imaginative variation, or
by means of the meanings he apprehends through written language and
not that he is merely present to words on a page.

2) The researcher reads the same description more slowly and
delineates each time that a transition in meaning is perceived with
respect to the intention of discovering the meaning of learning. (the
research example discussed) After this procedure one obtains a series
of meaning units or constituents. A constituent is not an element;
the former means differentiating a part in such a way that one is
mindful of the whole, whereas the latter implies a contextless dis-
crimination.

3) The researcher then eliminates redundancies, but otherwise
keeps all units. He then clarifies or elaborates the meaning of the
constituents by relating them to each other and to the sense of the
whole. This process also clarifies why the specific meaning units
constituted in Step 2 were perceived.

4) The researcher reflects on the given constituents, still
expressed essentially in the concrete language of the subject, and
transforms the meaning of each unit from the everyday naive language
of the subject into the language of psychological science insofar as
it is revelatory of the phenomenon of learning. In other words, each
unit is systematically interrogated for what it reveals about the
learning process in that situation for that subject. It is at this
point that the presence of the researcher is most evidently present,
but he is needed to interpret psychological relevancy.

5) The researcher then synthesizes and integrates the insights achieved into a consistent description of the structure of learning. The structure is then communicated to other researchers for purposes of confirmation or criticism. (pp. 74, 75)

Giorgi's description parallels closely the steps of explication as outlined by Van Kaam except that he does no longer consider it fruitful to attempt any form of quantification in terms of frequencies of statements, nor does he think it necessary to collect data-descriptions from a large number of subjects. As a matter of fact, the actual description of the qualitative research method provided (1975b) tells us how to read and work with the individual protocol in its biographical integrity, in its situatedness. Unlike Van Kaam who pools his data after he has identified the "experience moments," Giorgi keeps the "meaning units" he identifies in each description together for each subject and then explicates that in terms of a "situated structure" (see below).

It is not surprising, therefore, that Giorgi presents a single case study of learning in his paper: "An Application of Phenomenological Method in Psychology," (1975b). Giorgi differentiates several levels of reflective analysis:

> The end result of the application of this procedure is one of a number of descriptive statements that capture the naive description in a more clarified and more psychologically relevant way. The descriptive statements can differ in terms of level, e.g. a Situated Structure of learning, which presents the situation as learned by the subject in concrete terms, or a General Structure, which describes the learned situation irrespective of concrete situations in which the learning took place. Each level of description has both strengths and weaknesses. The descriptive statements may also differ with respect to type. That is, most concrete descriptions fall between the universal and the individual and cluster at a level of generality that can be differentiated with respect to type, e.g. bodily language vs. cognitive learning and each type would necessitate a different descriptive statement. In sum, each descriptive statement, ideally, should both comprehend a large set of facts as well as deepen the understanding of the phenomenon under investigation. (p. 75)

Thus we obtain results on **two structural levels of meaning and generality** as **Situated Structure** and as **General Structure,** both answering "What is it?" questions and several **Types** of Structures answering to "How did it take place?" questions.

1) **The Problem and Question Formulation: The Phenomenon.** The research example presented comes from a research project on learning (Giorgi, 1975b):

> The basic idea is to try to discover exactly what constitutes learning for ordinary people going about their everyday activities and how the learning is accocmplished. (p. 84)

The eliciting question to obtain experiental data was:

> Could you describe in as much detail as possible a situation in which learning occurred for you? (p. 84)

2) **The Data Generating Situation - Descriptions.** In the actual research presented by Giorgi, the narrative description in response to the cited question, was not elicited in writing (as written description) but through an interview procedure with a lead-off question, i.e. by means of **"questioning dialogue."** This dialogue of the researcher with the subject was tape-recorded and then transcribed. This transcription constitutes the "data." In Table 4, Columns 1, 2, 3. and 4 (below) we present a juxtaposition of the various phases and types of data and results reported by Giorgi, including their transformations from one level of language into another, in a side-by-side presentation, so that the relationships between questions, descriptions, meaning units, and levels of structures become easily visible.

3 & 4) **The Data Study Procedure (Explication) and the Presentation of Results (The Formulation).** Giorgi writes:

> First one reads through the protocol to get the sense of the whole. The first step of the analysis itself is to try to determine the natural "meaning units" as expressed by the subject. The attitude with which this is done is one of maximum openness and the specific aim of the study is not yet taken into account. After the natural units have been delineated, one tries to state as simply as possible the theme that dominates the natural unit within the same attitude that defined the units. These results are presented in Table (4) 1.

(The Natural Units of Description and the Central Theme for each Natural Unit). (p. 87)

The issue of natural "meaning units" deserves some reflection and discussion. It is not clearly specified by Giorgi, but it involves the articulation of the **theme** - a verbal statement formuulated by the researcher that states the essence of meaning of the unit.

Cloonan (1971) in his thesis-work on decision making under Giorgi, has discussed this concept under the title of: **Intentional Units:**

> By 'intentional unit' is meant a statement made by the S which is self-definable and self-delimiting in the expression of a single, recognized aspect of S experience. For example, a S might reply to the question of how he arrived at choice of preferred task (e.g. math), 'Since I have always enjoyed working at numbers, I derive pleasure from math logic problems, reasoning problems that involve numbers, and math brain teasers.' The intentional unit here is: 'S has always enjoyed math problems.' This statement contains the essence of the statements thus far; it is not a reduction of S's experience. Where S to have added, 'I also find math challenging,' this would constitute a second intentional unit. An 'intentional unit,' therefore, is a statement of subject's experience in which there are collapsed redundancies of an aspect of S's reported experience. Every aspect of the experience is an 'intentional unit'. (p. 117)

Cloonan refers to lecture notes class (1966) to establish a reference. Over the years, however, natural "meaning units," Giorgi's coinage (1975), has become the preferred and unquestioned term used. It remains a problematical issue: What do you consider to be an **aspect of an experience?** Is it a unit of the behavioral act-intention, is it a psychological act? What kind of event is a "meaning unit"? The methodological step involved represents a transformation of the narrative first person experiential report into a declarative third person summary statement in the researcher's language formulation which becomes the basis for further reflections aiming at higher levels of universalization and more abstract meaning-comprehension.

Giorgi (1975b) continues with the delineation of the steps of the analysis and explication procedure:

The next step is to interrogate Table (4) in terms of the specific purpose of the study. If a study has a number of questions, these questions should be put to the data consecutively and should not be confused. To demonstrate this, let us first ask the question -'What is learning?' and then follow up with 'How was learning accomplished?' Therefore, the second step of the analysis is to look at the themes and the raw data from which they were taken with the specific attitude that asks 'What does this statement tell me about learning' or 'How does this statement reveal significance about the nature of learning?' If there is nothing explicit about learning within a given natural meaning unit, which is possible, then one simply leaves a blank. For some purposes it is important to know the meaning of the statement anyway or what function it serves in the total narrative, but this step is not followed here. The results of these interrogations are presented in Table (4) II (Expression of Central Themes in Terms Revelatory of the Structure (What) and of the Style (How) of Learning). (pp. 87-88)

Once the themes have been thusly enumerated, an attempt is made to tie together into a descriptive statement the essential, non-redundant themes. This can be done a number of ways, but it seems that at least two ways are valuable for general communication. One is a description of what we can call the situated level which means one that includes the concreteness and specifics of the actual research situation employed. The second one is a description at the general level. The general statement leaves out the particulars of the specific situation and centers on those aspects of learning that have emerged which, while not necessarily universal, are at least trans-situational or more than specific. These two sets of descriptions are presented in Tables (4) III and (4) IV. 'Structure' is the term used to describe the answer to the 'what is learning' question and 'Style' is used to describe the 'how did learning take place' answer. (p. 88)

For Giorgi, the systematic elaboration and answering of these two reflective questions: 1) What is the essential structure of. . . (Structure) and 2) How did this experience take place. . . (Style), constitutes the work of explication by means of which we arrive at the "final identification" (Van Kaam) or the "synthesis and integration into a consistent description of the structure of learning." (See Table 4)

Comparing Giorgi's approach to Van Kaam's, we can note the following: Giorgi does not use any quantification of his data nor inter-judge reliability checks. He engages, like Van Kaam, in a series of steps of explication from data to themes or "meaning units" ("experience moments" in Van Kaam's language), to structures. These steps constitute linguistic transformations of the materials from the subject's own words into professional psychological and explicitly phenomenological language. The description and rationale for this reads:

> I tried to read the description provided by the S without prejudice and tried to thematize the protocol from her viewpoint as understood by me. The interrogation that provided the above tables proceeded within the same phenomenological perspective. For me, again, this means that there were certain kinds of meaning that I allowed to emerge, and that I expressed these in the nascent language of phenomenological psychology (e.g., structure, style, meanings, situation, etc.), with all of the nuances implied by that particular context. Thus, these factors do not vitiate the findings but rather set the limits of the context in which they are valid. (p. 95)

While Van Kaam proceeded immediately from many descriptions to one general characterization to which all of the original descriptions contributed, Giorgi introduces several intermediary steps in order to distinguish the levels of situated structure which respects the integrity of each individual, and general structure, which characterizes the implicit universal structure of meaning true of all the individual descriptions. While this is plausibly demonstrated by Giorgi using a single case which is an account of a personal situated experience, it remains unclarified and undemonstrated how this two-level analysis is to be done beginning with several descriptions, a procedure often recommended and insisted upon in order to achieve representativeness and redundancy and to provide the opportunity to differentiate sub-types or varieties of types and styles of experiences reported by different contributors.

Comparing Giorgi's way of studying human phenomena with that of Colaizzi, we find that there are several differences: Giorgi is concerned with Fundamental Structures (FS) arrived at by means of Empirical Phenomenological Reflection (EPR), but he does not explicitly use Individual Phenomenological Reflection (IPR). In recent discussions Giorgi proposes the use of imaginative variation (part of EPR) in addition to structual analysis, although he has not explicitly operationalized this procedure.

## T A B L E  A :  G I O R G I ' S  E X P L I C A T I O N

| Instructions & Questions | Table I: The Natural Units of the Descriptions & The Central Theme of Each Unit | |
| --- | --- | --- |
| | Natural Unit | Central Theme |
| Could you describe in as much detail as possible a situation in which learning occured for you? | 1. The first thing that comes to mind is what I learned about interior decorating from Myrtis. She was telling me about the way you see things. Her view of looking at different rooms has been altered. She told me that when you come into a room you don't usually notice how many vertical and horizontal lines there are, at least consciously, you don't notice. And yet, if you were to take someone who knows what's going on in the field of interior decorating, they would intuitively feel there were the right number of vertical and horizontal lines. | 1. Role of vertical and horizontal lines in interior-decorating. |
| | 2. So, I went home, and I started looking | 2. S. looks for vertical and horizontal lines in her home. |

| Table II. Expressions of Central Themes Revelatory of the Structure (What) and the Style (How) of Learning | | Table III. Descriptions of Situated Structure and Situated Style of Learning | | Table IV. Descriptions of General Structure and General Style of Learning | |
|---|---|---|---|---|---|
| Central Themes Expressed as Revelatory of Structure (What) | Central Themes Expressed as Revelatory of Style (How) | Situated Structure | Situated Style | General Structure | General Style |
| 1. The awareness of vertical and horizontal li and ther importance for interior decorating as described by a friend was the content and one of the goals of the learning experience.

2. The subject looks for the lines in her | 1. Through a friend, S. becomes aware of lines.

2. S. begins to look for and finds a number of | S. becomes aware through a friend that rooms have vertical and horizontal lines and that these lines are important for interior decorating. Having acquired this knowledge, S. looks for and perceives the lines in her own living room and rearranges furniture | Through a friend S. becomes aware of the role of vertical and horizontal lines for interior decorating. Her friend provided S. with this knowledge and gave her a number of examples which enabled S. to perceive the lines for herself and to rearrange her own room in terms of them. S., | Learning is the ability to be present to, or exhibit the new according to the specific context and level of functioning of the individual. this awareness of the new takes place in an interpersonal context and it makes possible the sustained apprecia- | Learning for S. happened when she obtained knowledge from a significant other and concrete demonstration of this knowledge that related to a problem that bothered her for a long time. When S. found she could apply this knowledge to her own situation in her own way, taking into |

| Instructions & Questions | Natural Unit | Central Theme |
|---|---|---|
| | at the lines in our living room, and I counted the number of horizontal and vertical lines, many of which I had never realized were lines before. A beam . . . I had never really thought of that as vertical before, just as a protrusion from the wall. (Laugh) | |
| | 3. I found out what was wrong with our living room design: many, too many, horizontal lines and not enough vertical. So I started trying to move things around and change the way it looked. I did this by moving several pieces of furniture and taking out several knickknacks, de-emphasizing certain lines, and . . . it really looked differently to me. | 3. S found too many horizontal lines in living room and succeeded in changing its appearance. |

| Themes as Structure (What) | Themes as Style (How) | Situated Structure | Situated Style | General Structure | General Style |
|---|---|---|---|---|---|
| home and perceives and counts them. That a real perceptual change takes place can be seen from the fact that a beam is transformed from a protrusion to a line. | vertical and horizontal lines in a new situation, her living room. | in the room in accordance with her perception of the lines. Afterwards the room really looks different to her and this fact is confirmed by her husband, who, however, does not know why the room | however, was bothered by this problem for some time before her friend provided her with the knowledge. Then S. creatively applied the knowledge to her own situation (living | tion of a situation in a fuller way, or the emergence of behavior that reaches a different level of refinement in a sustained way or both. | account all the contingencies that the new situation offered, she felt that learning had been achieved. Thus S. learned by being attentive to another, |
| 3. The subject recognizes what is "wrong" with her room and rearranges it according to her perception of the lines. Once again a real | 3. S. sees what is "wrong" with her living room and rearranges it. | looks different. S. describes her own learning as knowledge application, and a certain way of looking and implicitly acknowledges that there may be levels of learning. Explicit | room). Application implied that knowledge was general but that she could effectively change the arrangement of the room within practical limits. | | plying for herself that knowledge which she received, with approval from a different significant other. |

| Instructions & Questions | Natural Unit | Central Theme |
|---|---|---|
| | 4. It's interesting because my husband came home several hours later and I said, "Look at the living room: it's all different." Not knowing this, that I had picked up, he didn't look at it in the same way I did. He saw things were moved, but he wasn't able to verbalize that there was a de-emphasis on the vertical. So I felt I learned something. | 4. Husband confirms difference, not knowing why. |
| What part of that experience would you consider learning? | 5. The knowledge part that a room is made up of horizontal lines. The application of that to another room: applying it to something that had been bothering me for quite a long time and I could never put my finger on it. I think the actual learning was what was horizontal and vertical about a room. The learning that was left with me was a way of looking at rooms. | 5. S. says learning in terms of interior decorating consists of knowledge and application. |

| Themes as Structure | Themes as Style | Situated Structure | Situated Style | General Structure | General Style |
|---|---|---|---|---|---|
| change is evident because the furniture is rearranged and the room appears di fferent to S.

4. Husband confirms change in room but is not aware of how or why.

5. S. verbalizes her learning exper ience in terms of knowledge, of vertical and horizontal lines, the application of that knowledge to another room, and a certain | 4. Husband confirms for S. that living room looks different and his inability to express why also confirms that she has learned.

5. By means of knowledge and application to something bothering S. for a long time that she could not figure out. Looking confirms she has learned. | awareness of specific criteria for determining the proper room arrangement were not present; only the general intention to rearrange the room. The readiness to learn about the relationship between lines and interior decorating made possible the recall of relevant past experiences about European cathedrals and their lines. | | | |

| Instructions & Questions | Natural Unit | Central Theme |
|---|---|---|
| Are you saying then that the learning was what you learned from Myrtis, what you learned when you tried to apply . . . ? | 6. Since I did apply it, I feel that I learned when I did apply it. I would have thought that I learned it only by having that knowledge, but having gone through the act of application, I really don't feel I would have learned it. I could honestly say, I learned it at that time. | 6. S confirms learning at level of knowledge, and affirms it more strongly in in terms of application. |
| Could you say in detail something about the application? Do you remember some of the things that were going on when you were working with your living room? | 7. I had counted the number of horizontal lines and I found there were too many. . . . | 7. S speaks about identifying lines in a room and gives example. |
| Could you specify more exactly what it was that Myrtis gave you? | 8. She gave me specific knowledge: "the horizontal and vertical lines." But had she stopped there I don't think I would have gone on because . . . she used an example of her room and we went through that together. She pointed out what parts of her room were horizontal and vertical and what points are often missed. | 8. Friend gave S knowledge of lines plus many examples of them. |

| Themes as Structure | Themes as Styles | Situated Structure | Situated Style | General Structure | General Style |
|---|---|---|---|---|---|
| way of looking. | | | | | |
| 6. S. affirms that both knowledge and application may be learning, with the latter more firmly confirmed. Implication of levels of learning. | 6. Once application was attempted it was considered decisive for learning. Before application S. thought knowledge was sufficient and would have called it learning. | | | | |
| 7. S. gives example of "new way of looking" that enables the knowledge of lines to be applied to her own room. | 7. S. creatively applied knowledge to her own room, e.g., she was not afraid to let rug be dominant horizontal line because she noticed it first. | | | | |
| 8. Via a friend's demonstration S. saw how one could | 8. Friend's demonstration of how knowledge of vertical | | | | |

| Instructions & Questions | Natural Unit | Central Theme |
|---|---|---|
| You could see it when she brought it up? | 9. Right. Actually, visually see it. The first thing that I did was go back to my room in the office and take a look around, but I didn't do any application there until later. My own home came first. | 9. S affirms it was possible to see the room lines visually. |
| By application you mean. . . ? | 10. Changing the lines. Changing what were on the horizontal and vertical lines. It was a matter of practicality: some things could be changed and some could not. One thing I actually did was take all the pictures down, and I looked at the walls. I had my lines, and I knew what I wanted to do, which was to have more vertical lines and fewer horizontal. Even walls have verticalness and horizontalness. | 10. S interprets application in terms of "changing" lines and describes how she wanted lines changed. |
| Did you have specific criteria? | 11. I could have had criteria - I could have measured the number of inches. I didn't do it. I just looked. | 11. S didn't formulate criteria although she could have. |

| Theme as Structure | Theme as Style | | | | | |
|---|---|---|---|---|---|---|
| move from knowledge of lines to concrete application. | and horizontal lines, including subtleties, could be applied was critical for learning. | | | | | |
| 9. Actual perception of lines precedes application of knowledge. | 9. S. could "see" lines never seen before. | | | | | |
| 10. The meaning of application specific to S.'s task is experienced and accomplished. Application means ability to transform a situation according to the knowledge acquired within practical limits. | 10. By concretely applying her knowledge to a real situation application meant changing lines with practical limits. | | | | | |

| Instructions & | Natural Unit | Central Theme |
|---|---|---|
| | 12. In another specific instance I didn't bother putting the picture up to see how it would have looked. I would have had to hammer a nail in. So there I had to imagine what it would look like. I had trouble imagining it and therefore I abandoned that idea. | 12. Imagining lines was more difficult for S. |
| When you first noticed the lines, what kind of balance did you want? | 13. I could not predict what goals I had in mind specifically, at all. I just started moving things. I knew my major goal, which was to change the balance. I could not have told you specifically, how much I wanted to change it or when I would be satisfied. After several of these moves, I saw that I was slowly accomplishing the goal, and . . . I stopped when it was aesthetically pleasing to my eye. | 13. S had only vague sense of goal that that became clear gradually and she stopped arranging the room when it was aesthetically pleasing to her. |

| Themes as Structure | Themes as Style | | | | | |
|---|---|---|---|---|---|---|
| 11. * | 11. * | | | | | |
| (12.) 11. Imagining changes not as easy as perceiving them. | (12.) 11. Imagining lines not as successful. | | | | | |
| (13.) 12. S. knew only major goal: to rearrange room so that it would be more aesthetically pleasing. Specific goals within that context were not posited and only emerged with the actual doing. | (13.) 12. Application means "knowledge" of only general goal, not of specifics. | | | | | |
| (14.) 13. S. can select significant aspects | (14.) 13. Selection of relevant past experience helps com- | | | | | |

| Instructions & Questions | Natural Unit | Central Theme |
|---|---|---|
| | 14. I remember once before in my life having been made aware of the fact that vertical lines do something, and that was in Europe touring all those different churches and it being constantly pointed out that the spires go up and try to reach the heaven. They're to go in an upward direction and this itself, just the lines, gives you a feeling of peace and trying to communicate with God, get up there, you're going into the spiritual realm of things, and . . . I never did apply that to any specifics. | 14. Information on European cathedrals from a prior trip comes to mind. |
| | 15. Yet now I can retrieve that incident because in a way it's similar to this. Now I'm ready to learn this. Before I didn't have an apartment to fiddle around with. | 15. S recalls earlier experience because she is now ready to learn it. |

| Themes as Structure | Themes as Style | | | | |
|---|---|---|---|---|---|
| of the past experience and relate to current situation. | prehend meaning of vertical. | | | | |
| (15.) 14. Readiness to learn about verticality and horizontality because of current situation makes specific recall possible. | (15.) 14. Readiness to benefit from past stems from present situation. | | | | |

* The situated and General Structure for meaning unit 11 are not printed in the text. Therefore, the numbering here in parentheses differs from the original.

Giorgi does not sustain the level-of-discourse distinction between Fundamental Description (FD) and that of Fundamental Structure (FS). Giorgi's Fundamental Themes are analogous to description on the FD level, but themes focus on part-meanings within the implicit context of the whole, and not on the integrated meaning description itself as in Colaizzi's FD.

Giorgi brings in another important distinction and order into the methodology by identifying the **Situated Structure,** and the **General Structure.** He works with individual experiences and protocols until he reaches the level of articulation of situated structure. Only then does he "universalize" or "essentialize," i.e. transcend the existentially situated specificity in favor of an essential trans-situational understanding. Another far-reaching change and feature of Giorgi's methodology is its emphasis on **life-world experience.** He studies learning as it happens to persons in their unique life-contexts, as a natural biographical task and experience. Using this approach the importance of the intersubjective dimension or the interpersonal context of learning has emerged as an important facet and structural feature of the phenomenon. As Pollio (1981) states regarding Giorgi's work:

> Learning 'happened' for E. W. when she was directly told something quite specific by an important other person about a problem situation that had been bothering her for a long time. The learning took place when she could apply that information to a new situation after having seen a few prior examples.
> Even though E. W. is only one person, a careful reading of her approach to learning yields some interesting results. For one, the interpersonal nature of human learning comes through loud and clear: Not only does E. W. learn about vertical and horizontal lines from her friend Myrtis, she finds confirmation for her new way of looking at things by comparing it with her husband's less precise statement that the 'room looks different.' A second important point is that learning is sensed by the learner as a 'new way of looking at things' that leads to new, previously impossible changes. Learning, from a first-person point of view, always seems to include a person's experiential history, for 'a new way of looking at things' implies that there was an 'old way.' In addition, learning outside the laboratory always seems to involve an interpersonal context. For learning to have occurred, the learner must perceive or behave in a new way with respect to his or her own personal history, a way that was not previously possible. (p. 163)

Giorgi's multi-level analyses are quite complex. In his view (1975a) they closely parallel the complexities of the multiple quantitative analyses that can be conducted in terms of numerical operations: as statistics, which yield "measures." The various qualitative analyses occur in terms of linguistic operations: as explications, which yield "end products." As Giorgi (1975a) says of this parallelism:

> I would describe what I have done as the development of a phenomenologically based procedure for the analysis of linguistic descriptions - as opposed to numerical descriptions. If there is a parallel with the achievements of numerical procedures it would be because a phenomenology of mathematics would lead to similar findings. In other words, the root or ground of both linguistic descriptive analysis and numerical descriptive analysis are ultimately in the perceptions and thoughts of man. It is this reflexive or self-referential movement that phenomenology tries to comprehend. (pp. 78-79)

Developing the implications of this parallelism, it would seem that the type of statistic used - the level of qualitative analysis pursued - would depend on the intention of the researcher and the "appropriateness" to the problem studied. In the quantitative paradigm this depends on the "design of the experiment," set up as the procedural guideline designed in order to answer questions and test hypotheses. In the qualitative paradigm it depends on the guiding questions that the researcher already has about the phenomenon he investigates, i.e. what he considers most important about the process under investigation: the phenomenon. We have to distinguish two levels of questioning:

(1) **The Data generating questions**: This is the question asked of the subject: What description is to be about. What phenomenon is to be selected and described.

(2) **The Explication-guiding questions**: This refers to the set of questions that the existential-phenomenological researcher addresses to the data, that guide his reflective questioning of the data, i.e. **explication.**

The different researchers presented in this section ask different questions on both levels. They are interested in different phenomena and they do explications differently.

Van Kaam (1966) asks:

1) Does this concrete, colorful, formulation by subject contain a moment of experience that might be a necessary and sufficient constituent of the experience of really feeling understood?

2) If so, is it possible to abstract this moment of experience and to label the abstraction briefly and precisely without violating the formulation presented by the subject? (p. 323)

He calls the answers to this: "Necessary Constituents." Van Kaam then composes a "synthetic description of the experience," his "end product."

Giorgi's (1975a) explication-guiding questions are:

1) What is learning? What does this statement tell me about learning? How does this statement reveal significance about the nature of learning? (p. 88)

This leads to two-levels of descriptions of structure: "Situated Structure" and "General Structure."

2) How did learning take place? (p. 88)

The answer to this question is given the term: "Style." It is also written for two levels: Situated Style and General Style, depending upon whether the specifics of the subject's existential situation are taken into account or not.

## §4.--ON THE EXPERIENCE OF BEING ANXIOUS: W. FISCHER.

W. Fischer in his book on the **Theories of Anxiety** (1970a) attempts an integration of anxiety theories. In his phenomenological characterization of the "faces of anxiety" (1970b) he presents a free-flowing informal but carefully argued report on his phenomenological reflective analysis of an actual report of "healthy anxious experiencing" and an imaginal example - created by W. Fischer himself - of "neurotic anxious experiencing." He analyzes both examples through a palpating reflective questioning in which he highlights the significant phenomenological themes and structures in dialogue with the descriptions. There is at this stage in Fischer's work - around 1970 - as yet not a full formalization of the method in specified steps which, however, emerges fully articulated in 1974, and in 1978.

W. Fischer, "On the Phenomenological Mode of Researching 'Being Anxious,'" (1974), provides us with another explicit example and chronicle of doing research in a phenomenological mode in a more clinical psychological context. He studies the phenomenon of "Being Anxious."

Fischer (1974) explicitly acknowledges a close collaborative relationship with the method worked out by Giorgi:

> Casting about for a place to begin, I discovered that Giorgi (in press) had already described, at least in its basic outlines, a three-stage method for analyzing qualitative, experiential descriptions or protocols. While the method that I came to use and am still evolving is not an exact, carbon copy of his, it is certainly based upon his suggested procedure to a significant degree. (p. 410)

(1) **The Problem and Question Formulation: The Phenomenon.** Regarding his general approach to research as a phenomenological psychologist Fischer states:

> One of the more important implications of all this is that every research enterprise, every effort to systematically understand and/or explain some phenomenon, becomes graspable as a project that actually seeks to further some perspectival access to that phenomenon. The researcher utilizes his own, as well as others' experiences of the researched, in order to bring to increasingly articulate intelligibility his own already operative, personally evolving, semi-articulate preconception of the researched. Thus, the history of the researcher's relations with the researched is an unfolding, evolving dialectic, one pole of which is constituted by the researcher's presuppositions and preconceptions pertinent to the researched--what Giorgi has called his approach - while the other pole consists of the researched content, that is, the phenomenon that is under study as it has been solicited, illuminated and articulated by the researcher's questions and methods. (p. 408)

In his research Fischer reports on two related studies: one on the experience of one's being anxious and the other one focusing on "the experience of another person being anxious." In this report we will limit ourselves to a discussion of the first: "One's own being anxious." He formulated the following question to gain access to the experience of being anxious:

Please describe in detail a situation in which you were anxious. To the extent that you can recall it, please include in your description some characterization of how your anxiousness showed itself to you as well as some statement of how you were, that is, what you experienced and did, when you were anxious. (p. 408)

(2) **The Data Generating Situation: Descriptions.** Regarding the situation in which the data-descriptions for the research were generated, Fischer reports:

I asked the students in my undergraduate personality theory class - about seventy per semester - to submit, as their term papers, descriptions of situations in which they themselves had been anxious. Needless to say, all the students were told in advance that I was interested in the phenomena of being anxious and that I wanted to read descriptions of other peoples' experiences with this human possibility. Further, all the students were asked if their descriptions could be read to others and/or used for publication. (p. 408)

Fischer thus obtained a large collection of descriptions of the experience of being anxious from college students in a psychology class. The demand-character of the situation was that the descriptions served as a term-paper, in the context of an evaluative classroom situation. The students presumably made their best effort under those conditions, and, indeed, as we look at the single case example of a descriptive narrative reported by Fischer (See Table 5, below) we find an unusually articulate, perceptive, and dramatic rendering of an experience of being anxious, an excellent protocol.

It is clear that the richer, the more detailed, the more dramatic the experiental descriptions are, "the better the data," the better will be our opportunity for explications on the basis of these data. Existential-phenomenological empirical researchers are very much aware of this issue and the methodological problems associated with this. Giorgi (1975a) comments:

Lastly, I would like to say a few words about description itself. All approaches in sympathy with phenomenology agree that one must begin with naive description. The discipline enters in when one has to analyze what has been described. Secondly, from a phenomenological perspective, description or language is access to the world of the describer. Descriptions, of course, can be better or worse or even enigmatic, but they always reveal something of the world of the describer, even if it is only the fact of an enigmatic world. The task of the researcher is to let the world of the describer, or more concretely, the situation as it exists for the subject, reveal itself through the description in an unbiased way. Thus it is the meaning of the situation as it exists for the subject that descriptions yield. While detailed knowledge concerning the criteria for better or poorer descriptions would be helpful, it is equally clear that good descriptions communicating the intentions of the describer do exist. (p. 74)

In our own work we have found it most congenial and productive to begin with written descriptions in the context of an explicit invitation into a collaborative research venture and then, in a second step called: "Collaborative Dialogue," to engage in a clarifying interview-dialogue with the contributors so as to amplify the personal meanings expressed in the initial descriptions (von Eckartsberg, "On Experiental Methodology", 1971). We thus start form a twofold "data-base": description plus interview transcript.

    3 & 4) **The Data Study Procedure. Explication and the Presentation of Results: Formulation.** Fischer comments upon his explication procedure in a first characterization:

    Each student's description was a relatively circumscribed chronicle; each characterized the unfolding of a particular event - the person's own anxiousness or his experience of another being anxious - from a particular perspective. (p. 410)

He then gives the full protocol of one particular student (see below Table 5). Fischer comments:

    As I continued to read and reread this, as well as other protocols, I gradually realized that each consisted of a series of interrelated scenes, that is, shifts in the focal attention of the one providing the description. Further, the central themes of each of these scenes was derived from and yet uniquely contributory to the overarching sense of the whole event that was being described and unfolded. In other words, each protocol constituted a structure; the meanings of the whole were given in the meanings of the interrelated parts or scenes, but the meanings of these were dependent upon the sense of the whole to which they pointed. Finally, I could see that the meanings of the whole were given in the ways that the successive scenes blended one into the next." (p. 413-14)

Proceeding with the work of explication Fischer reports:

> I took as my first task an articulation of the central themes that characterized the respective, unfolding scenes of each protocol. Further, wherever possible, I tried to state these themes in the student-subject's own language. Thus, in this manner I began the process of trying to situate myself vis a vis the totality of each protocol's structure so that it would speak to me in its own terms, so that it would show me all of its constituents, and so that in the unfolding of its scenes, I might grasp its inner logic and sense. (p. 414)

He thus articulates the descriptive narrative, the "chronicle," the series of "interrelated and successive scenes" in terms of Central Themes (see the side by side listing below in Table 5).

Although Fischer reports that he "tried to state these themes in the student-subject's own language," a look at the wording of the central themes shows that he actually first transformed the characterization from a first person singular "I-report" (Actor report) into a third person singular narration, i.e. into a psychological scientific observer report: S did this and this. . . . However, Fischer closely retains the narrative sequence and the variety of described experiences well articulated in the rich protocol that served as the starting point for the explication.

Continuing the work of explication - now working with the central themes as representative of the original protocol - Fischer reports:

> Having thus articulated the central themes that seemed to characterize each shift in focus, that is, each scene of the protocol, I turned my attention to an explicit interrogation of the meanings of being anxious that were lived, experienced and described therein. The questions that oriented this reflective enterprise were: what was the anxious situation that this person found herself in, and what did it mean for her to live that situation anxiously? (p. 416)

The aim of these explication guiding questions is to arrive at a characterization and "understanding of the meanings of being anxious as she lived, experienced and describes them." Fischer comments upon the difficulties involved in moving from the subject's descriptions to a characterization of the situated meanings of what Giorgi calls the "situated structure."

At this juncture, I must disappoint those readers who are looking for some procedure that would be analogous to traditional experimental design or statistics. I cannot offer a method of analysis that allows one to proceed strictly by the numbers. Instead, I would suggest that the movement of my reflections was quite similar to that which is utilized in the following everyday life situation: imagine that a person is seeking to secure from his friend a characterization of a particular other whom the friend has recently met. The friend is graciously willing to repetitively describe his experience of this other without limit. However, despite the person's persistent questions, the friend confines himself to the exact same words. Still, to the extent that this description is broad and yet detailed, there begins to emerge a more or less coherent sense of the other. In going back to the friend's words again and again, the person eventually came to realize a stable, though perspectival grasp of the other.

In going back to this student-subject's description again and again, I was able to achieve the following understanding of the meanings of being anxious as she lived, experienced and described them: (see below Table 5). (p. 416)

The next move in explication, in the method Fischer describes, is to go from situated specifity of a unique person's existential situation to the level of "essential or invariant meanings," to the "General Structure." Fischer reports in this context:

While the foregoing constitutes a characterization of the meanings of being anxious as they were lived, experienced and described by a particular person in a particular situation, the ultimate goal of my phenomenological analyses is to move towards a description of the essential or invariant meanings of being anxious as a fundamental human possibility. Thus, by analyzing instances of being anxious in their particularity, I hope to come to an understanding of being anxious in its suchness, in its universality. To this end, I took the characterization of the meanings of being anxious as they were lived by that particular girl in that particular situation, and I brought it together with other such characterizations based upon other protocols. Reading and rereading these, I sought to describe what seemed to be essential meanings of being anxious as they were revealed through the variant characterizations of these particular instances.

Again, I cannot say that I followed some straight-forward, mechanical, by-the-numbers procedure. However, I would ask the reader to think about what he sometimes does when an other asks him to describe, for example, a humanist, or a behaviorist, or a psychoanalyst, or a schizophrenic, or a representative of whatever group he might like. When he responds positively to this kind of request, he soon becomes involved in an inductive movement that cannot be adequately characterized as a simple abstracting of common elements. Rather, in gradually coming to a sense of a particular kind of person, in his or her typicality, he imaginatively and creatively re-understands and surpasses his own characterizations of the various styles of being anxious that were revealed in the descriptions.

Similarly, my efforts at illuminating the essential or invariant meanings of being anxious are based upon my readings and analyses of how this fundamental human possibility has been incarnated in the particular instances that were described by the student-subjects. In each of their respective protocols, meanings of being anxious were discovered as more or less explicit themes. As an increasingly articulate sense of this phenomenon began to emerge, it was seen that these themes, incarnated in the variations of each protocol, constituted the skeletal cores or infrastructures of the respective protocols. Hence, in reading and rereading each student-subject's description, as well as my own characterizations of the various styles of being anxious that were revealed in the descriptions, I came to realize the following sense of being anxious in its suchness: (pp. 417-418) (See Table 5)

In his "portrayal" of the essential invariant meanings of the experience of being anxious, Fischer distinguishes "two varying modes" or "types." While he does not comment on the exact origins of this differentiation, it appears from the context that all the descriptions studied - "about 70 per semester" - follow either one or the other mode.

TABLE 5:

## W. FISCHER'S STEPS OF EXPLICATION

| Instruction | Description |
|---|---|
| Please describe in detail a situation in which your were anxious. To the extent that you can recall it, please include in your description some characterization of how your anxiousness showed itself t you as well as how you were, that is, what you experienced and did, when you were anxious. | 1. I have been commuting to school by bus for three years now. And I hate it. I dread waiting for them. I detest riding on them, being pushed and shoved, crowded and having to make polite conversation about the weather or the price of things these days with my seat-sharer when I don't feel like talking at all. I hate trying to stay alert and watching for my stop because the constant grinding noise of the motor of the bus, plus the squeaking of the brakes on and off, provide an adequate lullaby for me. I almost always fall asleep while on my way to school or home. I become numb. But the worst part of the whole commuting process is waiting for my bus to come. Merely waiting for the bus to come is a vacant occupation of time. This waiting restricts and alienates me. It confines me to that one spot where I must stand in order that I might catch the bus that will take me to my destination. I must wait there regardless of my personal feelings. If it is ninety blistering degrees or sub-zero, I must brave the weather and stand at the designated spot. It is a very alien and unfriendly state. I witness the honking, screeching of cars and bus brakes and the on and off clicking of the corner stop light. The shuffling of hurried feet pass me by as I am fixed in my stationary, confined position, pushing and shoving, rushing ahead of others scurring around. Busy chatter, idle giggles, hearty laughter, children screaming and crying as they are dragged behind by the rests of their bargain anxious mothers, sophisticated, dignified discussions, current popular transistor tunes and the mutterings and mumblings of an old "bum" all pass me by. All the downtown street sounds surround me while I wait for the bus. I am caught in the middle of them. These sounds are alien and uncomfortable for me. I feel very uneasy in the midst |

| Instruction | Description |
|---|---|
| | of them.  This uneasiness and uncomfortableness of really being confined to that one spot was insurmountable one day while I was waiting for my bus to come.

2. This day was unlike the rest that I had known while waiting for the bus to come. It was a happy day. The sunlight was strong and brilliant. It illuminated the street and pavement. The light blinded me for a few seconds as it bounced off the shiny hoods of cars passing by. Every so often a cool breeze blew by not to make this warm light impose and dominate the day. The street sounds were radically and unusually hushed it seemed. I was in the middle of the city that afternoon, but yet I was in a balmy, breezy country too. Everything seemed serene and quiet and it was good.

3. As I was enjoying this abnormality, I was distracted by a figure that was coming closer to me from behind on my right side. The figure was that of an elderly black man. He approached me from behind, asking me, almost begging me to take his hand and hold it. At the same time he was telling me that his hand wasn't any different than mine, for me to take his hand and look at it.

4. I was stunned and shocked for a few minutes and then I retreated and thought, "Okay, the joke is over now, please leave, you old drunk."

5. But the joke wasn't over, it wasn't a joke and he persisted. I became increasingly more uncomfortable and helpless as he insisted that I take his hand. I felt the easiness and happiness of the day slipping away from me when he continued to remain on that sidewalk with me.

6. I never looked at him face to face because I was standing on the edge of the curb so that I could see my bus coming. But at a side glance I saw an older black man in his early or middle seventies, maybe older. He was pitifully shabby |

| Instruction | Description |
|---|---|
| | with an old shapeless cap, a heavy, dirty, torn tweed coat and heavy, hard-toe shoes, creased with grime so that every time he moved, they made a slow, muted shuffling sound. I can't remember his facial features except for the white whiskers that he had scattered over his deep pourous cheeks and chin. They didn't form a beard, but rather gave the impression that he hadn't shaved for a few days.<br><br>7. I can remember the hand coming around me for my right side, going and reaching for my hand. It was unlike any hand I had seen before. It seemed to be foreign, inhuman. Then hand was yellowish brown, the skin was extremely dry and cracked so that it almost looked as if it had scales on it. The four fingers were long and fat and curved outward all in the same direction. The thumb stuck inward opposite the four fingers. All were edged with thick whitish-yellowish nails. I was repulsed by this hand, I didn't want to touch it. Every time he spoke to me and mumbled the same words, "Take my hand, it's the same as yours," I became further and further removed from him.<br><br>8. Bodily I could not move. I became frozen stiff. I was not there really and concretely. I didn't exist at that bus stop and in that short time that he was there, I was invisible. I could feel my face becoming hotter and hotter, redder and redder. My eyes began to ache, they felt like they would explode. My hands became icy and wet and limp. As far as shaking or trembling, I couldn't move my body: I could not move my body: I couldn't even turn my head to look at the man. It was as if someone kept turning a key in my head and every muscle and nerve was so taut and strained that I couldn't budge from my position, standing slightly turned away from him. Every time he spoke, asking me to take his hand, these feelings increased. My eyes burned; my hearing became clouded. The sounds I heard were not clear and distinct, but rather muted and distant. I felt a thin covering being |

| Instruction | Description |
|---|---|
|  | pulled and stretched over my ears. I could actually feel my ears closing. My eyes bulged, my cheeks were hot, my head and whole body pounded rapidly; my hands were two icy dead weights and my throat felt pulled, twisted and sore. I knew I should do something. I wanted to do something so that he might leave, but I was afraid to do anything.<br><br>9. Every time he spoke I kept hearing what different people's reactions would be when I described the situation to them. It was realizing what these reactions would be that held me back from acting. I wanted to take the hand and smile and say, "Yes, it is like mine," giving him the affirmation that he wanted, but I was afraid of what he might do once I gave him my hand. I was also afraid of being ridiculed by passers-by. I could hear these strangers to this situation saying, "After all, a young white girl holding an old black man's hand, what's this world coming to?" I knew that physically if I didn't do something, I would soon drop dead because I felt that I was a time bomb pounding my existence away as each second passed. But I couldn't do anything. All the while he mumbled, I could see myself describing this experience to my mother, father, and aunt, hoping to find refuge in their advice. But my actions were restricted by their speech and I could do nothing. I could hear my mother saying, "You didn't take his hand, did you? God knows where his hands have been. You didn't touch it, did you? Wash your hands immediately; don't touch anything!" My father would say, simply and calmly, "Well, Mary, the next time anything like that ever happens all you have to do is. . . ." But this wasn't the next time, it was now. I could see my aunt and she told me very defiantly, "You should have stood up to him and said, 'Hey you, who do you think you are? You had better get out of here.'" I didn't want to disappoint my family. I didn't want to touch that old hand. I didn't want to be called dirty by any stranger who might see me as a young white girl holding hands with an old |

| Instructions | Description |
|---|---|

black man. I was afraid of who might see me. I
didn't want any disapproval, any disgusting remarks or any repercussions as a result of my
reactions to him. So, I didn't do anything. I
wanted to do what was right; I sincerely wanted to
take the hand as a kind gesture and make something
nice out of an ugly situation. I went over the
possibility of his being truly sincere and merely
wanting an affirmation of his hand being like mine
- for whatever meaning he needed from that affirmation. Butn I doubted if I was right in my decision and I also doubted that man and the possibility of his being sincere. I was afraid of what
might happen to me. So, I did nothing. As I said
before, even though mentally I was going over
these possibilities or alternatives, I couldn't do
anything. Bodily, I became further and further
removed from that instance, from that bus stop,
and from that man.

10. Finally, I saw a bus approaching. I had decided to get on it even if it wasn't my bus. It
was mine and I boarded it, leaving the old man
just standing there. In those explosive, pregnant
few minutes, I never felt more inadequate. I was
unable to act. I was unable to put an end to that
experience. I was relieved to be on the bus, to be
safe and out of the situation. Slowly, my body
regained its normal pace and my hands began to
become warm again.

| Themes | Situated Structure | General Structure |
|--------|--------------------|--------------------|
| 1. S. had been commuting to school for the past three years and she hates everything about it, e.g., having to wait for the bus, riding on the bus, being pushed, shoved and crowded, expected to make polite conversation, having to stay alert to watch for her stop, etc. S. emphasizes that the worst part of the whole routine is the waiting at the bus stop, an activity that she experiences as confining, restrictive, vacant and uncomfortable. | Her anxious situation was one in which she found herself called upon to do what she felt was right, but, at the same time, anticipating that if she did, others, whose opinions mattered to her, would be disappointed and might hold her up to ridicule. Being anxious in that situation meant explicitly imagining and being utterly immobilized by the expressions of ridicule and disapproval that others were expected to manifest. It meant feeling alone and inadequate in an increasingly foreign world. It meant intensely experiencing an | An anxious situation is one in which a particular problematic possibility of my project to be an adequate, competent human being announces itself and solicits me to responsibly confront it; an anxious situation is one in which I am called to thematically rediscover that the who and how of my life really matter, that they are without guarantees or unquestionable justifications, and that for this realization, they may depend to a considerable extent upon my effortful commitment. Three variations of this general characterizatio |
| 2. The day in which S. experienced herself being anxious was unusual, i.e. it was happy, serene, the sun was shining, there was a cool breeze, and everything seemed quiet and good. | | |
| 3. Waiting for her bus, S. became aware of an elderly black man who was aproaching her. In a voice that was almost pleading, he asked her to take hold of his hand, to look at it and to see that it as no different from her own. | | |
| 4. Stunned and shocked, S. tried to recover her composure by thinking the whole thing a joke and by waiting for the man to leave. | | |
| 5. When he persisted, S. became increasingly uncomfortable, was unable to act, and felt the easiness and happiness of the day slipping away. | | |

| Themes | Situated Structure | General Structure |
|---|---|---|
| 6. As the man continued in his request that S. take hold of and look at his hand, S., through a sidewise glance, saw that he was an old, shabbily dressed, apparently unshaven, black man.<br><br>7. Suddenly, S. realized that his hand was reaching for her. In repulsion, she experienced it as foreign, inhuman, yellowish-brown, dry and cracked as if it had scales. As the hand came to her, the old man mumbled, "take my hand, it's the same as yours."<br><br>8. In the face of this hand and its plea, S. felt frozen, stiff and invisible, no longer at the bus stop. Her face felt flushed, her eyes ached, and her hands were limp, wet and icy; her body felt so taut and strained that she was unable to even tremble; her hearing became clouded and her whole body pounded. She knew that she should do something, but she couldn't; she was afraid.<br><br>9. As the man persisted in his request, her thoughts raced to her family; she sought advice in their anticipated reactions, but the words that she heard them speak negated her own promptings to "do the right thing," to give him the affirmation he wanted. She didn't want to disappoint her family, she was afraid of what he might do if she took his hand, and she was afraid that passers-by might see her and ridicule her as a white girl holding hands with an old black man. She | inner demand for some transforming action that would break the binding character of the situation, but feeling helpless, filled with doubts and unable to act. Finally, it meant thematically discovering different parts of aher body in their affected, alien suchness. | may be delineated:<br><br>In the first, the particular possibility that I am called to face and own is one that I have already been living, either directly or indirectly, as never-to-be-true-of-me; in the second, I am called to do that towards which I am already moved, but anticipating that if I do, others, whose opinions are very important to me, will disapprove of and even condemn me; in the third, I am called to explicitly face the possibility that as the project to become a certain kind of person, I may be a failure. |

| Themes | Situated Structure | General Structure |
|---|---|---|
| felt that she had to act, but she could do nothing.<br><br>10. Having decided to board the first bus that came, S. left the old man without a word or look. On the bus, she wondered as to her sense of relief and realized that she had never felt more inadequate in her life. | | Initially, becoming and being anxious in the above-described situation means being suddenly distracted, even torn away from my everyday unreflective orientation towards and involvement with people, things and possibilities of my world. No longer able to attend undividedly to whatever I was doing I am momentarily suspended in my living; there is a kind of inarticulate confusion. Breaking through this, my body, or part thereof, intrude themselves and call me to discover and immediately understand their affected, alien suchness. I find myself |

| Themes | Situated Structure | General Structure |
|---|---|---|
| | | moved to "see" myself, to bear a critical, evaluative witness to the me that is now congealed and totalized in the threatening meanings of a particular emergent possibility. In being anxious, I am unreflectively impelled to do something, to perform some self-saving act that would cut through the encroaching oppressiveness and would enable me to regain my world.<br><br>Beyond this general characterization of being anxious, two varying modes are discernable: in the first, I can find nothing to do and further, am uncertain of my ability to do |

| Themes | Situated Structure | General Structure |
|--------|--------------------|-------------------|
|  |  | anything; moreover, I am fearful that whatever I would do, it would only make matters worse; hence, for the moment, I am immobilized; ultimately I flee in the face of a potentially responsible confrontation with the threatening meanings of the problematic possibility; I refuse any genuine and explicit reflection upon the who and how of my life. In the second mode of being anxious, I ultimately speak to and affirm the problematic possibility as also mine; in uncertainty and trepidation, I appropriate it and resolve to be myself. |

Fischer found it necessary to distinguish two modes or types of being anxious to account for the full existential spectrum of situated experiences of being anxious.

Reading Fischer's characterization of "being anxious in its suchness," i.e. in terms of its "general structure," its "skeletal core" or "infrastructure," it is very noticeable that the final version is written from the personal, actor-perspective, i.e. in the first person singular: I am. . . I do. . . my. . . etc. Who is I? Presumably the universal human, "homo universalis." It is as if the reader, when he reads this description, is talking to himself about himself. Indeed, if the description has achieved universality of meaning, then it must be possible to say it in the manner of a "universal I." This is a rather interesting and powerful narrative device, and it avoids the implied distance and observer-orientation that inheres in any third person singular structural characterization, i.e. a structural description in the voice of the scientist, speaking about the subject matter over there, speaking "objectively" about it (which is another form of narrative manner, another level of discourse).

If we look a little more closely at the metaphors used by Fischer, both in his descriptions and his characterization of the work of explication: "Chronicle," "scenes," "successive scenes," "protrayal," the "event organized in terms of scenes," etc., we find literary metaphors and the imagery of literary criticism. A type of analysis and formulation presents itself that speaks in terms of actors, of situations and scenes, themes of moves, of decisions, of responses, of attempts, and failures. It is a characterization in terms of dramatic action, much as one would describe the unfolding of a plot in a novel or in a play. We would like to suggest here that the underlying and implicit motif of the characterization of the experience of being anxious is to disclose the **"psychological plot"** of the experience, the "essential experienced story-line" that makes being anxious what it is.

We want to make another observation concerning the internal organization of Fischer's general characterization of being anxious. In comparison with the summated situated description, the final characterization is much more elaborate and informed by a strong implicit theory of personality and motivation from within the existential-phenomenological tradition. More specifically, it is the utilization of the notion of one's personal existential project (Sartre: **Existential Psychoanalysis**, 1953), "my project to be a competent human being," to "become a certain kind of person," "effortful commitment," "to perform some self-saving act," that gives

Fischer's characterization its dramatic power, its internal cohesion and psycho-logic, which blends nicely with the choice of the grammatical "universal-I-form." Every person can recognize himself in this familiar psychological plot, provided he is familiar with the literature of pheno-menology and phenomenological ways of speaking. The level and type of language in which the characterization of the "essential or invariant meanings" are couched is of a professional and phenomenological nature and goes beyond common sense contents of everyday language.

We already referred to Giorgi's statement that explication, parti-cularly the step of "reduction" (a la Van Kaam) involves a translation from the "everyday naive language of the subject" into the language of psychological science. There are many schools of thought in psychology each with its own specialized conceptual framework and language. Giorgi also states that it seems inevitable that the existential-phenomenological researcher expresses meanings he discovers in the "nascent language of phenomenological psychology (e.g., structure, style, meanings, situations, etc.)." Thus, we cannot really escape our approach, "where we are coming from," our theoretical preconceptions. This means that as part of our approach we bring with it always an implicit conceptualization of "Who is man?", i.e. personality structure and "What makes man move?," i.e. motiva-tional dynamics. "Man as existential project" is a core-theoretical con-cept of existential-phenomenology, a real theoretical contribution, the discovery of a hitherto neglected phenomenon in the light of a new star-ting point, a new view of man, which elucidates the meaning of our ex-perience in general, and our experience of being anxious in particular.

In the research by Giorgi, reported before, it was the notions of "awareness" (of the new), "meaning," "interpersonal context," that consti-tuted the core-insight and line of articulation of the experience of learning. Again it was the utilization of core-concepts of existential-phenomenology - awareness, meaning, level of functioning, consciousness, interpersonal context - that opened up the understanding for us. However, Giorgi utilizes a more common sense level of everyday language to express his existential structure, although his way of speaking is complex, in-formed by a phenomenological approach. For Van Kaam the guiding notions are: "perceptual-emotional Gestalt," "co-experience," "personal meaning," "relief from experiential loneliness," "experiental communion," which place him in communion with the existential-phenomenological framework of thinking and languaging. We cannot escape our theoretical pre-suppo-sitions, our "approach." All we can do is to try to make our approach as exlicit as possible.

Approach always implies a theoretical pre-conception, an implicit operative hierarchy of what we consider most important and illuminating. This is expressed and revealed through the particular psychological concepts employed. In this sense existential-phenomenology is not "a-theoretical" but self-consciously theoretical. As Van Kaam (1966) states:

> Observation is thus really perceiving what is 'out there.' But observation is also perceiving according to a theory of an observing subject. Therefore, existence as observation is necessarily theoretical and empirical at the same time. (p. 88)

## β 5.--ON PRIVACY: C. FISCHER

Connie Fischer, in her article: "Toward the Structure of Privacy" (1971), came to her research being puzzled about the reality and meaning of the experience of privacy. "There is much talk and struggle about the right to privacy," she said, "what is it we are trying to protect? What about it seems valuable to us?" (p. 149) Qualitative research into the experience seemed called for, beginning with the description, questioning, and study of her own experiential involvement. The phenomenon, privacy, revealed itself to belong to the larger dialectic process of **privacy - disrupted privacy**, i.e. being, finding oneself in a state of privacy and then being disrupted, pulled or pushed out of privacy by another who breaks in on our experience.

C. Fischer also discusses another dialectic of the experience of privacy in terms of the attitudes that one can hold toward privacy as either **pro** or **anti**. One can argue for it but also against it with good reason. These considerations and personal reflections on her experience led C. Fischer to the following research-guiding questions:

> When is privacy? Then: Which futures are available when it is? In other words like all human phenomena privacy is constituted of the experiencing person within some particular context. In still other words, it is his relations with a complex of circumstances. . . .
>
> Our answer to the question "What is privacy?" will not be a simple one: it must specify that matrix of human intertwinings with circumstances. That is, our description of privacy must take the form of: Privacy is, when: (such-and-such a matrix exists). From this we can see what privacy allows and what it precludes, and we can then point to both its desirable and undesired aspects. (p. 149)

This expresses C. Fischer's approach and pre-comprehension of her phenomenon in an evaluative, i.e. diagnostic context. She views her phenomenon
in a functional and value-engaged way: what does it allow or preclude, as
one would evaluate any constellation of circumstances according to one's
goals and purposes. C. Fischer emphasizes a thoroughgoingly "contextual-
izing approach": "Privacy is when . . . and will not be when . . . (disrupted privacy is when . . . and will not be when . . .)." It seems that
C. Fischer is intrigued with how a changing set of circumstances can lead
to a particular type of experience although her research emphasis is on
the description of an experienced psychological state which is said to be
contextually co-constituted. It is a dynamic way of viewing a phenomenon
as a "moving into and out of."

C. Fischer can also be seen to have a practical, we might say clinical interest in the value of her research findings. Her research is designed to arrive at a clarification of the meaning of the phenomenon that
can allow one, as a clinician or "assessment-person," to recommend moves
and strategies to change the constellations so as to change the phenomenon
in a desired direction. She seems concerned with how to change the "experienced state" as which privacy shows itself in the inter-human context
of assessment or therapy in which this dialogal explication takes place.

I will restrict my review to the first part of the experienced dialectic: Lived privacy, to indicate the way in which this research was
done. Methodologically C. Fischer proceeded "empirically" from multiple
situated descriptions of her own experience of lived privacy and disrupted
privacy, a type of "empirical individual phenomenological reflection." She
wrote up several events from recall - in retrospect. The actual data-
generating question is not specified in the report, but it must have been
something like:

> Describe several experiences in your life in which you have
> experienced privacy and then the disruption of privacy. Describe also
> the context or circumstances in which this occurred.

C. Fischer says of her method:

> My method was first to recapture many of my own experiences of
> privacy, which I wrote out in detail. As I wrote, I found that
> experience Y recalled aspects of experience X that I had not recalled
> when I first recorded it. Through the writing exercises, ongoing
> reflection, and attention to occurring privacy for myself and others,

I eventually grasped the beginnings of the structure of privacy. That is, I found certain components and their relationships that were present in all cases of experienced privacy, but not in other experienced states. (p. 150)

This is a shorthand description of a complicated process as we have seen in the previous section. The "Steps of Explication" by means of which C. Fischer arrived at the preliminary structural characterization and the nature of the explication-guiding-questions are characterized only in a most general way. The intellectual processes used: "writing exercises, ongoing reflection, and attention to occurring privacy" can be roughly described as a kind of multi-dialogal self-involvement with the data. The **"initial structural description"** that was the result of the procedures described so far and based on the reflective study of the descriptions is itself not presented in the text. Four descriptions ("data") are provided as "samples" of which one, the third, reads as follows:

I'm lying in bed reading **Newsweek.** Or I was, now I'm gliding among reveries about a Utopia in which all people participate in basic forms of work and thus share broader perspectives and possibilities for peace. I haven't formulated the details; they are to come later, after I prereflectively soak up unverbalized wanderings. It's a rich landscape, inviting my attention in all sorts of promising directions. My husband remarks that he thinks the shower floor leaks. "Uh huh," I say, easily flowing along my landscape. But now he's discussing what should be done about it. I mumble some more, trying to stay within my territory, but I must also listen to what he is saying. Finally I hear the irritation in my mumblings, and toss aside **Newsweek** and my lost unretrievable world. Now we discuss plumbing costs, remaining vacation time, etc. I wonder abstractly what I had been so caught up with before." (pp. 152-53)

In this description we see the dialectical process-character of the phenomenon. The experience of lived privacy: finding oneself in it and then being disrupted. These descriptions served as the basis and beginning points of several other phases in the research-process which include face to face dialogal transactions in the **explication process itself.** It can thus be said that C. Fischer's reflective dialogue with her own experiences and meanings and her dialoguing of that experience and its structural characterization with that of others in a face to face classroom situation made her research "dialogal-phenomenological." She reports on the "moves" she made after her initial structural description:

> Then I moved to another phase. I asked a group of six under-graduate students to carry out the above exercises with their own experiences. Examining these, I found them to be consonant with my own work. Moreover, various examples and analytic remarks allowed me to become aware of additional components and nuances. And sometimes a student hit upon a word that described our common experience better than mine. Finally, I presented my refined grasp of privacy, and together we dialogued it with further instances of privacy and non-privacy, until we felt assured that although further nuances and components would probably evolve through repeated exercises, at that point the grasp did definitely at least roughly fit our experiences.
>
> This type of dialogue was repeated with several individuals and with a class of ten graduate students. In all, the process has been going on for over a year. While there is still much to be done, the present results can be said to be significant at the .0000 level! That is, with subject-researchers being earnest and starting together from the realm of lived, everyday experience, we came to totally consensual findings. (p. 150)

In other words, C. Fischer engaged in a progressive dialogal involvement with concrete others and their experience in order to arrive at a "refined grasp of privacy" that did "fit our experiences."

The steps of this more dialogally oriented process cannot be pre-scriptively stated in the same way as we can the cognitive steps of empirical reflective phenomenological explication as shown before. Dia-logue, if it is genuine, is mutually creative and open-ended. It is for-ever new and surprising and cannot be identified beforehand as a necessary series of explicit methodological steps. Dialogue seems to require some "indeterminancy" or "fuzziness" as to steps of explication. Even the explication guiding questions seem to change as dialogue continues. Dia-logue is an inter-human event of mutual and shared exploration whose future horizon is always open-ended and unknown. It may be better charac-terized by the metaphor of a "shared journey" (a la Marcel) or by the technical metaphor of a "hermeneutic circle" (a la Heidegger) rather than by Step 1, Step 2, Step 3, i.e. as a series of differentiable, sequential, cognitive operations.

As to the "results," the findings or the formulation, C. Fischer reports:

> Back to the consensual results. We find that they are of two orders. The first is the description of the experience of privacy in terms of its phenomenal earmarks - the aspects to which we readily say, "Yes, yes, that's true of my experiences; that's the way I've been - although I wasn't particularly aware of it at the time." The second order is more distant, reflective one. There we ask of the pattern of earmarks its connections with other human phenomena and circumstances. In so doing, we discover still more components and refinements of the earlier description, we find that we must use more and more abstract terms that somehow often fail to "call up," to immediately connote, the lived phenomenon. So here we must move more slowly, trying to be sure that we don't dictate abstractions to our data, and that we are all referring to the same thing.
>
> It is especially this second order of fuller structure that always requires further refinement and extension, particularly in the case of the present analysis. However, it is apparent that we have a clear focus on the structure of the phenomenal order of privacy, and the fuller structure is emerging in definite directions. These already have important, socially relevant implications. (p. 151)

In terms of its dialogal-hermeneutical orientation C. Fischer's research on privacy could be placed in the part on "hermeneutical-phenomenological studies; actual life-text studies," in this book. C. Fischer's way of doing research anticipates and is akin to de Rivera's approach entitled: "conceptual encounter," which we discuss later.

Thus C. Fischer can be said to speak of "consensus results" which refer to the notion of inter-human truth which is the fruit of dialogue. She also uses "phenomenal earmarks" or "patterns of earmarks" to refer to the structural components of the experience. The **validation** of these earmarks is done in terms of an appeal to the personal experience of the reader: "Yes, yes, that's true of my experience." Personal experiential and existential involvement becomes part of the research process both as a starting point and in terms of validating return to personal experience.

The collection of experiential protocols and personal reflection on personal experience (Individual Phenomenological Reflection) making one's own implicit living explicit, yields intuitive insights and formulations that can then be communicated and offered to dialogal response and criticism. In the final results C. Fischer (1971) presents her formulation of the phenomenon of "lived privacy" (in retrospect) in summary form:

> In Summary, Privacy is When: the watching self and the world fade away, along with geometric space, clock time, and other contingencies leaving an intensified relationship with the intentional object. The relationship is toned by a sense of at-homeness of familiarity, and its style is one of relative openness to or wonder at the object's variable nature. (p. 154)

C. Fischer's structural description uses both conceptual - on a fairly universal level - and metaphorical components. The essential-universalizing characterization uses the context of phenomenological ways of speaking: "relationship with intentional object" as well as a metaphorical way of speaking about the quality of the experience referring to a "sense of at-homeness or familiarity" and "openness and wonder at the object's variable nature," i.e. using metaphors of everyday experience themselves in need of clarification but existentially suggestive and inviting.

In summary, C. Fischer uses a multi-phasic and multi-level approach. Her research can be said to constitute an exercise in multiple level discourse. She uses description of her own experience and that of others. She uses individual reflection on her experience as well as dialogue with others about their descriptions and theri reflections. She arrives at a structural description in contextual terms: "privacy is when. . . ." Her method can be seen to lend itself especially well to a clinical and particularly to an assessment orientation because it serves an evaluative and prescriptive intention and gives the subject-researcher, the co-researcher or client a voice in the formulation of the results. There is also a strong emphasis on personal growth and deepening of one's own experience through doing this kind of research. In her validating appeal to the reader's own experience, C. Fischer addresses herself to the universality of personal experiences and their clarification through reflection and discourse which is a dialogal style of communication on the part of the author.

B.

# EMPHASIS ON PROCESS

## HOW DOES IT HAPPEN?

In this section we discuss a research which emphasizes the unfolding nature and process-character of psychological phenomena: reconciliation. The main concern in this research is the understanding and articulation of "how it happens for the person." A diachronic view is presented, as contrasted to the style of structural articulation in the previous section which is synchronic or configurational in nature (Ricoeur, 1979).

In the process-oriented view we follow the unfolding inner meaning and "psycho-logic" of the experiencing and acting individuals as they confront their challenge and future without the benefit of hindsight. Thus we become attuned to the importance of decision-points, of periods of hesitation and refusal, of the quality of lived time. Retaining process-focus also preserves the dynamic and dramatic, and tensed quality of living experience: **dramatic intentionality.**

It involves the tracking, scanning, and mapping of that event. Via such reflection experiactions are able to configure themselves into meaningful psychological moves and to be revealed in relation to a discriminable "existential plot." The explication guiding questions which discloses the **existential process structure** reads: How does the description reveal the psychological movement(s) of **this person** over time? This experienced meaning process becomes disclosed in response to the question: How does it happen? How is the event manifested for the person? These questions yield the existential process structure of the event.

In taking this research stance, the phases of an irreversible psychological process become highlighted and thematized. The **order of events** itself becomes an essential feature of the constitution of the phenomenon. Hence we speak of the **process-structure** of the experience and of **existential process.** Kierkegaard (1846/1868) emphasizes the importance of this concept - existential process: "Because abstract thought is sub specie aeterni it ignores the concrete and the temporal, the **existential process,** the predicament of the existing individual." (p. 267, my emphasis)

Plot becomes the chief metaphor in the articulation of the existential process structure. This is in line with Ricoeur's view (1979) who considers plot to be the link between the **episodic** nature of an event viewed diachronically and the **configurational** comprehension of an event when viewed synchronically. The plot of an experiaction can be articulated either way. One of my main interests as a social psychologist is relationship-building and its associated phenomena. The process of reconciliation is central to relationship-building.

### §6.--ON THE EXPERIENCE OF RECONCILIATION:
### R. von Eckartsberg

I initiated a collection of stories concerned with reconciliation. I chose one of these protocol stories to illustrate my approach to the study of the **existential process structure** of the phenomenon, i.e. how it is an unfolding experience for the participant. After I obtained the story in a classroom setting, we engaged in dialogal elaboration through class discussion (von Eckartsberg, 1979; 1985). After this I began the explication and interpretation by identifying and naming the chapter headings of the sub-phases and sub-events. The explicit explication-guiding question in this step of the interpretation was: "What are the chapters and sub-phases or episodes that constitute the plot of reconciliation and how can they be named?"

The second step was to formulate the psychological meaning contained in each phase of the story as an experienced existential process. The explication-guiding question of this step of the reflection was: "What is happening in the experience of the protagonist? What concrete existential process is experienced by the actor in the story in the exact sequence of its occurrence?"

These questions about what happened in terms of the protagonist's experience emphasize her **psychological moves** sequentially. My reflective work consisted in articulating my view of this unfolding process, preserving its chronological character as an unfolding plot. Table 6 presents the results of this reflective work.

The chaptering, sub-phasing, and episoding summarized in Table C reveals my own process of comprehension and interpretation. I see the story as a long drawn-out personal struggle by Terry to save an important relationship, a long-standing mutually satisfying love-mentor relationship.

| TABLE 6 : von Eckartsberg: Steps of Explication | | |
| --- | --- | --- |
| Original Story | Chaptering and | Existential Process Structure |
| I. We have known each other many years, - in fact she had been my teacher in junior high school. We had more than a teacher-student relationship even when I was in Junior High. As I became older we shared more and more and discussed things I needed to sort out. She always had the gift to not give me direct answers to my questions and problems but rather could give me information to work with to formulate my own answers. I became close to her husband and three | I. From Teacher to Mentor  How, over several years, the relationship between Terry and Anne, her Junior High School teacher, came about and what it meant.  1) Their Initial Relationship:  How Terry and Anne came to know each other and established a more than teacher-student relationship: discussing things Terry needed to sort out. | I.  Terry, a young girl, meets a woman- teacher, Anne, in Junior High School with whom she establishes a personal relationship of the mentor-type. The teacher makes her feel welcome and encourages and guides her to always find her own solutions. Anne becomes important for Terry, and Terry also becomes friends with Anne's husband and three children. Terry keeps in touch with Anne over the years by occasional visits and communications and considers herself in a stable and rewarding relationship with her. |

children also,
and, although I
saw them infre-
quently I kept in
touch by letters
and phone.

2) **Anne's Gift:**

Anne's gift
for Terry: to help
her find her own
solutions. A men-
torship develops.

3) **Terry and
Anne's Fami-
ly:**

Terry became
friend's with
Anne's husband and
three children
also and stayed in
contact over time.

II.

When I sent her a
Christmas card a
year ago she
called and told me
that she had moved
out of the house
and was living in
an apartment with
another woman. I
had met this woman
before met this
woman before and
Anne said enough
for me to get a
vague feeling for
what was going on
without bluntly
stating it. She

**II. Complications
in the Relation-
ship: Precipi-
tating Event.**

How, a year
ago, Terry
realized Anne's
change to a homo-
sexual life style.
Serious complica-
tions arise in the
relationship.

**The News:**

A year ago,
news of change in
Anne's life and
moving in with

II.

A crisis occurs for Terry
in the relationship a
year prior to the report
while Terry is a junior
in college. The crisis
arises for Terry through
a hint in a Christmas
card sent by Anne indica-
ting that she was now
living with another
living with another woman
whom Terry also knew.
Terry suspects it is a
homosexual bond. Terry's
relationship to Anne be-
comes problematic for
Terry and leads to a
serious struggle with

invited me over to the apartment. And several weeks later I did go. On the way over I had a pretty good idea of what to expect but I kept telling myself that it was easier for her to live in an apartment while going to school. After spending the day with her and Jane, there was no longer any denying the fact that she had left Bill for a different life-style.

another woman comes by way of Christmas greetings exchange. Terry writes - Ann calls.

2) **The Telephone Call:**

Terry knew the other woman and was suspicious about what was going on. Terry gets invited to visit.

**The Visit:**

On the way over, what Terry expects to find and how she makes up her mind about it.

4) **The Realization:**

After the day's visit Terry concludes: Anne is homosexual!

herself. She experiences the emergence in her of a social moral attitude and a stereotyped view of such a life-style within her. But Terry is curious and wants to see for herself and test out what this relationship is like and she accepts an invitation to visit Anne in her new home several weeks later. She realizes during and after the visit that Terry is indeed living a homosexual life-style and she finds herself bewildered and confused.

### III.

On the way back to the bus I found myself with half a smile on my face, thinking: "Well, now you know, kid, what are going to do about it?" I didn't honestly see anything wrong with homosexuality, but from the little bit I heard I felt obligated to find something wrong with it. So I found my point of attack in: "What about the kids?" It certainly wasn't original, but it sufficed to get me worked up enough to condemn the whole thing. The easiest thing to do is just to forget it ar.d since I was involved in other things I managed to somewhat. But I could not deny my feelings for her. I knew I had a very dear friend

### III. Crisis, Avoidance, Conflict.

After the visit Terry lives in conflict and avoidance of Anne and the issue for several months.

1) **Terry's first thoughts:**

Now you know, what are you going to do about it?

2) **Feels obliged to take a stand:**

Terry feels socially obligated to reject and condemn homosexuality and justifies it by a stereotyped response.

3) **Condemnation of Anne:**

Terry works herself up to condemn the whole thing.

### III.

Terry is now forced into a moral dillema and feels that she has to make a choice: for or against Anne. She cannot come to a decision in a purely rational and deliberate manner, once and for all. She becomes entangled in the conflict and resolves her ambivalence and confusion by condemning Anne, rationalizing her stance in a selfrighteous but stereotyped manner. It takes months for Terry to find a way out of her pattern of projection of blame and denial. She "forgets" by keeping busy with other things and avoids the issue. Yet from time to time her continuing positive feelings for Anne and her appreciation of her as her mentor surface and Terry cannot deny them to herself. They are in gestation and work underpsychically. Yet she continues to avoid coming to terms with the relationship and with Anne.

and I loved and respected her.

IV.

It wasn't until the following summer, when during an argument (with mother) I blurted: "You only love me when I live your way," did I realize that that was exactly what I was doing with Anne. I sat down and really thought about it and then I wrote her a letter. Although I didn't

4) **Terry's avoidance:**

She keeps busy and forgets, almost; she avoids.

5) **Terry's Love for Anne surfaces again.**

6) **Terry's hesitation:**

Terry reasserts her love and respect for Anne to herself, but she hesitates.

IV. **The Turning Point in their Relationship.**

Terry has the insight and resolves to confront and live through her conflic and ambivalent feelings.

1) **Terry's insight:**

Last summer Terry realized her onesided intolerant reaction

IV.

After six months of avoidance, of denial of being anxious, of experiencing conflict and just letting time pass and keeping busy in other directions, Terry finds herself confronted with the issue of conflicting life-styles in another relevant social context in a confrontation with her own mother whom she accuses in a spontaneous outburst of anger and frustration: "You only love me when I live your way!" In a

say flatly what I was trying to say, she understood and within a week I received a reply from her. Her letter sounded jubilant. She sounded jubilant. She was so happy with the new house she and Jane had bought, being enough for the kids to really enjoy and other developments in her life. But more importantly because she knew I had worked through the situation and my love for her hadn't changed.

V.

In the meantime, I had read everything about homo-

regarding Anne in an encounter with her mother.

2) **Contact again:**

Terry writes an explanatory letter to Anne.

3) **A Positive reply:**

Within a week Anne writes back jubilantly.

4) **Good news:**

Good development; new house with Jane and kids.

5) **Ann still her mentor:**

Anne "understood," helped her find her own solution again. Terry's love for her had not changed.

**V. The Blessing of Reconciliation.**

Terry overcomes her stereo-

moment of deep emotional agitation Terry makes the connection to her own attitude toward Anne and comes to an insight about her own style of denial which had made her suppress her love for Anne as her friend and mentor. This insight re-configures her understanding and she acknowledges to herself that she had avoided the issue by projecting the blame. Accepting responsibility for her actions from that moment of recognition forward for her own self-deception and self-justification and for denying her deepest feelings and genuine love and respect for Anne, she makes a moral decision to respond, to face up to her true feelings, to live authentically and to risk herself and her meaning-making habits. She takes courageous action to confront her own unknown leanings and uncertain reactions by initiating personal contact again with Anne and to explain herself to her. She first writes a letter, and receives an encouraging, understanding and im-

sexuality that I could get my hands on, even law books, and I was amazed that my original response was so stereotyped and narrow-minded. When I finally saw her again, I told her all the research I had done and how I felt. Somehow during the discussion we fell into a serious gaze and our hands fell into each other's. I leaned forward to her and we embraced and I began to cry silently. When we looked at each other we were both crying but at the same time smiling gloriously. There was a special beauty in our silence and a special meaning, which language cannot begin to touch.

typed ideas and fears, makes contact again with Anne, and a deep reconciliation and reunion ensues.

1) Homework:

Terry reads up on homosexuality and gains insight into her own past narrow-mindedness.

2) Their reunion:

As they meet again they have a deep personal exchange. Terry confesses her doubts. They have an emotional reconciliation in which they find themselves genuinely close and moved and they firmly reestablish their mutual love and respect for each other, their inspired fellowship.

plicitly forgiving reply from Anne within a week.

V.

Before seeing Anne again Terry studies up on homosexuality and now fully realizes how narrow-minded, stereotyped, and defensive she had been. When they finally meet again face to face, they both experience the blessing of reconciliation after the following happened: a kind of confession of sins on Terry's part, a making speakable between them what had not been shared and not been shared and the granting of mutual forgiveness in a tender moment of mutual recognition beyond words in which they are both moved to tears and embrace. Terry realizes that Anne has been acting as her mentor all along allowing her to come to her own insights and decisions, to make her own mistakes, and being accepting of her, concerned and always encouraging and welcoming her being without pushing her or forcing the issue.

The relationship of Terry and her mentor Ann had fallen into some neglect over the years but continued underground because it seemed an important milestone in Terry's early development, a lasting bond of what I call "inspired fellowship." This is a sub-form of a love relationship in which two people, one older and more experienced, mutually encourage and elevate each other in thinking, feeling, being creative, and valuing. They "bring each other out," help each other grow spiritually as persons, and even challenge one another.

A crisis occurs for Terry in the relationship through the disclosure that Anne is living in a homosexual way. The disclosure leads Terry to a struggle with herself and her socialized moral attitude stereotypes toward such a life style. She is forced into a moral choice - for or against Anne. she cannot come to a decision in a purely rational and deliberate manner, once and for all. She becomes entangled in the conflict and it takes a long time and some fortuitous circumstantial happenings in Terry's life for her to find a resolution which leads to reconciliation.

After a sequence of particular psychological moves (being anxious, doubting, delaying, avoiding, feeling conflict and letting time pass) Terry is confronted with the issue in another social context, the relationship with her mother. In a moment of deep emotional agitation, she comes to the insight about herself that it has been her own warding off style of denial which had made her repress her love for Anne as a person and mentor. Accepting responsibility for her own self-deception and denial of her deepest feelings and values, she makes an essentially moral decision to respond, live authentically, and risk herself by facing up to the conflict. She takes courageous action to confront her own unknown leanings by establishing personal contact again with Anne, to see for herself first by letter, and then face to face, on which occasion the "blessings or reconciliation" is experienced by both. This includes a kind of confession of sins, a making speakable between them what had not been shared. The airing of Terry's loss of faith in Anne, her suspicion, erecting psychological barriers, moral condemnation, and anguish helps to re-establish and strengthen their relationship. In retrospect, Terry comes to see Anne's handling of the crisis as another instance of her concern for Terry as a mentor, thereby allowing Terry to come to her own decision.

We do not have to move very far into a meta-level of theoretical understanding and discourse to account for the motives operating here. One could attempt a Freudian rendering in terms of latent homosexuality, a Jungian translation in terms of the "wise old person archetype," or a social learning interpretation in terms of the reinforcement and deconditioning of parental stereotypes. We are here taking an existentialist position, i.e. the perspective of **responsible personal agency** which holds that people create relationships with each other through acts of moral judgment and commitment in the context of chosen value orientation.

We can add another step to our reflective work and try to characterize the a-chronological configurational meaning of the phenomenon as the **essential meaning structure.** In this structural configurational attitude, the plot or **meta-story of reconcilation** turns out to be the following:

## The Essential Meaning Structure of Reconciliation

An ongoing interpersonal relationship of intimacy and mutual importance is ruptured due to a falling out between the partners over an issue and made problematic. Ongoing face to face contact is disbanded and a self-righteous construal of the reasons for the break is formulated, which typically projects the blame for the break on the other partner. There is much denial. A precipitating event or crisis typically occurs in one of the partners which disrupts the stalemate and reminds that partner of the continuing claim of the relationship, of the living in tension, and in mutual rejection. Bringing the relationship to renewed awareness forces also a reconsideration of one's attitudes, values, and involvements. If one of the partners has a change of heart and/or insight into the situation and can dislodge his or her frozen and stereotyped perceptions and evaluations, owning up to and assuming some of the responsibility for the rupture, then movement toward renewed contact and conciliatory actions become possible, i.e. imaginable and actualizable.

Once initiated, the peace-making overtures must be acknowledged and reciprocated by the other so that a crucial face to face exchange can occur. Such an exchange involves confession of sins and stupidity, expression of regret and sorrow, and the asking of forgiveness in so many words and gestures, in a situation and moment of great vulnerability, openness, and risk. The other, when approached, has the right and choice to refuse. The accepting response of the other seals the reconciliation in a dramatic moment of mutual recognition and ongoing shared intimacy and co-creativity can resume its course in a strengthened relationship.

This characterization of the essential meaning struture of the experience of reconciliation is a provisional statement subject to confirmation, challenge, and modification by further work on other stories. It is subject to revision through further data and research even though there is a presumed shared consensus of meaning tied up in the very concept: reconciliation. We know the verbal and experiential meaning of this word in a general way but not as a detailed psychological configuration in all its nuances. It is only by using an existential-phenomenological approach that we can articulate both the unfolding of the **existential process** over time and the **essential meaning structure** of the phenomenon as an idea.

When we emphasize **process,** i.e. when we are guided in our examination and explication of the story by the question: How does it happen?, we imaginatively place ourselves into the "shoes," body and experience of the actor, the narrator. What is it like to go through this experience? The story portrays a person in psychological movement, a person deliberating, waiting, making decisions, undergoing shifts in feeling, in uncertainty, hesitating, avoiding, a person ongoingly responding to and creating her life in the specificity and sensoriness of this relationship. This happens in **episodes,** one event after another, in the real and concrete fabric of personally experienced time, in the full tension of past and future in this named person's fate. The story takes us into the unique, named, and dated reality of social living. Proper names characterize the level of existential process. This is what happened to me. We obtain an account of the psychological moves of the actor.

The story is the life-text of the event for the actor. It discloses a meaningful narrative and it invites reading "between the lines," entering into the subtexture or "subtext" of the reported and experienced event. As listeners and readers we respond and elaborate and add to the manifest story focussing on the tacit connections, the implied motives and struggles and pre-reflective decisions accomplished by the actor which hold the episodes of the event-story together. We want to empathically understand the hero and comprehend this persons' particular way of dealing with this situation which we calla reconciliation.

In characterizing the process or the process-structure of the experienced event we emphasize the importance of sequence and of time-span. An individual's experience is a "time-gestalt." My experience has n irreversible episodic and unfolding nature. This is an essential, i.e. structural characteristic, of personal experience. It is also concrete, i.e. sensory and personal and historical and this means that it is characterized by proper names of persons, places, and dates. This makes it part of the genre of biography, of case study. Our life texts are autobiographical documents, stories of our life. When we listen to such stories we imaginatively relive the events with the actor and we are moved by the account in our heart. These stories are self-justifying and self-explanatory. We become emotionally affected. But we also understand and make sense of what happened in an intellectual way, in terms of naming the motives and reasons, the value- and moral choices that were made. We judge the person in some way, as a hero or a coward, maybe, as somebody with a problem, as somebody I would like to get to know better or as somebody to be careful about or avoid.

We can also transcend our personal concerns and relationship to this person and treat the life text as a collection of facts and statements about the human condition in general, as data that disclose the meaning of the human plot of reconciliation. As a research psychologist I am professionally interested in the phenomenon of reconciliation. It is an important interpersonal reality. If we could understand and verbally articulate its meaning-structure, its essential constituents and key constellation as well as its dynamics, then we could make a contribution to the field. Reconciliation thus becomes a cognitive object of professional interest. The plot of reconciliation is a certain configuration of experienced meanings and actions. Knowing the meaning-structure we can then test and assimilate many specific reconciliation-stories into the universal meaning-matrix and dialectically change the structure as new evidence demands. Articulations of essential structures of phenomena are forever provisional and subject to review and reworking. They serve as "hypotheses" for further investigation "until further notice."

Both modes of explication, that of process-structure and that of general structure are valid and necessary articulations. In its emphasis on the unique person and the "case" the process articulation is essential to psychotherapeutic procedure. As therapists we have to enter into the temporal and internal, i.e. private, working dynamics of the client's experience and construal of his or her reality. This is what needs to be made speakable between client and therapist: How does it happen? In the therapeutic context we do not generally aim at a working-though on the universal level of What is this phenomenon in general? The vantage point of cognitive distance required for a universal characterization is typically too great and too objectivating for clients. It requires a different kind of involvement, one of contemplative dispassionateness. This does not mean, of course, that **universalizing understanding** is undesirable in therapy. On the contrary, "insight" into one's existential situation and maneuvering is the great desirable. But the aim for **personal insight,** for insight into my situation so as to enable and empower me to cope more effectively and more responsibly in my life, is of primary importance. Also, in therapy the client selects and presents the problem or phenomenon to be addressed, in research it is the investigator's professional interest.

The empirical phenomenological work of producing general structural characterizations of phenomena is important to the therapist because it provides a systematic presentation of human phenomena as lived structures of consciousness. The problem with some of these characterizations in the literature and in dissertation work is that they are expressed in the idiom of phenomenological concepts which is a language that is difficult to understand and which presupposes a detailed familiarity with the phenomenologial literature. This sometimes prevents the fruits of empirical existential-phenomenological work from being enjoyed and appreciated by a wider audience.

My research effort has been to 1) stay with a particular person's story, 2) elaborate the **existential process** which the protagonist experiences and enacts in its temporal sequence and span, 3) to go beyond the single case and to articulate also the most universal and generally valid features and constituents, including its dynamics, of the phenomenon of reconciliation and to do this in non-technical terms as much as possible. By focusing first and primarily on the question of: How does it happen? and by articulating the elaborated dramatic narrative we invite fidelity to the happening and an appreciation of the subtleties of the experienced existential process and thus of the **intergration** of life-world experience.

# C.

# VALIDATING

# PHENOMENOLOGICAL CONSTRUCTS

There seems to be a third broad category of doing empirical existential-phenomenological research. In this mode empirical data are collected to be analyzed and to be used in validating or critiquing phenomenological constructs. Psychological research is undertaken in order to engage in a dialectic with the fruits of philosophical reflection in order to provide an empirical basis for phenomenological constructs. Richer's research is of this type.

Keen works somewhat differently. He uses phenomenological constructs initially to organize his data-material but he then also relies on his descriptive data to extend and differentiate as well as to illustrate the meanings of phenomenological constructs.

There is, of course, a large body of phenomenological research in clinical psychology and psychiatry (May, et al., 1958) called "categorical analysis" (Ellenberger, 1958) which utilizes the basic conceptual framework of phenomenology to clarify clincial phenomena:

> Categorical analysis takes a system of phenomenological coordinates, the most important of which are time (or rather "temporality"), space (or rather "spatiality"), causality, and materiality. The investigator analyzes how each of them is experienced by the patient, in order to achieve, on this basis, a thorough and detailed reconstruction of the patient's inner universe of experience. (p. 97)

Discussion of this large body of literature lies beyond the scope of this study.

## §7.-ON THE PERCEPTION OF AFTER-IMAGES: P. Richer.

Paul Richer in his phenomenological study of the visual after-images (1979) introduces a variant of empirical phenomenological investigation which he calls: "Dialectical-structural analysis" following Ricoeur (1966). He dialogues the phenomenological structual characterization of concrete object perception of Husserl (1962) and Gurwitsch (1964) with its "modalization" or alteration as after-image. He states:

> The after-image was not investigated for its own sake; it was investigated in relation to ordinary thing-perception for the sake of furthering an understanding of perceptual positionality in general. The phenomenon was viewed "diagnostically," as a deviation which, as deviation, necessarily implies another structure." (p. 164)

Thus Richer proposes that through studying deviations, errors, illusions - in a previous study Richer (1978) has published work on geometric illusions using the same methodology as will be illustrated here - and after-images we can shed light on, challenge, confirm and disconfirm eidetic phenomenological formulations of thing-perception.

> In a phenomenological analytic the ordinary material perceptual object reveals itself to be the unity or organization of an infinite multiplicity of anticipated possible perspectival views or "noemata." Any given view implies or "intends" the system in which it participates; this is to say, any given view is of an object. (Richer, 1979, p. 166)

Richer's aim was to empirically study the experience of perceiving a perceptual illusion and to place the results of such a study in critical dialogue with the philosophical phenomenological structural formulations.

Regarding method, Richer collected free descriptions of the experience of watching an after-image from 25 subjects:

> Twenty-five participants were invited to report their experiences of an after-image. They were chosen largely on the basis of their naivete with regard to the psychology of perception and phenomenology. Each participant stared binocularly into a bright light source placed about 1 meter from the eyes for two minutes. The source consisted of a 250 watt bulb placed several centimeters behind an aperture 1 centimeter in diameter. After the light source was extinguished, observers were asked to describe their experiences of the after-image as completely as possible "so that someone who has never experienced an after-image would know exactly how it looks just on the basis of hearing your description." Further: "You can't give too

much detail." In various previous studies that particular wording has proven to yield the richest descriptive protocols. (p. 163)

These protocol-data were approached and analyzed in the "peculiar stance of the psychological-phenomenological reduction" and viewed by the researcher in such a way that constitutitive questions could be asked. The actual structural analysis was conducted in 2 phases:

1. Analysis was initiated by uncovering essential themes common to the protocols, "which were either explicit - stated outright - in the subject's words or hinted at directly, or "only implicitly present but supported by the overall structure of the protocols." Thus "constituent themes as well as illustrative examples of observer's comments are summarized below prior to the structural analysis."

2. After themes were extracted, a formal structural analysis began. The configuration of interrelations and mutual implications between themes comprises the structure of the phenomenon, but from the start this structure implied another structure so that analysis was dialectical. (p. 164)

The themes with illustrative quotes from the descriptions were:

1. The after-image is a sensuous appearance but not an appearance of a material thing.

It's not really there. It is projected out there like a movie.
It's not really real. I see it but it's not really there.
It looks like a vision.
It looks like a ghost.
I saw this image but it did not seem real.
I knew I could not reach out and touch it but it was floating in
    my space.
It's sort of like a profile with no thing.
It's just an appearance but not really there.
It was a light but not from anything real.
It's just a brightness.

2. The after-image is only loosely coherent. It is largely unpredictable and flighty.

It's gone and then comes back and I never know.
It changes all the time and I can never figure it out.
If I blink it changes all different ways.
It has free will, like something from outer space floating.
I lose it, then get it again.
It's always changing unpredictably.
It's psychedelic.

3. It has no depth in space. Spatially disparate perspectival views are not possible.

You can never see around it.
It doesn't take up any real space.
It didn't appear to have any depth in space - just a flat splotch floating in the air.
There aren't any sides to it.
There's no backside.
It's flat, a filminess I would say.

4. Attempts to focus or fixate the after-image are abortive.

You can never really look at it. You see it because you see something else.
I can't get it in focus.
If you try to stare at it your eyes blur.
The harder I look at it the worse it gets.
It won't stay long enough for me to catch it, like.

5. The after-image creates - or is - a hole or rupture in material perceptual objects.

I stuck my hand out and my hand appeared to go through the dot and then disappeared for a second.
It blocks vision everywhere you look.
It makes a colored hole in things.
The disc is a kind of elusive discoloring of whatever I look at.

6. The after-image does not participate in the causal nexes of material objects.

The pattern is sort of free of gravity.
It seems to be just floating there.
The spot was abstract. It was removed from the world.
It doesn't bump into things.
It is a light that doesn't light anything up.
It gets darker in the light.

7. The after-image experientially and thematically implicates the perceiving eye, and its place is fixed in the visual field.

It's everywhere you put your eyes.
It follows you around everywhere you look.    It comes and goes in the middle of wherever I look.
It's just a trick my eye is playing.
You would say it's a brightness in my eyes. (pp. 165-166)

In the discussion section of his paper, Richer then develops an articulation of the essential structure of the perception of after-images in close dialogue with the analysis of the structure of thing-perception developed by Husserl, Gurwitsch and Merleau-Ponty which he presents first, followed by the structural characteristics of the after-image by contrast:

In the case of the after-image, apparently the perceptual flow does not concatenate such that the concatenation strains beyond itself as it does in ordinary thing-perception. . . . On the other hand, in the case of the after-image, the Gegenstand (object) does not overtake the appearances; the latter do not concatenate sacrificially. . . . It is critical that the concatenation gives rise to an inner horizon that is not made up of spatially disparate perspectival views. To see a three-dimensional material thing is to anticipate though any one view a whole organized series of different perspectival views. The after-image neither allows nor promises views from other angles. . . . In addition to lacking depth, the image lacks weight. . . . At the perceptual level the after-image cannot be focussed; it eludes perceptual exploration; it cannot be fixed. . . . The after-image does not relate to the rest of the world as things do. It is more like an intrusion than like one object amongst others. . . . The after-image seemed to create a hole or gap in things, to rupture them momentarily. . . . As an interference the after-image takes its place in the world "negatively." It relates to surrounding material things as an absence, an impediment to their perceptual constitution. . . . The after-image is an absence in relation to other observers as well as in relation to other things. No one else can see it. . . . (pp. 166-170)

So far the structure of the after-image phenomenon was clarified in a negative sense, what it is in contrast with thing-perception. What is the positive sense of the phenomenon? Richer proposes a thesis on the basis of his experiential evidence: "that the after-image positively reveals sensuous material of 'hyle'."

Again Richer proceeds dialectically. First he reviews the understanding of "hyle" in Husserl, concluding that "hyle is linked to subjectivity. It is noetic. Hyle must be reunderstood as 'act material,' the very stuff of the subjective acts of perceptual consciousness in and through which noemata are constituted." (p. 170)

Richer makes a case from his data and the abstracted themes, that the experience of after-images provides experiential evidence for the existence of hyle. He argues that hyle is perceptual subjectivity disclosed:

Apparently when consciousness intends the after-image as appearance, when it cannot leap through and far beyond appearance, it tends spontaneously to "regress" and implicate the very subjectivity (the noetic factors) out of which the appearance itself is constituted.

The after-image "regressively" implicates the perceiving body experientially and thematically. The backward reflection to subjectivity is at once a reflection of perceptual body-subjectivity and a reflection of perceptual hyle. (p. 171)

Richer thus presents us with an interesting variant of empirical phenomenological psychology. He uses experiential data from a variety of subjects which he reflectively articulates and thematizes, and which he then uses as evidence for or against the adequacy of the structural charactizations presented by phenomenological philosophers. In a sense, Richer attempts to validate phenomenological constructs and theory. But it is also more than validation and/or criticism. It is a challenge to the philosophical work to become more complete and reality-adequate by taking more relevant life-world situations into account. The **psychologist** (Richer) points to important human phenomena of incomplete or distorted or "aberrant" perceptual phenomena and collects experiential data and evidence about them with which to challenge the claims of "apodictic certainty" of Individual Phenomenological Reflection and the philosopher's eidetic analysis which has tended to disregard or de-emphasize the noetic, immanent, subjective dimensions of perceptual experience. Richer says:

> Phenomenology also has tended to pass over these phenomena in favor of the thing, and, consequently, it has given an incomplete account of perception. A return to immanent "reell" hyletic analysis in an intentional framework, the "subordinate" task of psychology. . . will help to complete the perceptual analytic in ways that Husserl might not have anticipated. (p. 173)

An empirical psychologist enters the philosophical discussion with phenomenological-psychological methods and data and evidence, in order to contribute to the **common ground of phenomenological discussion** - in which both philosphers and psychologists dialogue frequently - about the nature and structure of human consciousness and, specifically, perception. This variant of empirical phenomenological psychology methods holds promise for closer cooperation between psychology and philosophy, both focusing on the **reflective analysis of life-world** experience.

What is new and different in Richer's method is that he does not work his themes into a structural generalizaton of the essence of the phenomenon empirically arrived at, but that he brings his structural themes into direct dialogue with the philosophically articulated essential structural characterizations of phenomenology, in order to contribute to their understanding and clarification through life-world examples.

## §8.-ON THE EXPERIENCE OF A FIVE-YEAR OLD: E. Keen.

In this study Ernest Keen (1973) uses phenomenological constructs to elucidate an experienced situation bringing phenomenological thinking into dialogue with lived experience. He describes the experience of his 5 year old daughter as she prepares to go to her first overnight visit with a neighbor girlfriend, how she changes her mind once she gets there and returns home content to go to sleep.

> Let us watch my five-year-old daughter. She is carefully putting her pajamas, hairbrush, and favorite doll into a large paper sack. After this packing is done, she waits eagerly by the telephone for her friend to call to say that her supper is over and that they can now begin their overnight together. The telephone game comes. She is eager and happy as she puts on her coat, then grabs her sack in one arm and my hand with the other hand in order to walk to her friend's home, two houses down the street. The two girls giggle when they see each other, and together they run off to the bedroom.
>
> Three quarters of an hour later we receive a phone call from her friend's mother. My daughter has been crying uncontrollably for half an hour and wants to come home. There is no apparent reason for this behavior; all she can say is that she wants to go home. As I bring her home, her tears subside, and when we come through the front door she grins. Even though we send her right to bed, she is glad to be home, and she does not cry further or demand a snack or a story. She goes right to sleep. (p. 3)

He interprets this episode phenomenologically following its unfolding movement step by step in order to explicate the meaning that the situation must have had for her. He does not interview his daughter in order to find out exactly what happened in her experience, he does not elicit a proto-col. Rather he approaches and analyses the episode in a reflective manner, inquiring into its conditions of possibility phenomenologically in terms of the essential dimensions of space and time, of memories and antici-pations. He reflectively reconstructs the changes that the experience of his daughter has undergone and he does it using a phenomenological way of describing the unfolding meanings. While Keen uses phenomenological con-structs to help him articulate the meaning of his daughter's experience, he also tests and validates these concepts and their fruitfulness on the basis of real life experiaction, of her comportment in the situation.

Time: Keen represents the structure of the experience in a graphic form, as a series of diagrams, in order to illustrate the interdependency and contextualization of its dimensions at the important turning points and phases of the episode. During the phase of packing everything fell against a backdrop of anticipation which, in turn, was thematic against the common stock of memories, the realm of the familiar which surrounds and permeates all of our experience.

After she was at her friend's house, she changed her mind. Her **experience** changed. All she could say was that she wanted to come home. Was she frightened that something would happen at her friend's house? Probably not, for she had been there during the day many times and had always seemed to enjoy it. If she was frightened that something would happen, the fear was not present while she was packing. Indeed, it did not seem to be the future that flavored her experience after she changed her mind; it seemed instead to be the past. Home. She remembered it, and she wanted to be there. Its safety and familiarity seemed to call her back. (p. 5)

In changing her mind the quality of her experience, its meaning, changed. The events were meaningful to her in terms of the "backdrop" against which they appeared, in terms of past - present - future, or expressed as psychological terms, memories - perceptions - anticipations.

If we thus look carefully at the temporal context of experience we discover complex dynamic and interchanging structures that help create the meanings perceived.

The term "backdrops" of anticipation and memory is merely a way of indicating how those temporal contexts enter into the fabric of meaning - not as focal points, but as ground against which figures appear, as in visual perception (p. 9).

It is important to see that when times zones are backdrops, future and past prenetrate the present in much more complex ways than we have yet described. My daughter's anticipation of a fun-filled overnight was based upon memories, like the good times she had with her friend and what she recalled of her friend's room, where she was looking forward to sleeping. What she was looking forward to appeared in her experience against the backdrop of what she looked back to: events against the backdrop of anticipations and anticipations against the backdrop of memories - a complex structure, but entirely relevant to our task of understanding her behavior in the first stage of the evening.

As she was crying, wanting to come home, her memory of home made the sack, the bed, and the room appear lonely, alien, unwelcome. But the memory of home loomed only because of a further backdrop of anticipation - of going to sleep in this alien room. She had been in the room many times before and had not found it unbearable. But knowing that she was supposed to go to sleep there made the room appear an empty place, a cold place, in contrast to her memory of her own warm bed at home. She would not have remembered her own bed except for the prior anticipation of sleeping in this one. Events against the backdrop of memories and memories against the backdrop of anticipation also provide a complex structures. (pp. 6-8)

**Space:** Keen also describes the episode in terms of **experiential space.** He focuses on two aspects in this context: 1) the "social field" in which she was engaged while packing, and 2) the "spatial field" of the relationship of "her house" and the "friend's house." We can say that the experience of the child undergoes a shift in focus, a "gestalt-switch." First, her fantasy partner was part of her personal field, then her father replaced the fantasy partner. Her social field has become transformed and reorganized.

While she was concentrating on her packing, she was quietly talking to herself. Her face was going through a series of expressions, as if she were in a conversation. Suddenly she noticed me looking at her, her "conversation" stopped, and she gave me a big grin - only a little embarassed that I have been watching her. Here we can see two distinct spaces, within which she "staged" her experience, one after the other. At first, the placing of articles within the bag occured within a space occupied by herself, the task, and at least one other person, who was present to her but not to me. The "fantasy other" may have been her friend, her mother, or even her future husband. We wold not know who it was unless she were to tell us, but it is clear that she was construing her actions according to a **social field,** a space structured by 1.) herself as worker on the task, 2.) the task itself as a display for the other, and 3.) the other as an audience and fantasy commentator on her performance. She was very much involved in the dynamics of this space when she suddenly noticed me watching her. (p. 9)

With regard to the **spatial field**, while she was waiting for the phone call the two houses represented opposite poles in a two-pole field. Initially the friend's house was attractive and pulling but once in that house the value shifted.

> The friend's house became alien, and home was "home." The pull was in the opposite direction. When we ask why she "changed her mind," we must specify what changed in her "mind" before we can broach this question. One of the things that changed was the structure of the space that included the two houses. The attractive one became unattractive, and the unattractive one became attractive. The experience of the friend's house, upon her first arriving there, fell against the backdrop of space as originally structured. Later her experience of the same house was utterly transformed. The shining rooms shone differently; they looked different, felt different, and had a different meaning. That difference was possible because the structure of the space against which they were experienced had become reversed. The rooms that had been shining promises of fun became alien territory.
> The changing of her "mind" was a changing of all these things at once. What is critical is that events, objects and people came to **mean something different** to her; the origin of meaning in experience is the context within which events, objects, and people appear - the backdrops that allow them to stand out and be experienced. In understanding her change of mind, we are therefore seeking to understand her change of meanings, and, in understanding her change of meanings, we seek to articulate the experiential contexts of events from which meanings emerge. (pp. 12-13)

Keen does not answer the **why question.** Phenomenologists don't. Why did she change her mind? He does not do so because he believes that it is not a matter of causality but of intentionality. The behavior is initiated in response to a perceived situation and the meaning of a situation can suddenly change in the experience of a person.

After he has analyzed the episode from the point of view of the child's experience Keen compares and contrasts this characterization with that of an adult's experience, expanding his phenomenological work, and even venturing into "why-territory."

But what is the difference between my daughter and myself? The impoliteness of her behavior did not impress her; she did not experience her behavior as impolite. Why not? Because she characteristically structures her experience differently from the way in which I structure mine. Her way of experiencing herself in space and time "permits" such changes of mind, whereas mine does not. The difference is twofold, temporal and spatial. First the temporal: My anticipations of fun would have made the experience more fun than it was for her. My remembered anticipations ("I recall how I've looked forward to this") would have colored my seeing the expected rooms, providing my experience with more ballast than was available to her. Furthermore, I would be "ashamed of myself" for changing my mind, which she obviously was not. Anticipating that I would remember the incident (anticipated memories) and continue to be ashamed of it would have deterred my behaving as she did. So, in relation to both anticipated memories and remembered anticipations, meanings in my experience would have been more stable. (pp. 13-14)

Keen uses a very suggestive metaphor: "ballast" in the above description to indicate that the availability of the further horizons of anticipated memories and remembered anticipations tend to stabilize the meaning of events.

Shame requires the existence and awareness of an interpersonal space, a space "in which there is at least one whose judgment counts." Although the child was not incapable of experiencing shame,

she was not ashamed that she had changed her mind as she did. Such a space was not a relevant context for, and it did not determine the meaning of, her decision to change her mind as she did.

Therefore, it is not the absence, but rather the relative weakness, of this experiential structure that makes her different from myself and most other adults. (pp. 14-15)

Her experience had neither the stability of adult experience lent by the complexities of remembered anticipations and anticipated

memories, nor the stability lent by a more or less constant context
of interpersonal contracts and agreements in which the other's point
of view is part of what events meant to us and we assume that the
other's point of view is stable. (p. 16)

Keen's method is that of doing a **situation analysis** in phenomenological terms. He uses insights gained by reflective phenomenological work
concerning the essential structures of consciousness and he applies them
to a clarifying description of an everyday situation. He demonstrates that
the phenomenological reading articulates implicit experiences and realities that were involved in the event and which contributed to its unfolding meaning.

Keen makes these reflective comments on his method and the meaning
and fruitfulness of phenomenological research:

> It is interesting to note that, whereas our phenomenological
> analysis has given us a pretty good idea of **why** my daughter changed
> her mind and **what** changed when she did, we have really discovered
> nothing that we did not already know. Yet at the beginning of the
> study we were puzzled in a way that we are not now puzzled. The fact
> that I already "knew" everything written here is relevant in my im-
> pulse to try to correct the awkward situation created by the inci-
> dent: the impulse to say such things as "What will the neighbors
> think?"; "How have you made your friend feel?"; (the social context
> of behavior and experience); "You will be sorry tomorrow!" (antici-
> pated memories); "An hour ago you could hardly wait!" (remembered
> anticipations); "Don't you want to be a big girl?"; "Don't be a
> baby!"; (self-definition as meaning producing contexts). This impulse
> was to make her see the matters as we do, implicitly knowing that she
> was experiencing it differently. We knew it all, but we did not know
> **what** we knew or that we knew it. For that reason we were puzzled.
>
> Phenomenology does not yield new information in the way that
> science pushes back the frontiers of knowledge. Its task is less to
> give us new ideas than to make explicit those ideas, assumptions, and
> implicit presuppositions upon which we already behave and experience
> life. Its task is to reveal to us exactly what we already know and
> that we know it, so that we can be less puzzled about ourselves. Were
> it to tell us something that we did not know, it would not be telling

us anything about ourselves, and therefore it would not be important. (p. 18)

Keen thus concretizes our understanding of a phenomenological way of seeing and speaking, and he enriches our self-understanding by providing us with descriptive phenomenological constructs and "handles" with which to touch our own experiencing and enhance our explicit awareness of what is happening. Keen's work shows how phenomenological analysis can make the implicit explicit, the hidden manifest.

Keen's analysis also corroborates the value of phenomenological constructs such as intentionality, temporality and spatiality. Keen practices a brand of empirical existential-phenomenological psychology which critically examines, illustrates, and empirically validates the work based on reflective philosophical activity.

PART  II


CONDUCTING

HERMENEUTICAL - PHENOMENOLOGICAL

RESEARCH

# A.

# ACTUAL LIFE-TEXT STUDIES

The data-base for hermeneutical research is typically wider than that for empirical existential-phenomenological studies. They range from personal documents, to literature, to works of art which present themselves for interpretation. There does not seem to be a set starting point or a clearly outlined procedure to follow in hermeneutical-phenomenological investigations. One embeds oneself in the process of getting involved in the text, one begins to discern configurations of meaning, of parts and wholes and their interrelatedness, one receives certain messages and glimpses of an unfolding development that beckons to be articulated and related to the total fabric of meaning. The hermeneutic approach seems to palpate its object and it makes room for it to reveal itself to our gaze and ears, to speak its own story into our understanding.

In hermeneutic work we grope for the single expression that will do justice to the integrity and complexity and essential being of the phenomenon. We become spokespersons and messengers for the meanings that demand to be articulated. We become intrigued and entangled in the webs and voices of language and its expressive demands. In hermeneutic work we become engaged in an expanding network of meaning-enrichment contributing new meanings to the ongoing dialogue. It is a process of contextualization and amplification rather than of structural essentialization. Hermeneutic work is open-ended and suggestive, concerned with relational fertility.

In a more formal characterization we can say with Ricoeur (1971) that the hermeneutical approach to the social sciences utilizes the notion of the **text** as the basic paradigm. Human action and all other products of human activities as **expressions** - art works, rituals, institutions, etc. - can be understood as "text-analogues" in need of interpretation.

Titleman (1975) discusses the relevance of Ricoeur's work for a hermeneutic phenomenological psychology. As compared to actual situated experience, as in a face to face dialogue **action as text** has the following four discernible characteristics:

(1) **The fixation of meaning:** We need some record or "protocol" of experience or some transcription or trace with which to work, whether it

is produced from personal experience by direct investigation or taken from works of creative imagination.

(2) **The dissociation of the mental intention of the author from the text:** In contrast to the face to face situation of dialogue the **text** is independent of the author's consciousness. It stands in a new communicative situation. The intentions of the author have to be inferred and reconstructed by the hermeneutic investigator, they cannot be ascertained by asking the author. The text stands on its own.

(3) **The display of non-ostensive references:** As Titleman (1975) phrases this concern:

> The meaning of a subject's descriptive protocol(s) cannot be comprehended by analyzing and reducing them atomistically into separate and unconnected parts; rather, the meaning of the subject's described experience(s)/behavior(s) must be understood in terms of the relation between the constitutive dimensions. . . . The descriptive protocol is more than a linear succession of sentences - it projects a **world,** a cumulative and holistic process, the structure of which like the text, cannot be derived from or reduced to the linguistic structure of the sentence. (p. 186)

(4) **Its universal range of address:** The text is open for everyone who can read and gain access to it. Unlike the directed speech of two partners in a situated speech event, the text is there to be taken up and read in any way whatsoever.

> Like a text, a descriptive protocol can be read by an indefinite range of possible psychologist-readers. The descriptive protocol, like the text, is an "open work" that awaits fresh interpretations from different perspectives and as history, in its unfolding, sheds new light on the experiences and events that have been described. The meaning of a text-analogue is in "suspense" in the sense that its meaning is never totalized. The description of human experience and behavior, like a text, is open to everybody who is capable of reading. (Titleman, 1975, p. 186)

While Ricoeur presents a generalized theory of **action as text,** Titleman's paper relates this work directly to the problems of a phenomenologically based psychology concerned with the analysis of life-world experience.

Another central issue in hermeneutical work is the so-called "hermeneutic circle." This thought-figure describes the open-ended and continuously spiralling nature of the hermeneutic inquiry and sense-making process. We have a fore-knowledge about most aspects of life. We come to any phenomenon with a pre-comprehension of its meaning, yet in search for deeper understanding and more precise differentiation. As Titleman states this:

> The circularity of the hermeneutic endeavor is not vicious in that it involves a passage from a vague pre-conceptual understanding of the meaning of a phenomenon to the explicit seizure of its meaning. There is no entrance to the hermeneutic circle, no beginning point. The psychological investigator must "leap" into the circle in order to elucidate it. (p. 187)

The hermeneutic stance acknowledges the perspectival nature and biographico-historical involvement of the researcher and makes the investigation of the implicit pre-comprehensions of the researcher part of the interpretative process.

An important consideration in all hermeneutic work is the problem of the validity of the findings. How can we evaluate the truth claims made by the various interpretative readings? Titleman (1975) discusses this issue in the following way:

> The validation of the particular interpretation in the area of the social sciences is not like proving a conclusion in logic, but rather it is closer to a logic of probability than to a logic of empirical verification. Showing that a particular interpretation is more probable, given the available knowledge, is different than proving that a conclusion is true. (p. 190)

Ricoeur (1971) seems to regard hermeneutics as an argumentative discipline, as a subspecies of rhetoric when he says:

> Like legal utterances, all interpretations in the field of literary criticism and in the social sciences may be challenged, and the question "what can defeat a claim" is common to all argumentative situations. Only in the tribunal is there a moment when the procedures of appeal are exhausted. But it is because the decision of

the judge is implemented by the force of public power. Neither in literary criticism nor in the social sciences, is there such a last word. Or, if there is any, we call that violence. (p. 553)

The validation of interpretation is a difficult issue. Ricoeur thinks that a new type of logic is involved here, a "logic of uncertainty" and of "qualitative probability."

For Gadamer (1960) the "hermeneutical experience" is one of becoming involved in a dialogue or a dialectic of question and answer. Its primordial medium is language or "linguisticality," the saying power which creates the world within which understanding and disclosure take place. Worlds appear between persons in dialogue and rest on the common ground of our tradition as shared language. In the hermeneutical experience and situation an encounter takes place between the heritage which is sedimented in the text revealing a world made text from a perspective through a particular experience and the horizon of the interpreter. Author and reader belong to the language but differently through the distance of time and perspective. A "fusion of horizons" takes place in which the reader becomes a servant of the text, open to hearing what is said and articulating the message.

As Palmer (1969) states this issue in commentating on Gadamer's work:

He is not so much a knower as an experiencer: the encounter is not a conceptual grasping of something but an event in which a world opens itself up to him. Insofar as each interpreter stands in a new horizon, the event that comes to language in the hermeneutical experience is something new that emerges, something that did not exist before.

The method appropriate to the hermeneutical situation involving the interpreter and the text, then, is one that places him in an attitude of openness to be addressed by the tradition. The attitude is one of expectancy, of waiting for something to happen. (p. 209)

All human understanding is historical, linguistic and dialectical, each disclosure contributes to the task of developing our effective historical consciousness. According to Gadamer (1960) the task of hermeneutics is:

> to bring the text out of the alienation in which it finds itself (as fixed, written form) back into the living present of dialogue, whose primordial fulfillment is question and answer. (p. 350)

In organizing the research examples of hermeneutical-phenomenological psychology we set up two divisions: (a) **Actual life-text studies:** In this group we present work that creates data -life-texts- by tape recording actual verbal expressions in situations, ranging from a "speak-aloud" protocol on the situated stream of experiaction (von Eckartsberg, 1972), to the study of therapy transcripts (Fessler, 1983) to research on interview transcripts from a professional role-ensemble and clients (Kracklauer, 1980), to dialogal research in the framework of a "conceptual encounter." (de Rivera, 1981)

(b) **Studies of recollection and literary texts:** In a second group of hermeneutical-phenomenological studies we present work that draws on personal experience in an intuitive and illustrative way to engage in hermeneutical reflection (Buckley, 1971), work that utilizes established masterworks of dramatic literature as texts (Halling, 1979), hermeneutical work on the meaning and origins of the theoretical attitude which guides our activities as researchers and scholars (Jager, 1975), and hermeneutical reflective work on a theme in a historical context. (Romanyshyn, 1982)

## §2.-ON THE SOCIAL CONSTITUTION OF THE STREAM OF EXPERI-ACTION: R. von Eckartsberg.

Our awareness of our ongoing stream of consciousness, of experience and action, of "experiaction," is a fascinating phenomenon. We are, always already, bodily involved in a here and now situation. Experiaction is situated. Some awareness has to be used by a person to relate bodily to his or her physical environment, but our experience or conscious awareness also transcends the situation in order to make present other domains or landscapes of consciousness. Through our modes of psychological access: to remember or to anticipate, to imagine possibilities, to reconstruct, to think and reflect. In experiaction we are not limited by or exclusively bound to the physical situation at hand. We live in a psychological life-space mediated by experiactions of which we are partially aware. We live in a mappable "psychocosm" (von Eckartsberg, 1981) or a personal "life-scape."

We can research the constitution of the psychocosm by collecting samples from the experiactional flow of a person. We select and specify the situation and duration of the observational period which sets limits to what and how we can record the experiaction. We can make concurrent recordings in the form of tape-recordings of behavior and dialogue and we can create "speak-aloud protocols" by asking our respondents to verbalize everything that occurs to them in conscious awareness. In situations in which the researcher is alone, this poses no particular problem, although at first it feels unusual to audibly verbalize all of what goes through "one's mind" in a monologue. Speak-aloud protocols (Klinger, 1978; Aanstoos, 1983; Wertz, 1983) are difficult or impossible to obtain in interpersonal situations except under special circumstances or in psycho-analytic work. Interesting attempts have been made to sample the stream of experiaction by the creative use of kitchen-timers (Leary, 1970) and by random electronic beeping (Csikszentmihalyi, 1978) alerting us to what we experience at the moment.

In this hermeneutical research the focus is on a solitary situation in which I let my experiactional stream unfold itself without censorship, such that it can reflect underlying personal concerns and social determinants. I just recorded about 20 minutes of my own experience as a reportage on a Sony audio tape-recorder. I speak the experience as it happened to the extent that I was capable of doing this: voicing my experience.

In the situation it was me sitting alone on our sunporch. I felt that it was a very everyday event, nothing "unusual" happened. I think I was my "usual self," whatever this means. Whenever I sit down by myself, some such train of thought and experience unfolds, although, naturally, it is always different. That particular day, as I started speaking out loud, however, my experience quickly became oriented and organized around a particular focus: I had to give a lecture about Experiential Psychology at New College, Florida, two weeks hence. This anticipated task and event became the major organizing principle - the theme - that shaped my experience during these 20 minutes. This is what happened, in verbatim excerpts selected in terms of the relevance to the topic: how an antici-pated event enters and co-constitutes the flow of experience and how a social determinant, i.e. the demand character of the social situation of giving a public lecture exerts its shaping influence on the personal stream of experience. Although being alone, social reality nevertheless permeates and shapes my "private" experience influences.

## Transcript from Recording

It's Easter Sunday. . . just around noon. . . and I'm sitting
here in my sunporch. . . gorgeous day. . . quiet, very quiet. . .
looking out over the golf course there. . . sun is bright. . . can
see the green, just starting. . . . The lawns are just beginning to
be green here in Pittsburgh. . . Pittsburgh spring is late. . . . Now
looking down there. . . see the Steel Building. . . U. S. Steel
Building. . . just a massive. . . gray and brown. . . slab there,
iron. . . steel slab. . . . Now I'm thinking about, uh. . . just
sitting down. . . thinking about experience. . . just tuning in to
experience. . . my own experience. . . what's happening right
now. . . just this next few minutes. . . just settling down now. . .
sort of have to relax, just sort of quiet. . . and uh. . . . What
comes to mind is uh. . . that I have to go to Florida. . . and give a
talk there at the New School. . . at the uh New College. . . . I got
this letter. . . Dave, Dave Smillie. . . he called up and asked me
to come down and speak. . . and uh speak about experience. . . what
I'm doing, studying experience, experiential psychology. . . and uh.
. . New College. . . I get drawn into that. . . . What is that? I
only have an image of that; I have some knowledge of what this means.
. . but looking forward or just thinking about it. It's just a
concept more or less. An image, maybe faintly. . . New College. But
this is sort of an image, visually. I know about it through Dave. . .
Smillie who came down there, to teach there, two years ago. He
visited, he told me a little bit, he called me up for this talk. . .
and uh. . . from the conversation I got a feeling for. . . New
College, a small school, bright students, very bright students - I
heard that also, from a colleague of mine, Jack Rains. We've had a
few conversations about New College, nothing specific. I don't have a
specific image, but this concept  now fills up - New College, small
school, very bright students, interesting faculty probably. People
who want to get close with students, work intensively with students.
I know what that's like. That's what we're trying to do also. . . at
Duquesne. I know what that is. But when I turn and think of what is
my knowledge, what is my experience. . . of New College, looking
forward. . . empty. . . anticipations. . . just pointers, just. . .
inklings. Nothing substantive, no concrete experience. And uh. . . so

I can just flow with the idea of Florida, knowledge. . . . New
College, how a concept. . . fills in. Here I got lost. . . .
     But somehow I come back to this talk, because uh. . . I'm tuning
in to this talk. I've been thinking about what I should be doing. I
haven't written out anything yet. I made a few sketches, in my diary
a couple of weeks ago. . . having to do with knowledge and uh. . .
objective knowledge, subjective knowledge. I was reading Rozack then,
the counter-culture and . . . about the myth of the objective consciousness. . . and uh. . . tuning in and going around consciousness,
more as personal consciousness, private consciousness, the flow just
as I've been describing. How unique this is, how uh. . . you know,
interwoven, intermeshed, flowing, jumpy, a little bit. Just going
along. . . I was thinking a little bit about that. . . yea. . . So
I'm drawn back to: I have to give this talk. So uh I've been
thinking, here and there it comes up. I sit down, I think about it.
Anytime it comes upon me. What am I gonna do there? And uh as it has
shaped up, Experiential Psychology, this, this is the title. Dave
asked me for a title, what shall I talk about. . . and I said Experiential Psychology. That's, that's the term I use now for doing
what I'm doing. . . I'm recording it as it happens right now and. . .
you know, my eyes sometimes drift off, swerve off the thrust of
attention that I had focussed on this talk and. . . and. . . then I
shift back into, let my eyes connect me with the world, because
that's what I'm talking about, the. . . you know, what I'm conscious
**of**, the intentional aspect of consciousness, as phenomenologists
would say. . . that consciousness is **of** something, it's always what
you pay attention to as it presents itself, and it presents itself in
different. . . levels, guises. Close up, I'm connected. I'm in touch.
. . with the eyes, hands, sitting in this blue chair, heavy, I'm just
relaxed, sitting, and. . . I can feel my body, my arms on the chair
here and. . . looking out, that view, I like that view; that view
called me so I was getting away from. . . describing what I was
doing, recording the experience, just giving an account just like a
radio announcer who would describe an event, so I was describing the
event of sitting here in this room right now. . . quiet, as I said,
you know, it's this atmosphere and. . . I let my mind go, you have to
just, just let it glide, let it flow, let it go around and in doing
so it's an exploration in experience, it's sort of like the movement,
a journey, an experiencing. It always comes back to: I'm thinking

about this talk and. . . how I'm recording it now, because that's one of the things I came up with. . . just thinking about what I should do, why not record experience, and then comment upon it, the second stage, and reflect upon it, take it into a more thoughtful, reflective generalizing stance, and then those three steps would be what I would present - not talking about Experiential Psychology. I don't like the about, talking about something out there anymore. I'd really like to just get into it. So, so this is, I feel, getting into it. Just a short recording, a few minutes. It's only been ten minutes or something. Just a few minutes and then uh I'll take this as the data and begin to talk about it, think about it, show how consciousness is manifested. It's just an everyday event. . . . so much for the structure of this. . . .

But what intrigues me is the knowledge, the way in which I am connected. . . to. . . New College - people here, the ideas. I have sort of two personal connections - Jack Rains. . . and Dave Smillie - conversations that continue with these two, which put me in touch with this place there and. . . . It's at a distance, and how we know at a distance, and. . . how we really know at a distance. . . through the experience of other people. . . it's through these conversations that. . . the world becomes richer, it grows, it's challenged. There's a dialectic there so that. . . experience. . . it is not just personal but it involves others. It's interpersonal experience basically. And so even sitting down here by myself with this Sony machine. Yet, nevertheless I'm also already anticipating this event in the presence of... this event that I have to perform, or that I have to be at, or that I have to conduct. So it's an interpersonal situation.

## Reflection

Now, I would like to go over this experience to amplify and to reflect upon it in a contemplative attitude of openness, of letting the phenomenon - the meaning constitution of my stream of experience - speak to me. The material is quite rich and lends itself to reflection in many different ways, answering many explication-guiding questions. I will develop one particular theme that has to do with the way in which a socially determined event - the task to give a lecture - in the future, as anticipated, enters and helps constitute the ongoing stream of experiaction in a meditative moment and setting. The future event seems to cast its "shadow" on the here and now. The task ahead exerts a demand character on me, it has a claim on me to heed it, and to fill my time in anticipation and preparing and structuring it in my consciousness prior to its enactment in tangible reality.

As I go along, reflecting on this experience, I try to discover essential or universal aspects of the process of experience. These are exemplified in this unique-concrete reported event but they can be said to be valid for experiencing in general. This constitutes the reflective work, looking back and thinking about this experience, discovering meaningful patterns and structures, universal features that are lived out concretely in a unique fashion.

This is perhaps a first universal we find concerning experiaction: that it is situated and hence in a close interface with the material-and meaning-organization of the situation. We cannot study experience apart from the situation in which it originates. As individuals we participate in a large, though never unlimited repertoire of situations and hence the domains of experience to be studied are quite expansive. In interpersonal terms, experiaction varies, of course, depending on who the people in dialogue are in relationship to each other. With an intimate friend you obviously tend to experiact spontaneously and in a spirited manner whereas with strangers a more formal style prevails.

Reflecting on the first part of my experience it became situated within the context of an implied presence of an audience - a sophisticated college audience in my anticipation as my movement into a thoughtful and psychological - experiential language indicates. Also, the choice of topics within the "monologue:" knowledge, concepts, images, conversational community, perspectivity - makes sense within the context of my en-visioning the type of my anticipated audience.

As we can readily see from this, my experience was embedded in multi-ple contexts of meaning, such as to "record an experience," "make it relevant to the talk," "something for the New College," "representing the approach of experiential psychology," which are all part of my definition of the situation. To be concrete and faithful to what happened I would have to differentiate the physical situation (sunporch) from the experi-action definition of the situation (recording an experience for my talk) which in a sense constitutes a situation within a situation. The experi-action is held together and derives its coherence and meaning from the future event (giving this talk) to which it refers and for which it is preparatory. In motivational terms we can speak of my "awareness and commitment of giving this talk" as being the project which then ties together many strands of my experience which contribute to setting up the event. With these experiences I prepare for the event.

Within the recorded experience I referred to the fact that I had thought of this occasion several times and that slowly a strategy had evolved. Recording my experience was part of the procedure. It makes sense only as part of this overall event that got set off in Dave Smillie's awareness before he called me on the phone, then entered my life through the call, has occupied my attention intermittently throughout this period. . . . involving sometimes sustained thought-work as I am writing this reflection here and now. It is entering a new phase right this moment-one week after the description - and it will continue to call my attention for some time to come, depending on what happens with it in relationship to other aspects of my living. Any event has its own unfolding life within the rest of a life.

Reflecting on this experience so far, I have highlighted how there is a situated context and focus and guideline that pulls the strands of experiencing together. This continued focus or project allows me to "stay on the track" and to become aware of distraction or detours that pull me in another direction. The implication for our understanding of the nature of experiaction is that experience is always something (the content of consicousness) which typically occurs in the service of something else, be it the guiding intention of the conscious person or the habitual and hence anonymous bio-social programming. We might call this the **double-intentionality** of consciousness. Naturally we may not always be conscious of our intention in this double sense.

Questioning the meaning of an experience leads to the widening of the horizon of understanding, to a broadening of the context. We see this particular situation in the broader context of an array of situations which is held together in its intermittent and yet continuous and sequential unfolding by an overarching intent or project. The ultimate context for an individual is his or her life-project (the way Sartre works this out in his existential psychoanalysis) and the projects that society and culture provide. Each moment of experience is, therefore, also embedded in a particular socio-cultural matrix of meaning. Let me reflect on how this works.

In my recorded experience, I accept the "social," that is "professional collegiate" definition of the situation to a large degree. I choose a certain level of language, I accept the etiquette of formal presentation I had been screening out imaginative variations. I tended toward the serious atmosphere prevailing in academic circles in my monologue; there was little humor which tends to sparkle easily in the presence of others and not so readily "in solitary." It seems that projects - not necessarily rational projects exclusively, to be sure - hold situations together and that situations are the matrix of all particular experiactions that may occur within them. But "situation" is itself a term that needs clarification. In the context of this recorded experiaction - this situated event - it becomes clear that we are involved in a complex structure. Using the thought-dimension of time we can see that my situation - sitting bodily on the sunporch in Pittsburgh - was transcended in awareness both **forward** in time to my anticipated-presence at New College in Florida, two weeks hence, as well as **backward** in time to my remembered-presence to conversations with Dave Smillie back in Pittsburgh a few years ago. In other words, any situated experiaction spills over its physical space/time dimensions, unless one is able to limit one's awareness by concentration. In experiaction we can move freely and usually extend ourselves beyond our bodily here and now. This is why an exclusive focus on the observer attitude is misleading to a large extent. We can describe this by saying that experiaction, even though it presents itself to us as orchestrated and unified, can be recognized as occurring at different layers. Psychological language has names for these different experiential processes, such as perception, thought, memory, anticipation, imagination, etc. Although it makes some sense to distinguish these levels or modalities of experience - particularly in view of the fact that we as persons have some measure of control over where to direct our attention, using what modality - there is usually a mixture of modalities occurring in any concrete experienced event. They run together. Going back to my recorded experience of last Sunday, it is apparent that in my experiaction I moved back and forth in time, and that I also moved from immediate perception to recalling to conceptualizing to questioning. In a sense, everything is connected within the unity of my own consciousness, and we are witnessing an organic process of interpenetration and growth with continuous evolving transformation - informed and shaped by efforts at making sense - giving rise to complex understanding and awareness of the functioning of consciousness. By comparison, computer-memories are terribly static and dead.

Human awareness as it is accessible to description and reflection is intriguingly complex, subtle, and challenging to understanding. If there are any root-motives to human life, certainly one of them is to understand and to make sense of experiencing one's world, although not everybody might feel this urge which is the beginning of scientific and philosophic interest.

Studying experience is different from studying physical or even biological reality out there. The moment people are involved - human experiaction - we are dealing with interpreted reality, with human meanings. For me it's the United States Steel Building the way I see it, in terms of what it means to me, and this is dependent upon what my extended relationship with the United States Steel building is, my knowledge, my attitudes, my values, etc. In one act of awareness, looking at this building - as I sustain my focus of attention, as I tune-in and just hold steady in this determinate direction - all my past and future involvement somehow assembles relevant experiences to fill in and amplify the meaning of what I am looking at. An organic structuring of the total stock of my experience occurs around the focus of my attention, the United States Steel Building.

In phenomenology we speak of experienced horizons which open out from the spectacle. The focus of attention acts as a sort of vortex or **vacuum-field** which draws into itself relevant items from our stock of experiaction established through previous contact. Thus, associated meanings are awakened and begin to dwell in the invisible and hovering presence around and through the topical focus of interest, modulating its meaning. For example, my wife and I looking at the same identifiable structure (U. S. Steel Building), nevertheless experience two different realities: what this spectacle means to her and what it means to me. We agree on the same object of reference - on this level we have common understanding - but we differ in what it means - in its idiosyncratic meaning. Using Gurwitsch's phenomenological language, what we are aware of is the total meaning co-constituted by the thematic object (the U. S. Steel Building) and the thematic field (The U. S. Steel Building meaning-horizons for me). Experience is thus a constantly changing and evolving cumulative meaning-manifold, shifting from aspect to aspect and from domain to domain. Yet in spite of the personal subtleties and nuances in the unique flavor of experiacting, there are the common foci about which we can establish consensus - what we are talking about - and there are universal shared features of experiacting - the way in which something appears to a person - always as contextualized, from a perspective, in time, etc.

The experiactional stream of a person can be seen to be organized. It takes place in situation as a "situated event." Events have a duration through time; they could be called: Time-Gestalten. Events (such as giving a public lecture) first tend to appear in the stream of experience in imaginary anticipation usually as a result of a social invitation or as a self-initiated project. In anticipatory experience projected events are developed, worked-on, thought about on repeated occasions. The event takes shape in experience as an anticipation (what I thought the lecture to be like) before it takes place (what it turns out to be in actuality). This has consequences and is important because strategy-decisions are made which actually create the future event. During the recorded experience I actually decided what I was going to do for the lecture. (Needless to say you can make mistakes and proceed from an inadequate anticipatory image. I imagined myself to be speaking to interested psychology students and the audience later turned out to be senior citizens in retirement in Florida who like to hear a lecture at the college on any topic. They were very kind to me.)

The meaning of this anticipated event which has personal (what shall I do) as well as social-professional horizons (what is expected of an existential-phenomenological psychologist and of a lecturer in a college setting, generally) sets limits to what is allowed into the imaginary anticipation or the projecting. They could be said to act as "charges" upon my experiaction here and now. It seems that the event in anticipatory elaboration is richer and allows more play in experience. As we approach the actualization proper (actually giving the lecture) the range of possibilties narrows. Anticipation has to become embodied: it springs into action and enters the domain of public and shared social reality. We enact and we witness the event.

Any component of the experiactional stream - particularly in the anticipating phases of event-structures - is built up in complex ways. This may be described as "interwovenness." Whatever we focus on (for example, the United States Steel Building in Pittsburgh, Pa.) can be seen to arise on a string of previous encounters reaching back into one's at bottom indeterminate biographical stock of experiaction. This stock hovers horizonally around the theme - what I pay attention to at the moment - and codetermines its meaning. This makes for idiosyncratic meanings. But our past experience is also in a good measure shared (social) because it is based on experiences of communication to which I had access through lan guage or images. To some extent, therefore, there is also a public and shared meaning to a perceived theme.

Components of the experiactional stream are also gathered up and connected through a higher and unifying intention, the project. We take many steps to actualize a project, and we also seem to have more than one project going on at any one time. This tends to "mix-up" our stream of experiaction in surprising and complex ways.

In this study I have taken a small strip (20 minutes of continuous experiaction: sitting down and recording what occurs to me) which turned out to be connected to the larger sequence of being involved in giving a lecture. This event as an over-arching project casts its shadow ahead of itself and colored my anticipatory experience in clearly definable ways.

The general structural features uncovered here through reflection were present and at work during my experiaction although I was not explicitly aware of them at the time, while living them out. Nevertheless, my pre-reflective experiaction turned out to have been structured and organized. In what I thought was a unique-private experience there were revealed and operative general-universal structures. The personal-existential and the general-phenomenological components are inextricably intertwined and collaborative in the creation of human experience in a particular situation. They constitute a tension inherent in the flow of experiaction. In living we constantly move between these levels and as researchers in this field we always try to bridge this "gap" that arises in understanding which dichotomizes "lived immediacy" and "theoretical understanding." Either extreme - "just living" or "just thinking" - if emphasized unduly is an aberration. The human way is to experiact and to make sense of it so that mere living-out is humanized into living-with-awareness. This can never be fully accomplished but is always in process, ongoing. Everyone has to unfold his own awareness and understanding, recognizing that the depth or ground of living eludes objectification and final conceptual grasp. We can only tune-in and become involved.

## §2.-PSYCHOTHERAPEUTIC INTERPRETATION:
### R. Fessler.

Research on psychotherapy that has employed the external view or "observer perspective" has not been able to do justice to the actual complexities of the lived experience of therapeutic involvement. The two traditional approaches: (a) the empirical study of psychotherapy from the perspective of the researcher as an objective external observer, or (b) the study of psychotherapy from the perspective of recollections and reconstructions of what transpired as formulated by the therapist, have failed to articulate the richness and complexity of the ongoing experience and meaning of both participants in the process.

In studies of the psychotherapeutic process and psychotherapeutic interpretation there always exists a gulf between the expectations derived from training, textbooks, and the claims of theoreticians that the novice psychotherapist carries into the situation and the actuality of therapeutic encounter and what research shows to be true. There always is a tendency to clean up the messiness and ambiguity and the inherent confusion that occurs in the midst of psychotherapy for both the therapist and the client and to retrospectively translate the actual events in terms of coherent conceptual categories and a reasonable logical account. As Fessler (1983) said, it is important not to forget that: " Our conceptual understanding of psychotherapy is the net product of a translation process rather than a reproduction of psychotherapy itself." (p. 34)

To a large part this is due to the one-sidedness of most psychotherapeutic research focusing either on the perspective of the psychotherapist or on that of the client. What if we try to ascertain what both the therapist and the client focus on in the same psychotherapeutic events and disclose their experienced meaning from the point of view of their own experience? This is the hermeneutical-phenomenological apparoach that Fessler (1978) took in his dissertation research, entitled: **A phenomenological investigation of psychotherapeutic interpretation.**

From existing research with audio- and audiovisual tapes of the therapy sessions we know that there is always more going on than what participants can spontaneously recall. Audio- and audiovisual recordings have thus become a valuable tool and aid in training and research regarding psychotherapy because they allow us to articulate and discuss the lived and pre-reflective dimensions of bodily expression and gestures. Retrospective accounts and protocols tend not to do full justice to these lived dimensions of interexperience and interaction. As participants we are only partially aware of the fullness of our involvement and we are subject to selective perceptions and even gross distortion.

All retrospectively constituted accounts have this difficulty. They are written in hindsight and from the point of view of completed action, i.e. from after the end of the completed event. Audio-visual recordings and speak-aloud protocols which articulate the ongoing process at each passing point are thus qualitatively different from retro-protocols and usually contain more detail and nuance.

If we combine the audio-visual process-recording and the retro-account and then combine them in some dialogal way we create a variegated and fertile data-base for reflective work. The combination of these two data-sources - process recording by audio-tape and protocol by retrospective verbal account - is one of the fascinating innovations in hermeneutical phenomenological methodology that Fessler introduces.

**Method.** Fessler (1983) obtained audio-tape recordings of therapy sessions by experienced therapists immediately after the sessions with clients who had been in therapy at least six months. He investigated three therapist-client pairs.

The researcher transcribed 5-10 minute segments from these tapes in which **interpretation** was perceived **by the researcher** to have taken place. He then returned the next day to conduct separate interviews with the therapist and the client regarding their experience of the session and the particular events under study.

First the subjects were asked to **recall** what had taken place. This verbal report was itself recorded. Then the segment of the tape-recording of the original session was played, a sentence at a time, while the subject read along from the transcript.

The subject was asked to try to recapture the experience that he had had at the time, sentence by sentence. What had he been trying to say? Why? What had he thought the other person was trying to say or do? Why? What thought had he had but not expressed? This way of proceeding produced an hour of elaboration on what the subject had experienced at the time. This elaboration plus the recalled account constituted the "data base" for reflection and comparison of the perspective of the therapist and the researcher, from the privileged vantage point of the researcher who was thus able to gain access to the actor-perspective of each participant (therapist and client) something that neither was privy to at the time.

**Results.** As I see it, the results of this investigation of the experiences of the patient and the therapist are discussed by Fessler in terms of three issues:

(1) **The difference between retrospective recall and audio-tape-assisted recall.** The research design and process generated new data and revealed the nature of the smoothing-over and cleaning-up of the original experience when it is rendered retrospectively as account. The original experience turns out to have been much more ambiguous, more detailed, more

confusing and, generally, more messy. The research subjects, by going over the experience again, sentence by sentence, now were able to see things which they did not see at the time they occurred. They became empowered - by the audio-feedback - to pay attention to their "horizonal experiences" which were not focal at the time but which became thematic during tape-assisted re-living.

The results were intriguing. In his recollection of the session (prior to listening to the tape) the therapist clearly remembered what he had tried to convey to the patient, how he had conveyed it, and how well he thought the patient had understood. He remembered the content of what he had said and described his delivery in ways that suggested that he had been very conscious of saying it in a way that the patient could hear it (i.e. in a way that would not arouse too much resistance). But when the therapist then listened to the tape recording of the session, he discovered that what he **thought** he had done was not what he had done at all. Reliving the session a sentence at a time with the tape and the transcript, he now remembered that in fact he had often been confused, floundering, vague about what he had been doing. The transcript was replete with half sentences, false starts, "ums" and "uhs" that he had forgotten in his recollection. . . . And he had **not** recalled a wealth of horizonal experiences that he had had at the time. His recollection had been a hindsight view, a retrospective, encapsulated version, which made sense of his **reflection** on the session but which did not include a good deal of the original experience.

A similar discrepancy was found between the recollection and reliving of the session by the patient. In his recollection...the patient described very little of the content of what had been said and remembered primarily a global experience of being either understood or misunderstood by the therapist. In reliving the session a sentence at a time with the tape and transcript, the patient **now** remembered that he had often been confused by what the therapist was saying. He remembered trying to get the therapist to be more direct and trying to correct the therapist when he misunderstood him. In this reliving, the patient still remembered experiencing at the time primarily the therapist's encouragement, support, understanding, or misunderstanding rather than the content of what the therapist had specifically said. (pp. 40-41)

(2) **The comparison of the experiences of the patient and the therapist.** Fessler's research method and double-perspective approach allowed
him to scrutinize what I want to call the process of "inter-under-
standing." From this privileged perspective of the researcher who gained
access to the "inner lining," i.e. the personal meanings of both the
therapist and the client, it was possible to discern when mutual understanding or misunderstanding occurred. Fessler was able to trace the
moment by moment unfolding of the meanings which the therapist and the
client experienced with regard to each other. On the basis of this micro-
analysis of elaborated statements Fessler came to the following conclusions:

> This comparison revealed that the therapists and the patients
> frequently had entirely different experiences of what was taking
> place during their session, and neither had been fully aware of what
> the other had been experiencing or doing. . . .
>     . . . What is expressed at any moment in therapy has meaning in
> a dual context - the context of the therapist and the context of the
> patient - and the meaning that they give to what is taking place is
> often quite different. (p. 41)

Fessler also presents a careful verbatim transcript of a 2 minute trans-
action which vividly illustrates the step by step unfolding of convergen-
cies and divergencies in meaning.

(3) **Unity in diversity.** In spite of the obvious divergencies of
experienced meaning of the same events there was an underlying or over-
riding unity of meaning in the discourse that revealed itself to the
privileged position of the researcher who had both perspectives in view.
As Fessler states it:

> Their separate profiles mesh. There is a unity to psychotherapy
> but it is a unity that is horizonal for the participants who are
> caught up in their conversation, and one that is visible only from
> within the privileged perspective of the researcher who has access to
> both participant's experiences.
>     Despite the difference in phenomenal experience for the two
> participants, there was a unity to what was taking place. The thera-
> pist and the patient do not take turns speaking and listening.
> Rather, they participate in a speech that is taking place between and

through them - a speech that is both spoken and listened to simultaneously. Each speaks in response to what he hears the other expressing, and each tries to express himself in a way that the other can hear and understand.... They may have completely different experiences os what is being said, but despite that each is led on by the other's words to a further elaboration and articulation of his own experience and to a further unfolding of what he thinks the other is trying to express. . . . Therapy is not done by one and received by the other; it is a shared speech that participates in the "sculpting" of a developing meaning for each participant - a meaning that does not originate in either one of them but through their parallel attempts to be heard and understood. (p. 44)

Fessler's creative research design, which he developed in collaboration with A. Barton who directed this Ph.D. research, combined written protocol, transcript, dialogal investigation and audio-feedback. It opens up a whole new area and method of investigation. It can be further elaborated on by the use of video-feedback as well. There are important and yet very subtle aspects of intersubjective dialogue to be investigated in this microanalytic fashion.

Each subject's expression is the "other side" of the other's experience. The patient's attempts to articulate his view are the other side of the therapist's experience of digression, and the therapist's attempts to bring the patient back are the other side of the patient's experience of being misunderstood. (p. 44)

We tend to assume that our experienced meaning is spontaneously shared by our partners in dialogue. Proceeding on this assumption of presumed congruence we tend to come together again sooner or later in a moment of mutually recognized congruence. But we also often fall out of sync and consensus into mis-understanding when we recognize that our presumed congruence was really a self-projected illusion which was not shared by the other. A recognizable rift occurs in the relationship which calls for attention and address.

## §3.-ON THE DRUG PROBLEM: C. Kracklauer.

The following example of a hermeneutical-phenomenological approach shows the potential for use in researching complex social events and community problems. Similar to much family research and family therapy findings, this approach provides access to the intricate variety and dynamics of social interaction. Such social interaction may be viewed as part of a complex social network which generates the ongoing realities of meaning and attribution in which we live and act.

In approaching the study of the "drug problem" (marijuana and LSD), Kracklauer (1974) focused on three young males. A professional psychologist identified them, respectively, as follows:

    (a) a drug abuser;
    (b) a drug user (recreational);
    (c) an abstainer.

These individuals' "drug problem" could not be seen apart from the soical network formed by family members and professionals who enact socially assigned institutional roles in relation to this "problem." Inspired by Berger and Luckman's (1966) social phenomenological work, Kracklauer recognized the social constitution of the drug problem. He interviewed professionals who fulfill the legal roles related to the drug involvement of youth, including those professionals who formulate drug related educational and judicial policy.

As lived out in early 1970's America, the following "cast of characters" composed this social and professional network:

    (a) a state legislator;
    (b) a police chief;
    (c) a drug attorney;
    (d) a judge of juvenile court;
    (e) a school psychologist;
    (f) a program director;
    (g) an assistant principal;
    (h) a drug abstainer;
    (i) a drug user (recreational);
    (j) a drug abuser;
    (k) the parents of the drug abuser.

Kracklauer referred to these people as part of the drug problem "language game." An office holder was interviewed in each of the preceding role-types. Kracklauer asked each group certain guiding questions. For the professionals, the questions were: (1) "If you believe that there is such a thing as an adolescent drug problem, how would you define it, or describe it; in other words: What is the problem?" (2) Given this understanding of the drug problem, what is your role in dealing with it, in light of your professional background?"

A more open-ended question was asked of the users and the parents: "How did you get involved with drugs? How do you live your relationship with drugs?" The "data" for reflection was thus provided by these tape recorded and transcribed interviews.

Kracklauer's **explication guiding questions** for the professionals were concerned with four dimensions of the data:

1. the understanding of the problem;
2. the underlying factors;
3. their role in dealing with the problem;
4. the solution to the problem.

Kracklauer explicated "various contradictions, idiosyncracies, and ideological stances" upon reading through the data numerous times. He described these characteristics as part of the **"contradictory perceptions of the drug problem,"** in this case held by professionals.

All of Kracklauer's subjects were apt to regularly identify their preceptions with one or the other side of the following viewpoints: the drug problem as. . .

a. unbounded epidemic vs. situated action;
b. use equals abuse vs. does not equal abuse;
c. marijuana - the domino theory vs. the model of alcohol;
d. the drug problem - critical vs. worthy of concern;
e. drug abuse - escape vs. illness.

Kracklauer next articulated the **"contradictory beliefs about the solution of the problem,"** as held by the professionals. Their proposed solutions included the following:

a. the law - necessary vs. irrelevant;

b. get the pusher vs. change the system;

c. agreement - the role of education;

d. the role of rehabilitation.

Kracklauer then studied how the professionals lived out and legiti-
mized these contradictory beliefs. He examined how these beliefs about the
drug problem solution are institutionalized. Each professional subject
gave a self-description of his role in coping with the drug problem.
Kracklauer summarized these self-descriptions as follows:

a. the response of the school psychologist and assistant principal -
in general, to press for the possibility of derepressing the communication
between themselves as adults and the young, by assisting the young in
coming to see that their problems are less indigenous to themselves than
the system within which they live.

b. the response of the legislator, police chief, and judge - in
general, to rationalize the behavior of the young in such a way as to
render it amenable to legal technical manipulation in the name of pro-
tecting them from the menace of the drug problem.

c. the response of the program director and grant writer - in
general, the same as "a" above, except that his activity tends, as does
"b" to perpetuate the problem by legitimating its reality through the
production of rehabilitation centers; he becomes coopted by the system.

d. the response of the drug lawyer - to participate in both approaches to the drug problem, by working in and through the system on
behalf of the people which the system might otherwise define as criminal.
His understanding is informed by the perpectives of both systems; and he
construes a case, within the constrained freedom of the law, that has the
best chance of winning acquittal for his client in an adversary trial. The
lawyer's loyalty is both to the client and to the stipulations of the law
as an autonomous body of rules.

Kracklauer was next concerned with understanding how institutionalized roles affect the users and influence their self-understanding. To
learn about this, he investigated young people's self-perception with
regard to their involvement in psychedelic drugs. These subjects were
approached by Kracklauer with three basic user-related questions:

1. understanding of drugs and relationship to drugs;
2. self-understanding;
3. parents' understanding of the user.

In closely studying the interview texts, Kracklauer also employed the interview questions as **explication guiding questions.** With such a reading, Kracklauer came to characterize what the drug problem meant to the users. Kracklauer articulated this meaning as follows:

. . . . The meaning of the activity of drug taking for the abuser and user is in terms of the **experience** induced by drugs, in particular the so called hallucinogens. In other words, they do not talk about chemicals as chemicals, but rather of the experiences occasioned by the use of chemicals. What emerges for both is a common kind of experience which experience is interpreted differently by each. This common experience I will call the experience of **self-dramatization,** and will characterize it by saying that it serves to mirror the psyche of the intoxicant to himself, with a kind of larger than life quality. There is little wonder that both subjects should share this experience, for the literature on the subject reveals it to be a common occurrence for most people who use hallucinogens.

What is different for each of the subjects is the way they interpret the meaning of this experience from the perspective of their normal experience. Another way of saying the same thing is that each of the subjects appropriates this experience back into his ordinary experience with quite different meanings. The drug abuser understands the sense of self he is while high on the drug to be both more real and more efficacious than his sense of self in ordinary experience.

The abuser tends to build his sense of self-identity out of those experiences of self he has while high on the drug. From the perspective of normal experience, the sense of self he recollects from his drug induced states is recalled as being more real and more effective to him than the sense of self he has in normal experience, which of course includes the sense of self he has while making this interpretation of his sense of self when intoxicated. Precisely because the drug induced sense of self is recalled as more real and effective, he choses to consider it his de facto real self. Within his particular relevancy structure, a sense of self as real and

effective is to be chosen over a sense of self as irreal and inef-
fective, as the sense of self out of which he should form his identity. (p. 101-102)

In a final comparison between the three subjects of this study Kracklauer
summarizes his findings as follows:

> The **abuser** experiences himself as either not knowing whether or
> not he can accomplish the things he wants to, or as simply not being
> able to accomplish them. When the latter is the case, it usually
> devolves to a belief on his part that he cannot do what he wants to
> because his parents are preventing him, or have prevented him in the
> past. As for his identity, the abuser feels he has no clear concep-
> tion of himself, and moreover, finds no models in the world for the
> sort of person he would like to become. He expresses this succinctly
> in saying that he is "totally fluid," that he is "not even his own
> idol." And, as was already suggested in our analysis of the meaning
> of the activity of drug-taking, the abuser's sense of his own, ordi-
> nary experience is that it is not quite real, that it is not to be
> totally trusted.
>
> The **user,** on the other hand, experiences himself as quite ca-
> pable of fulfilling the projects he sets for himself, even when the
> price for doing so may be withdrawal of support from significant
> others, i.e. his parents. He has, in addition, a clear sense of his
> own identity. He understands himself as someone who is about the
> business of discovering just who he is, as apart from being the sort
> of person his parents might have wished him to be. Hence, his sense
> of identity, or agency, are in no way fully delimited for him as he
> is still very much involved in a process of growth and self-dis-
> covery. Nevertheless, his identity as someone who is about the work
> of growth and self-discovery is very clear to him. In this respect he
> stands in marked contrast to the abuser. In the same measure, he has
> a healthy trust in his experience as a guide to his actions.
>
> Finally, there is the **abstainer** who has a definite conception of
> what he can do and who he is, yet experiences both as tenuously
> secured. Both his father and his grandfather eventually became "schi-
> zophrenic" and the subject harbors fear that he too may be travelling
> in the same direction. Hence, he does not take his competency and
> identity for granted, as the ground from which he moves into the

world, but monitors them closely for signs they may be deserting him. He experiences himself as being under great pressure to keep himself together for the sake of his family as well as himself, and believes that only his relationship with God and church is enabling him to carry on. This subject, however, does trust his experience as a guide to what he should do and not do, and as the general barometer of his psychic welfare. It is this experience of himself which leads him to believe he should not indulge in drugs, for example. The same experience tells him he is in danger of loing control over his emotional life; for as long as he keeps himself together, himself as the source of his own experience will not become questionable to him. (pp. 107-108)

This fascinating example of the application of a hermeneutical-phenomenological approach is especially relevant to community psychology. It points out the dynamic nature of social attribution as it is distributed in a role-defined community setting; it explores an ecology of role configurations understood in terms of an ongoing process of linguistic communication. Kracklauer's work illustrates vividly some of the essential dimensions of the hermeneutical space of a focused social reality.

There is also a large emancipatory potential in this research. It lays bare the effective communication and attribution channels, locates points of contradiction, and identifies barriers to changes in stereotyped views. Such knowledge can help the participants to arrive at a truer and more fully personal understanding of their complex placement in particular social realities. It can enable them to evolve strategies of action that would allow them to break out of false perceptions and ideological mind traps.

## §4.-ON THE CONCEPTUAL ENCOUNTER WITH ANGER:
### J. de Rivera.

J. de Rivera has developed an originary intersubjective approach to the study of human experience, an approach he calls "conceptual encounter." Conceptual encounter is a dialogal method for the exploraton of human experience which aims at structural characterizations of human events such as being angry. The two partners in this dialogal phenomenological approach are the ,investigator and the **research partner**: "Conceptual encounter refers to an enounter between the investigator and a person who has agreed to act as a research partner" (p. 3).

> . . . The investigator asks each of his or her partners to give a specific, concrete example of anger, love, or whatever is being studied, and to faithfully describe the actual events that occurred in as much detail as possible. (p. 3)

The research partner provides a detailed account of a lived experience of the phenomenon in question, either in spoken or written form. This concrete experience, as a story or as an account, is the "raw data" for the investigation. The intention of the researcher is to explicate the essential structure of a specific experience, in this way grasping its meaning:

> Conceptual encounter. . . asks how we can describe the meaning of an experience - the organization of a person's experience at a given moment, the person's way of being-in-the-world - the various choices that confront him as a creative participant in experience. (p. 22)

The method used by de Rivera is different from the ones discussed so far in three respects:

(1) He does not try to derive the conceptualization of the meaning structure primarily from the descriptions by explicating their inherent structure through meaning-unit analysis - i.e. in an inductive way. Rather, the investigator brings a provisional but explicit conceptualization called the "researcher's abstract conceptualization" to the research situation. This abstract conceptualization, of the researcher's own formulation, is then dialogued with the research partner's concrete experience.

(2) The process of reflective explication of the data itself occurs in an actual dialogal exchange called "conceptual encounter" between two social partners. They meet to work together on the structure. In this way we can characterize de Rivera's approach as dialogal-hermeneutical. The hermeneutic circle is accomplished in and through actual dialogue between research partners.

(3) The narrative descriptions serve as empirical data to test and validate the researcher's abstract conceptualization. This is akin to the empirical existential-phenomenological methods described earlier. It is

also related to the approach of "validating phenomenological constructs." It is de Rivera's working assumption to trust the process of genuine dialogue focused on a shared topic to produce intersubjective validity for a structural characterization. For de Rivera, conceptualizations develop through repeated encounters between the level of conceptualization and the level of experience, in mixed discourse dialogue.

There are basically four types of conceptual encounters:

(1) There is an easy fit between the conceptualization and the experience.

(2) There is a complete miss in the encounter between the conceptualization and the experience.

(3) The experience may force a change in the conceptualization, revealing heretofore unarticulated dimensions.

(4) The conceptualization may illuminate aspects of the experience which were previously not recognized by the research partner.

In the use of conceptual encounter de Rivera affirms a dialogal and hermeneutic orientation: a dialectic between inductive and deductive moments of meaning. The particular (lived experience) and the universal (conceptualization = thought) stand in a progressive dialectic relationship to each other. They mutually modify and enrich each other in an "inherent creative tension."

> Thus in the course of a series of encounters with different partners the conceptualization becomes more precise and acquires depth and generality so that it can illuminate some aspect of human experience. (p. 4)

> In one sense it (the structural characterization) can never be finished for there is always room for development in science, mathematics, and art. But there is a point where it is finished enough to share with others, a point where a product has been completed and publication is desirable. (p. 7)

As his criteria for evaluating the success of a conceptualization de Rivera names the following:

(1) The conceptualization must be true to experience. It must cover the available case examples and be successful in explicating what has previously only been implicit in the phenomenon.

(2) The conceptualization must be elegant. That is, it must be relatively simple rather than cumbersome. It must describe different aspects

of the phenomenon and, ideally, it should use concepts that are related to other investigations of interest to psychologists.

De Rivera is very much interested in the development of a comprehensive theory of intersubjective emotional relationship events (1977). He is guided by the assumption, which he shares with phenomenologists in general and more particularly with Heider (1958), that everyday behavior and experience is meaningfully organized and has a structure of meaning-relationships which can be articulated in a conceptual characterization.

De Rivera does not tell us precisely how, by what means or by using what steps he arrives at his original structural characterization. He is open to many sources for his "data-base."

> The investigator can draw upon his or her own descriptive skill, and knowledge of other examples, and of English literature, to offer literal or figurative statements about the experience which the research partner can recognize as applicable or inapplicable. (p. 11)

We can say that de Rivera is interested in an interdisciplinary and multi-access approach. He will use descriptions and conceptualizations wherever he can find them to help him in his "conceptual encounter work."

> It is desirable to have as many accesses to experiences as is possible, and if one wants to grasp the meaning of experience, one may well look for it in a work of literature or art where the essential features of an experience are sometimes captured with a minimum of confusing details. (p. 23)

Regarding the hermeneutical nature of the conceptualizations arrived at through conceputal encounter, de Rivera states:

> A conceptualization that accurately fits experience and that reveals a hitherto unexpected order is almost an artistic creation that can only occur after patient study of numerous instances of the phenomenon. (p. 6)

In this orientation de Rivera represents the hermeneutical pole of the spectrum of methods. He says:

Conceptual encounter is a powerful and highly sensitive method that can probably be used in any area of inquiry. However, its power is completely dependent on the personal qualities of the researcher and somewhat dependent on the personal qualities of the research partner. (p. 13)

An important aspect of conceptual encounter is its ability to accomodate itself to the different personalities and interests of different investigators. . . . De Rivera's predilection is towards the precision of mathematics. Hence, he tends to favor the abstract pole of the encounter - attempting to arrive at an almost geometric conceptualization of the experience of anger. (p. 29)

The various studies presented in the book **Conceptual Encounter** (1981) reflect the flexibility of the method and illustrate the varieties of outcomes based on research interest and personal style of approach.

De Rivera understands conceptual encounter to emphasize building upon prior conceptualizations. This method is one of progressive refinement of conceptualizaton by both empirical and reflective-hermeneutical means, i.e. by using multiple modes of access to an experience. De Rivera uses this "foreknowledge" or "forestructure" as the starting point for further dialogue and research. To make the structure more refined and reality adequate he engages in a dialectical circle of interpretation which has been called the "hermeneutic circle." De Rivera's approach thus stands in contrast to the empirical phenomenological stance which emphasizes the bracketing of presuppositions. In that view the data themselves, the descriptions, reveal their structural organization. In doing empirical phenomenology we do not start with a conceptualizaton but end with it. The general hermeneutic position, though, is that we always already have a pre-understanding which we can further clarify and articulate. De Rivera recognizes this hermeneutic epistemological attitude and operationalizes it by using actual dialogal research partners in the process of re-conceptualization.

In presenting his research de Rivera first offers the unfolding of his understanding of anger in structural terms - i.e. as an organized system of implicit concepts and experienced commands which rule the experience and situation of anger. He articulates the essential constituents, the necessary and sufficient conditions, that must be present for anger to occur.

Outlining the steps by which "conceptual encounter" occurs, de Rivera presents his results or findings, his conceptualization, to his research partners, to "colleagues and students," in order to "solicit critical responses" to the presented conceptualization - which is then modified in response to this challenge. Several rounds of critical dialogue take place. The last step in this sequence which involves students in psychology courses, is very explicitly described:

> In order to continue refining the. . . conceptualization of anger, I asked students in my classes to write short (3-5 page) papers based on an encounter between the conceptualization and their own personal experience of anger. (p. 51)

De Rivera encourages his student-research partners to go for an "exciting encounter" rather than a mild one:

> . . . An exciting encounter [is] where the power of the conceptualization reveals aspects of the experience that were previously unnoticed or the details of the experience forces a modification of the conceptualization. I made it clear that I valued exciting encounters more than mild meetings and that the former occurred when one went into the concrete details of some specific experience and pitted them against the specific terms of the conceptualization. (p. 51)

De Rivera then presents lengthy excerpts (2-4 pages) from four research partners who discuss their "conceptual encountner" with de Rivera's original formulation. De Rivera writes a commentary on each example, pointing out how it challenged and changed his progressive understanding of the phenomenon of anger.

Finally de Rivera procedes to summarize his findings in a diagrammatic representation which shows the explicated concepts and relationships which structure the emotional situations of anger, fear, hurt, and depression in their relationship. This is an expression and contribution of de Rivera's mathematical-geometrical inclination, his indebtedness and appreciation of Lewin's idea of life-space, and his underlying intentions as a psychological map-maker. He wants to map out the "experiential landscapes" of the different emotions and their interrelationships. De Rivera expresses his intentions in the following way:

I want to get at the essential nature of anger, at the meaning of the experience, in the way I imagine an early geometer wanted to get at the essence of a circle. (p. 35)

Following this outline of the steps in conceptual encounter, what are the **results** at each juncture in the dialogal-hermeneutic circle, of meaning-transformation? Examining instances of anger to see what they have in common, de Rivera first finds that:

In every case the person wanted to change the object of anger - to make it other than it was - to psychologically push away or **remove** the object of anger. . . . (p. 36)

De Rivera describes this as the "wish of anger" or the instruction which rules the emotion: **remove the object!** The emotion lasts and does not subside until the instruction is carried out. De Rivera notes in this regard how:

We can describe any emotion in terms of how a person experiencing the emotion must transform the world if the emotion is to disappear. And in the case of anger the instructional transformation is to remove the source of the anger. (p. 37)

In conceptualizing anger de Rivera also explicates the importance of a power dimension which he calls "could":

Anger. . . implied that the person felt he or she **could** somehow affect the other, that there was some sort of possibility that the person's anger could influence and transform the object at which he or she was angry. (p. 37)

The concept of "can" or ability and power plays a prominent role in Heider's conception of interpersonal relations, and de Rivera bases his own conceptualizations in significant ways on Heider's work.

**The Concept of Ought.** De Rivera thus "dialogues" on several fronts. He uses different "data bases" to inform and assist him in his conceptualization work. He turns to Heider for clarifying the meaning of "ought," a meaning which implies a force that is supra-personal.

What ought to exist is not just what some person desires, but what is perceived as required by some objective order of affairs. . . . For Heider, what a person desires at a particular moment may be related to what the person **likes.** What a person believes ought to be in any particular instance is related to what the person values. (p. 38)

Another aspect of ought is the necessity for some feeling of unity. Oughts bond us to particular "we's," i.e. within community bonds which exist between people who share common values. It is towards others whom we recognize as belonging to a shared unit or "we" that we become angry.

**The Concept of Challenge.** The concept of ought, i.e. that the other ought to change his or her behavior, was seen by de Rivera to be a necessary but not a sufficient condition for anger to transpire. There also had to be the experience of a **challenge.** As de Rivera puts it:

. . . The person always felt **challenged** - that is, the other was perceived as intentionally violating the ought and the angered person was involved yet lacked control. The person was involved in a situation where the other's behavior defined a reality that contradicted the reality of the angered person. (p. 42)

An essential conceptual aspect of anger, therefore, is a challenge to what a person believes ought to exist.

**The Concept of Assertion.** Another finding of de Rivera's is that to be angry means that the person must be able to **assert** his or her belief that an ought shared with the other has been challenged by the other and that this challenge must be removed.

The presence of anger implies that, in this contest, the person continues to will what he or she recognizes as existent and, hence, to determine what oughts apply in the face of the other's will to define reality differently. (p. 44)

Anger is thus understood to support a person's position.

De Rivera's initial conceptualization of the situation and structure of anger was thus stated in the following way:

It is now possible for us to state a conceptualization which may be the necessary and sufficient conditions for anger. We postulate: If an other (O) **challenges** what a person (P) **asserts ought** to exist, then P will be angry at O. And conversely, if P is angry at O, then O is challenging what P asserts ought to exist. (p. 46)

**Critical Dialogues in the Conceptual Encounter Process.**   De Rivera writes:

At this point in our conceptualization we had statements for the situation of anger and the "instruction" and response of anger (remove the challenge to what ought to exist). These statements were shared with colleagues and students and critical responses were elicited. (p. 47)

These dialogues yielded two questions or challenges to the conceptualizations: (1) What is the "embodiment" of anger or how does anger affect the body? (2) What place does anger, as a way of being, play in a person's life. What roles and functions does it have?
In responding to these challenges de Rivera modifies his conceptualization to read as follows:

We suggest that anger is a way of being-in-the-world in which the angry person's will is strengthened so that he can remove a challenge to what he asserts ought to exist, thereby preserving the unit between the angry person and the object of anger and the shared values of this unity. (p. 50)

Through this work on the specifics of anger de Rivera also comes to a realization and conceptual articulation of the structure of **any and all emotions** on a higher level of abstraction and universality.

We propose as a working hypothesis that **any** emotion is a way of being-in-the-world that functions to advance the projects to which the person is committed. . . and every structure may be conceived as composed of four interrelated parts: (1) a way of perceiving one's situation, (2) "instructions" how to transform one's situation, (3) a set of transformations that alter the person's body and its relation to the environment, and (4) its particular function within that person's life. (p. 51)

The results of his students' conceptualizations are first presented as excerpts from four of the student papers (who had written out their response). These papers combine experiential accounts with reflection and critical dialogue on the parts of the students.

De Rivera then writes what we might call a commentary on each example, picking out the relevant challenges and themes. He responds to them and then dialogues these findings with important and relevant psychological literature - e.g. Dembo - all in the service of "further development" of the conceptualization.

As the results of this phase of the conceptual encounter de Rivera says:

> We now see that almost every aspect of this structure needs to be qualified. . . . (p. 73) The concept of distance had to be clarified. . . .(p. 72) While a challenge often reflects an opposing will, it is sometimes merely an impersonal violation of how the world ought to be and sometimes constitutes a threat to the person's identity and values. . . . (p.73) In all of these cases the person is held in the situation where he or she is confronted with what ought not to exist, by some outer barrier that prevents the person from reducing tension by leaving the situation, restructuring, or distancing. . . . (p. 73) Distancing, in the sense of a transformation of psychological space, is not the only alternative to anger. Another possibility is to feel hurt. (p. 75)

The complexity of the structure of anger and its relationship to other cognate emotions is summarized by de Rivera in the form of a diagram. He constructs a map of this experiential landscape. In de Rivera's judgement and preference for a geometrical-mathematical form of metaphorizing emotion, and in lineage with Lewin's and Heider's diagrammatic heritage, he summarizes his work both in a diagram and in an explanatory text and legend as how to read this "cognitive map."

De Rivera's approach is one of doing phenomenology dialogally. It is also empirical and structural in intent. It is hermeneutic in that it operates within the dialogal structure of the hermeneutic circle and recognizes the reality of preconceptions which undergo refinement and transformation through discourse. De Rivera's work is theoretical in its intent and practice in that he wants to work out a comprehensive view of the organization and interrelatedness of all emotions as forms of human being-in-the-world. De Rivera's method is essentially open-ended, and invites participation and collaboration by fellow ,researchers. It is a multi-level mixed discourse approach that combines into a coherent process many of the other types of phenomenological research.

Another interesting feature of de Rivera's approach and method is its "emancipatory" potential. Knowledge and insight is co-created and shared in dialogue, with both partners benefiting from the growing conceptualization. To be a partner in conceptual encounter is to be immersed in a co-constituted creative tension in wich mutual illumination may emerge. The traditional division between research and therapy is thereby also undercut. As de Rivera himself states, the dialogal method of conceptual encounter can be applied in both types of settings although the goals of the interaction would differ.

> Conceptual encounter is a powerful and highly sensitive method that can probably be used in any area of inquiry. However, its power is completely dependent on the personal qualities of the researcher and somewhat dependent on the personal qualities of the research partner. (p. 13)

The implications of this hermeneutic stance for our understanding of human science research are radical indeed.

We have to acknowledge an idiosyncratic component in all hermeneutic work. As we move toward the hermeneutical-pole of this survey of phenomenological psychology research approaches, we find that the research becomes very much an expression of the personality and style of the researcher as well as of the working atmosphere of the investigating ensemble of co-researchers. Thus the work of disclosure becomes an **offering** of insight to the reader and participant rather than the necessary result of a structural understanding of a replicable method in the service of objectivity. The reader-participant is left to respond to and to take up this disclosure in an existential manner in the service of life change.

## B.

# RECOLLECTION AND LITERARY TEXTS

In this group of research approaches we find a style of free-flowing and spiralling hermeneutics leading to a multiple level reflective presentation. Various orders of discourse are brought into dialogue: personal experiences, literary references and quotes, criticism, philosophical reflection, historical sources and the professional psychological literature. All these sources are used to clarify the psychological meaning of the phenomenon.

The style of presentation which characterizes these approaches is itself spiralling, following the model of the hermeneutical circle in that it starts in the midst of a precomprehension and then engages in dialoguing this understanding with the various bodies of knowledge and discourse from an interdisciplinary matrix. Such continuing dialogue differentiates and deepens our understanding of the phenomenon and allows us to articulate the multiple facets and inner coherence of its lived meaning. This happens as an unfolding argument during which we also, as readers, become more in touch with our own relevant experiences and deepen our understanding of our own involvements.

The style of hermeneutical elucidation and of the presentation of the results or fruits of these researches follows no pre-established pattern or design. The approaches are very idiosyncratic and thus an expression of the personal style of the researcher, which one might be able to learn by some sort of an apprenticeship rather than "by the book" or "by the numbers." The procedural steps in doing these types of free-flowing and multiple-level-discourse hermeneutical-phenomenological investigations cannot be clearly enumerated in a linear fashion. They are the consequence and manifestation of a disciplined general attitude and openness to the phenomenon which lets the phenomenon speak and tell its story by itself and through its cloud of witnesses who constitute it in our tradition. These studies also have an exhortatory quality. They appeal to us, they show us who we are and can be, they point out our forgetfulness, and they call us into self-transformation, into opportunties for more resolute and authentic participation in life. The studies by Buckley on **at-homeness,** by Halling on **forgiveness,** by Jager on the **theoretical attitude,** and by Romanyshyn on the phenomenon of the **changing heart and the metaphorical**

**nature** of **psychological life** express ethical imperatives and normative ideals. They implicitly speak of a primacy of the ethical dimension in human existence: what the right action is! These authors seem to speak in an advocate stance, from a value-committed position. They regard the phenomena they study as crucial to human existence and in need of advocacy. Their engagement as spokesmen for the value of these phenomena is part of their meaning-elucidating work. They believe in a self- and life-transformative consequence of doing hermeneutical-phenomenological work. Such work is done not only in the service of cognitive comprehension but also in the hope of existential transformation and growth.

### §5.--ON AT-HOMENESS: F. Buckley

Frank Buckley in his article "An Approach to a Phenomenology of At-Homeness," (1971), presents his way of doing research. It is primarily with his own experience and within the context of the arguments of fellow existential-phenomenological philosophers that Buckley "dialogues," dwells with, "travels," lets himself be addressed and called forth to respond. He does not proceed empirically by collecting protocols from co-researchers, but he relies on his own "dialogal presence" to the phenomenon, his openness to its self-revelation in response to a "dwelling, abiding presence." We could say that Buckley uses the method of "Individual Phenomenological Reflection" (a la Colaizzi). For Buckley "presence to the phenomenon" itself carries a dialogal meaning and experience; it is an expression of a **dialogal existential attitude.**
Buckley says about his approach:

How approach the question?
In the face of an experience so **intimate** and so **central** and hence so mysterious as that which we can simply describe at the outset in the common-sense phrase of the **feeling of being at home** there can be no question of effort to explain or define, but only that of attempting to describe and understand. But how, even to describe? Literature abounds in concrete passages that give us the flavor and feeling of the place its persons can call home. And theology, philosophy and science have noted and pursued this question in terms of the All and the One, as in Plato, Augustine, Boehme, Pascal and Whitehead. Yet the experience of the search for at-homeness remains - indeed has become both more pressing and more crucial in

our times. Thus the need to move or travel further here, taking
"traveller" as a description of both my state of being and my method
of inquiry. . . and struggle, hence **along the way,** as it were, to
bring forth, in a real sense, to experience anew what may be viewed
upon further reflection as constituting the more everyday experiential components of this constellation. Or a symphony of what may even
initially be described as a coming-together, or even a falling together, and, in that sense, a **coherence** that partakes of creativity. A
coming together which really needs to be called the **happening** of
"home-ness." (pp. 198-199)

For Buckley, the familiar has to be dialogued again and again so as to
deepen one's presence to it. He begins his report by presenting his explicit pre-comprehension which he articulates at the beginning of his paper.
The themes and the metaphors which later constitute the "results" are
already there: "travel," "along the way," "to experience anew a coming
together, a coherence that partakes of creativity," "the happening of
homeness."

In Buckley's conception we always already know the phenomenon on some
level. We don't act as if we didn't know it, but we can always get deeper
in touch with it. We can, and in Buckley's view we even have to, always
deepen our understanding and our very existential presence and dwelling in
and with it. And this experience of discovery and re-discovery and indeed
this "existential struggle" has the dynamic quality of a venture, a journey, a moving together of an intimate dialogue with being.

With regard to his method and understanding of phenomenology Buckley
writes: "If phenomenology is, as I see it fundmentally to be, the **disciplined struggle** "to let be," to let being appear, or break through, then
we have nowhere to begin but at the beginning - and that is, as I experience this "manifestation," through my co-constituting, intersubjective, and reciprocal **presence** to it." (p. 199) At another place he characterizes his "dialogal method" in the following manner:

What is it, we can then say, as I strive to leave an opening for
this experience to speak to me, that it shows me? And how can I draw
out its central dimensions, and what later do I call these dimensions, and in what manner are they related in the more comprehensive
understanding? In this search as described in part earlier, I try "to
let be" the experience that can catch me up or give me a sense of

abiding, with some feeling of "restful achievement" (or a sense of the satisfaction which comes from a mode of awareful presence and participation in the coming-together). Is this a form of unity and even communion, with the **ultimate dwelling**, the origin and source of all phenomena (manifestations or otherwise discretely perceived entities)?

I would like to develop a bit what may be described as certain **struggles** and **transformations** of the experience of moving which I have recently engaged in. These I have attempted to intersubjectively question, and/or confirm through the at-homeness experience protocols and phenomenological descriptions of others who have attended to this. These could include certain descriptions in published literature (Marcel, Bachelard, Merleau-Ponty, Van Kaam). and some developed by associates and graduate students more recently. I intend to draw these up more fully in a later publication. The experience of this problem, and of this mystery - for it is both a problematic, and a mode of participation deeply wrapped in the mystery of being - needs to be further concretized. (pp. 201-202)

This expresses Buckley's understanding of any existential phenomenon as a mystery rather than a "solvable problem" that reveals itself to the researcher only if he assumes an attitude of respectful listening and abiding open presence. This revelation occurs as a dialogal experience, as a give and take or a spiralling movement of a journey of presence-to and reflection-on the phenomenon. Buckley also describes another dialectic, inherent in the phenomenon itself, that between being-at-home and the not-at-home experience, i.e. wayfaring, travelling.

Buckley's way, then, is to proceed by means of his own personal reflective palpitation of his personal life-experience - moving from one home and city to another - a concrete existential happening in his own life occasioning the reflective re-visioning of the phenomenon "in dialogue" with the ways of thinking and speaking of his preferred collegiate dialogal community - including students - but in particular Gabriel Marcel and Steven Strasser:

It is increasingly clear to those who have been engaged in the rewarding but always difficult task of "doing phenomenology" - (as the current pragmatic American phrase sometimes puts it in sophisticated quarters) in living, research, and psychological practice, that this cannot be really carried out with much success, which is to say authenticity and continuity, unless it is pursued through an ongoing, struggling, intersubjective sharing and, indeed, with some onto-logical weight utilizing an experiential-methodology; which a few are led recently to describe as dialogal phenomenology. Such a source and approach might be even preferably called a **living community of scho-lars** whose life and thought centers around their deeply and openly shared concerns (caring) and perceptions. (p. 201)

For Buckley methodology is conceived as a shared intersubjective and personal struggle for truth through and in dialogue. He rejects a prag-matic and problem-oriented approach and prefers to consider the phenomenon of at-homeness as an "existential mystery" that reveals its meaning to the person who sincerely struggles toward an authentic relationship with this existential theme in his own existence. For Buckley "research" thus seems to have **existence-transforming implications and conseqences.** "Under-standing" the phenomenon in terms of its central dimensions in Buckley's view seems to require a personal existential movement deeper into the very experience of it.

For Buckley the process of **explication** which is a cognitive reflec-tive operation thus becomes one of **existential transformation** for the person who undertakes the research, a transformation which can be retro-spectively articulated in the metaphorical or even archetypal context of man's traveller condition (homo viator). Buckley gives us a personal and reflectively deepened account of his personal struggle with the existen-tial experience (phenomenon) of at-homeness. It is the report of a per-sonal journey, the story of a personal event, the story of a concern lived out, an **existential involvement.** He does not specify any particular data-generating or explication-guiding questions applied to the data, nor does he delineate particular and sequential steps of explication in the manner of empirical phenomenological strategies. He can only give an account of his personal "dialogal involvement" with his own experienced struggle for at-homeness in the course of which several central dimensions began to appear:

> Each of which seemed to lead to the center of my own ex-perience(s). These included still more telling concretizations, too elaborate to develop in detail here, as we prepared to leave our house (now home) in Pittsburgh to return to our home (now house) in

Worcester. Also, as further ambivalent sequences of "now I am **here** - then I will be **there**" were allowed to emerge, and "received" in consciousness, without any prior expectations, I found, as others have, that this could not be even partially carried out without the pain of struggle. In attempting to wrestle out some continuity of openness to a dimension of life that exposes one to the reality of death - since every real separation is a prototype and foretaste of one's earthly end - we may find it extremely difficult to remain sufficiently open to invite our **real** feelings and thoughts to emerge; preferring, or simply **needing,** even phenomenologists!, to spontaneously erect a structure of defense which leads us to maintain "all is fine" and repress any contestations or protestations of feeling or spirit. When I do this, however, I discountenance most of my real experiences that have to do with moving, i.e. with uprooting, changing, leaving, dying, and lose the actual ever cyclic inter-subjective tension between nearness and distance, warmth and coldness, openness and closedness, intimacy and objectivity or, in a word, the experience itself of at-homeness. And, it would seem that, unless the actual individual living phenomenological psychologist or philosopher (**you** or **me**) can do this, there is going to be a rather limited phenomenology; though it may, of course, be carried out on a fairly verbal, intellectual, and systematic level, sufficient to satisfy our more importunate needs for survival, order, closure, self-esteem, theory and academic nicety. (pp. 205-206)

Buckley actively argues for his position while he presents it as a research report. Appeal is part of his communicative style, appeal to the depth and/or height-dimensions of experience and the play of resistances due to the pain of struggle. He also engages in a polemic against a narrow understanding of existential-phenomenology as a merely cognitive reflective enterprise. Arguing strongly for a dialogal stance it is paradoxical that Buckley himself does not actually engage in face to face dialogal interaction with others to do his research. However, he conceives of his very attitude of struggling personally for presence and openness to the mystery of at-homeness, which includes the experience of transcendence in a spiritual sense as a religious dimension and the closeness to one's own finiteness as death, as an essentially dialogal way of moving, letting yourself be addressed, listening and responding authentically to the call that emanates form the mystery: "Dwelling itself." For Buckley the understanding of existential-phenomenology is seen as a personal journey, as a personal quest, which leads to **existential transformation** which is also always a spiritual transformation, of the person who goes out on such a venture. It is not the production of essential truths as objective propositons about human experience but the promotion of inter-human truth of engaging in genuine dialogue, struggle, and openness to Being, generally, that characterizes Buckley's "epistemological concerns."

Buckley does not provide an explicit "result-section" or "formulation." His method and results intertwine in the account of his reflective dialogal journeying in the tradition of Individual Phenomenological Reflection. He says: "What is proposed then, as an approach to a phenomenology of at-homeness amounts to a kind of constellation of aspects each of which, in a related and underlying and, thus, unifying manner, may be thought of as leading in some meaningful and humanly satisfying way toward the realm of Dwelling itself." (p. 206) Buckley does not give an explicit summary statement of that constellation. However, the very chapter subheadings (themes) of his paper, if read as a continuous text (with commentary), do constitute a "formulation," a "constellation of dimensions," perhaps a general structure of the meaning of the phenomenon of at-homeness:

An experience of at-homeness
viewed as a coming together
through the experience of moving
(in) the traveller condition
(as) everyday being at home
(and as) beyond the everyday, a struggle for transcendence
(including) openness and enclosure, the experience of ambiguity
(and of) embodiment, intersubjectivity, and betweenness.

In comparison with the methods of empirical existential-phenomenology which are articulated in a sequential, step by step, one operation after another, kind of presentation, Buckley's report of his struggle for his own existential relationshp to "at-homeness" may seem unsystematic. However, if we see it for what it is: a disciplined account of a personal existential and dialogal struggle with a phenomenon, an existential life process, in order to learn to dwell deeper with it, in order to "live it out," then his account in the manner of a hermeneutic reflective spiralling in the tradition of individual phenomenological reflection has to show a dialogal, mixed-discourse style. It is the telling of a personal story, a venture, an adventure into the mystery of at-homeness combining concrete-experiential reporting with universal-reflective moves and insights in an admixture of multiple-level discourse which genuine dialogue always essentially is.

The style of this kind of writing is perhaps more intimately related to the genre of: **Clincial psychological case study** than to the genre of: **reports of psychological research experiments** which seem to silently rule the format of some of the works of the empirical existential-phenomenological psychologists presented here.

### §6.--ON THE UNDERSTANDING OF FORGIVENNESS: S. Halling

Steen Halling (1979) provides us with a genre and sample of hermeneutical phenomenology which we might characterize as "free-flowing hermeneutics," in that it interweaves narrative, critical, and reflective discourse into an ongoing argument of idiosyncratic style which progressively deepens our understanding of the phenomenon of forgiveness. The focus of the investigation is on the theme of forgiveness, the data are two O'Neill plays, and the "results" are the reflective meaning elaborations. The reader has to follow Halling's argument in its unfolding in order to appreciate the subtlety of the presentation, the rigor of the hermeneutical-reflective work, the sophistication of the scholarly context, and the persuasiveness of the emergent structures.

Halling organizes his paper in terms of:

Introduction;
Psychology's benign neglect of forgiveness;
Considerations of method;
The plays as task and material;
The plots;
O'Neill's understanding of forgiveness.

Halling's concern is the relative neglect of the study of forgiveness in the traditional psychological literature which he reviews briefly. He discusses also the existential-phenomenological literature (Kierkegaard, Minkowski, Buber, Tillich, Fromm, Becker) who have shown more interest in forgiveness and in related experiences such as despair, revenge, blame.

Halling chooses two of Eugene O'Neill's plays: **Long Day's Journey Into Night** and **A Moon for the Misbegotten** as the data and research focus of his hermeneutical study because they "involve the theme of forgiveness on two levels. First, the plots of both plays center around the intense conflict of a closely knit family, the Tyrones, and their struggle to move beyond blame and recrimination to forgiveness and understanding. On a second level, it is clear that in writing about the Tyrones, O'Neill was really writing about himself and his family in an effort to come to peace with the turmoil of his past." (p. 193) In his hermeneutical work Halling dialogues three bodies of literature: traditional psychology, literary criticism relevant to O'Neill's plays, and the existential-phenomenological philosophical and theological discussion related to the theme of forgiveness. He is interested in forgiveness from whatever source will shed light on it.

Regarding "consideratons of method" Halling emphasizes the problems in using literary art-works as data, stressing that although the artist may have great insight into human beings and their experience, this does not make him or her into a psychologist. Psychological work is still necessary.

> I will approach O'Neill's plays as a task and a material which calls upon the psychologist to make explicit and systematic whatever psychological insights they contain.
>
> Of course, I am not approaching the two texts with a blank mind. There are a number of writers, most of them in the existential or phenomenological tradition, who have written on issues closely related to forgiveness. I will use their insights to illuminate and critically evaluate O'Neill's perspective. My method will be phenomenological, loosely speaking. On the one hand, I will try to approach the plays in as unbiased a manner as possible, describing how the theme of forgiveness is portrayed in them. On the other hand, I will move toward an essential understanding of forgiveness through that use of the imagination which is called free variation. Basically, it is a matter of attempting to determine what is essential to forgiveness, whether it be lived out among Irish-Catholic New Englanders or in some other cultural and psychological context. (p. 195)

There is legitimacy in using literary works as sources of data if we assume that a play does "create for an audience a dramatic living expression of essential insights into the human condition." It can thus be used as data for reflective work. Halling pursues a twofold goal in this study: 1) To systematically elucidate O'Neill's understanding of forgiveness; 2) To criticise this understanding constructively from an existential-phenomenological perspective.

(1) Halling, in approaching the two plays, is guided by the following "inquiry-guiding questions":

(a) What makes forgiveness a viable and possible response to another person?
(b) In what circumstances does forgiveness seem impossible?
(c) What does it mean to forgive?

We will organize the "findings" and results of Halling's research under the same headings although he does not do so explicitly in the text. We want to emphasize that this is a summarization of Halling's work and does not reflect accurately the dialogal process-nature of his hermeneutical unfolding. Also, a detailed familiarity by the reader with the two O'Neill plays is a prerequisite to appreciate Halling's work as a creative and promising genre of hermeneutical-phenomenological research. We are lifting the themes and constituents from their embeddedness in his text.

a) A belief that people are responsible, at least in some measure, for what they do. In order for forgiveness to be possible, the past must be truly past, and there must be hope for the future. In order to be effective, forgiveness does not need to be offered by the person wronged.

b) Being accuser and accused, i.e. not being at one with oneself, is an obstacle to being forgiven. Revenge, blame, vindictiveness, and punishment are also all rooted in the recognition of our own and other's responsibility; revenge, blame and self-blame shed light on what makes forgiveness impossible, that is, a false sense of responsibililty; there are three themes which are incompatible with forgiveness but related to it: fatalism, blaming, despair. These themes are based on the refusal or inability to accept what cannot be changed and they fail to develop a proper perspective on the role of responsibility.

c) Forgiveness involves more than an act of will. Forgiveness enables the one forgiven to acknowledge the guilt and to own the guilty behavior. Self-revelation of being guilty leads to understanding and forgiveness.

Forgiveness presupposes a social context. We have to ask for forgiveness and be forgiven. When we forgive, we leave ourselves, we are reconciled with our world. It involves as much getting and giving. When we forgive we heal ourselves.

While these insights into forgiveness glimpsed from O'Neill's plays are illuminative and important they nevertheless also point up certain shortcomings of O'Neill's perspective: "So certainly we have to conclude that while O'Neill's understanding of forgiveness, and of human suffering, is one we can learn much from, his fatalism places a limit on the range of his understanding." (p. 206)

2) From the vantage point of an existential-phenomenological critique Halling finds that O'Neill lacks the dimension of hope and expectancy. "Minkowski (1970) argues that the future normally has two interrelated meanings, the possibility of the new and the coming of death. In O'Neill's life and plays, the latter theme predominates. However, from within that perspective forgiveness is more a matter of finding peace in the face of death than discovering the possibility of a new life in the midst of life." (p. 206)

From another source (Tillich, 1959) comes the insight that for forgiveness to occur those who feel guilty must come into "community with objective transpersonal powers of forgiveness," i.e. that it is a form of grace. Halling, following Becker (1964), also emphasizes the necessary role of love as a necessary social context for forgiveness. "Experiencing oneself as forgiven becomes possible when we accept the love of another, a love which accepts us as we are, and by receiving that acceptance we can also accept our own past." (p. 205) From this expanded view Halling gives us a summarizing characterization of the nature of forgiveness:

> It is hard to forgive those who throw us into despair, who unravel the very fabric of our lives and our identities. But insofar as we forgive, it involves a healing of ourselves, often made possible by those who through their love and concern allow us to rebuild the fabric of our lives. Forgiving another is not a matter of the righteous and the self-sufficient being gracious with those who are guilty or needy; rather, it is a coming to a reconciliation with one's world, oneself, and the other person. It is as much of an issue of getting as giving. Being forgiven is a matter of being freed from what Buber (1957) describes as the torrent of time experienced by the

guilty, and being able again to look for the future with hope and expectancy. (p. 206)

Halling's free-flowing hermeneutical approach is difficult to summarize because of the idiosyncratic nature of its style of explication. However, it demonstrates the fertility of using literary works as life-texts and the value of hermeneutic reading which dialogues different bodies of literature in order to deepen our understanding of a phenomenon.

## §7.--ON THE THEORETICAL ATTITUDE: B. Jager

Bernd Jager has developed an original hermeneutical approach to the study of essential human situations and activities focusing on journeying and dwelling. He manifests a strong similarity to Heidegger's way of meditative thinking, of thanking-thinking. It is an appreciative thinking. It is a thinking that moves backward to the origin and roots of our ideas and self-understanding within our classical tradition. Throughout his publications (1975, 1979) Jager pursues a discernible hermeneutical strategy, although his writing style is idiosyncratic and ultimately inimitable.

We will focus on one example of Jager's research (1975) on the phenomenology of the **theoretical effort**, to illustrate his approach. Jager begins by stating the aim of his research: To do an interpretative reading of the task of theorizing. He focuses on three central terms: theorizing, journeying, dwelling, suggesting that they are all metaphorically linked with the reality of the road:

> There appears to exist a persistent and deep inter-relationship between the themes of intellectual, theoretical or spiritual effort and those of travelling, exploration and sight-seeing. The very language of intellectual effort constantly refers us to the road. Thus we are said to make **progress** in our science, that we **advance** to, or **arrive**, or are **on the way** to new insights, that we work **towards** a new understanding, attempting to **reach** new conclusions, or hope for a **breakthrough**, all the while **keeping up** with the work of others, hoping not to **fall behind.** (p. 235)

Jager's opening hermeneutic strategy is always to systematically inquire into the etymology of the terms in order to discover and recover the original meaning of their first usage, as does the later Heidegger. Jager delves into the original contexts and roots of the relevant vocabulary, the first usages of the words. From this research into dictionaries and classical sources he derives suggestions for his contemplative reconstruction and elaboration of the unfolding of their meaning, historically, in sequence, as a fate in language. Jager studies the history of the words and thus the history of the ideas in the context in which they appeared. This context is typically the classical tradition of Greek philosophy, literature, the arts, and the field of historical scholarship of Western civilization. Proceeding chronologically and leading us gently to our contemporary situation, Jager commands and displays an impressive wealth of erudition and detailed scholarship when he illustrates how the meaning of these ideas undergoes changes during the march of history so that the original significance becomes covered over and changed, unrecognizable to the modern understanding and mindset. Jager articulates and recovers the original meanings in such a way that they speak to us and inspire us to a deeper vision of our theoretical task today.

Proceeding hermeneutically in this way requires a well articulated humanistic education and expertise in the history of ideas of Western and world civilization, in the areas of religion, myth, philosophy, art, letters, and science, a degree of comprehension of our cultural heritage that cannot be easily taught as a methodological approach or technique. From his complex stock of knowldge and humanistic scholarship, Jager researches the relevant thinkers and texts to recover their vision for us. In essence, he tells the story of theorizing and we become spellbound by the articulateness and eloquence of the diction, the wealth of descriptive detail and historical fact. We become fascinated by the unfolding drama of the "semantic drift" in which we are all involved. The dramatic narrative of the changing meaning of "theoria" restores the original vision and clarifies for us also the role of the activity and the actor in the life of the community which he or she serves.

It is difficult to abbreviate and to summarize Jager's argument and to do justice to his hermeneutical ways. The way he represents his research findings as a continuous narrative seems to require that we have to listen and repeat the process, to undergo the transformations of meaning as they become disclosed in order to appropriate the insight. Therefore, in the following I will quote Jager at length to convey his style as well as his findings.

An inquiry into the earliest usages of the words theorist and theory presents us with a wealth of suggestions for our inquiry. Probably the earliest use of the word theoros strongly evoked the components theo and eros to read approximately "he who regards and observes (the will of) God." It appears that the concept of "theorizing" originally emerged out of a context of a serving and observing presence to the divine. The Theognis of the 6th century B.C. makes mention of a theoretician whose function it was to visit the Delphian oracle as an official representative of his city. This theoretician must be absolutely incorruptible according to the poem, so that he may guard the word of the Pythia without distortion on his way back to the city. The first appearance of the word theoros in our literature immediately brings us within the sphere of objectivity. This first somewhat idealized description of a theoretician as a recipient of the divine message and as a faithful transmitter of this message back to the people comes to us already surrounded and interpenetrated with the spirit of truth and faithfulness. The foremost task of this first theoretician was to question and to faithfully transmit the response. But in order to hear the voice of god he had to venture out, to risk the perils of the road and to return to his point of departure. From the very beginning truth was a search. The life of the spirit required the road.

Approaching the fifth century B.C. the meaning of the theoros shifts or expands slightly. Pindar speaks of a theorion or a place where the theorists compete in the games. Koller shows in an unmistakable way that these early theorists are not mere spectators but rather actual participants in the religious celebrations. At this stage their function might be best defined as that of official participating delegates in the festivities attending a religious celebration in another city. The theorist remains a delegate, someone chosen by his people to represent them. He retains his religious function and he continues to be a traveler. He is both a participant and an observer, or rather his participation serves his observation and his observation is the measure of his participation. The word theorist or any of its close derivatives never is used by the ancient Greeks to refer to participation in a religious festivity in the hometown. From the beginning the theorist has to journey beyond the boundaries of his own city. From the beginning the theorist must move beyond the known territory into the new. (p. 236)

The key, here, is in the nature of the mission of a theorist. To receive a divine message, to bring it back home to the people who sent the person on this voyage. The message was to be found in the religious celebrations and mysteries of other people in another city or culture. Theorizing was to discover something from another world and from another realm, the divine. And there was to be a "homecoming" from the journey, a bringing back and a telling and sharing of the message. Theorizing was a social mission.

As Jager traces the mission of theorizing through history he first notices a shift in meaning away from its original religious implications:

> Gradually theoria comes to refer to the experience and knowledge one acquires while travelling. While a theoria becomes more and more associated with a mundane adventure, the qualities of the theorist are no longer that of someone skilled in religious observance but rather someone rich in mundane observations. The theorist becomes a sophos, someone clever, skilled, knowledgeable about the world, acquainted with a variety of people, customs, languages. Herodotus' description of Solon's journey, of his theoria, became the prototype for the study-tour which even today remains in vogue. (p. 237)

The meaning of theoria shifts toward the mundane and the secular, a "study tour," and loses its rootedness in the sacred dimension. After Jager has investigated the meanings associated with the idea: theoretical journey, he engages in a meditative dialogue between journeying and dwelling which stand in a mutually implicative relationship to each other. On the road when journeying, we recognize and appreciate the repose that dwelling offers, and at home, when dwelling, we appreciate the open-ended, unique and unpredictable adventure of the open road. Both shed light on each other as equally essential modes of human existence.

At the end of his paper Jager presents the results of his inquiry in a summarizing statement. It is formulated in terms of several "askeses," several task-imposed methodological disciplines or self-denials that the theoretician has to undergo in the right sequence. Jager presents these results as a **process**, as a progression, a series of steps of the theoretical effort:

> The first **askese** concerns the turning from the polis in the direction of the distant shrine. The second askese concerns the turning away from the shrine toward the city. In both cases the

ascetic turning does not constitute an absolute break but rather involves a losing of the past in such a manner as to regain it anew. The polis was constantly present in its absence during the first stage of the journey. The theoretic journey in fact constitutes a manner of presenting the polis to the deity. The second askese during which the traveler leaves behind him the sacred ground in order to return to the city performs a similar function. The homeward journey presents the sacred place and the deity to the city. The entire journey connects the human and the divine realm. In both cases the traveler cannot turn around except on the basis of an experienced fullness and of a sense of ripeness and completion. The turning is the fruit of a true mutual  presence. This turning is the mutual creation of the polis, the deity and the traveler. The journey back from the shrine to the polis speaks of the goodwill of the gods, the receptivity of the waiting community, the courage and the faithfulness of the theorist.

This last phase of the journey demands the faithful transmission of the message of the oracle back to the city; it requires the theorist to prepare for his audience, to recollect the major aspects of his journey, to bring order and relevance in a chaotic mass of events. The journey back to the polis is a labor of making visible and understandable, of mediating between the event and its audience. Homecoming constitutes the great reflective and hermeneutic task without which theoretical effort remains incomplete. At this stage of the journey the theorist places himself between the fullness of the events and the vivifying presence of an eager audience. If he positions himself in the right manner between these two forceful poles, he will be able to speak clearly and come to understand fully. (p. 259)

Jager's manner of writing is to take us through the material several times in a spiralling and continuously amplifying and also condensing mode of discourse that keeps uncovering and highlighting the essential contour and movement of the phenomenon of theorizing.

The ultimate concern of all of Jager's work seems to be the uncovering of the foundation for a "truly inhabitable world" in which we can dwell with passion and fully sensuous bodiliness in the mood of a festive celebration. Jager's project is to engage in a reflective meditation on the meaning of human embodiment and dwelling. Jager's stance and manner of proceeding is very kin to that of Heidegger's attitude of "meditative thinking" which discloses the Being of things. But whereas Heidegger focuses his attention and hermeneutic descriptive power on some of the **things** that make up our dwelling: the field path, the bridge, the jug, the peasant shoes, the temple. . . Jager concentrates his studies on essential human **situated activities** and our living through them: the journey, dwelling, theorizing, celebrating, the laboratory, the psychoanalytic situation, tracking their historical unfolding of meaning so as to recover the fullness and origin of meaning.

What Jager accomplishes is a concrete and historically grounded and psychologically differentiated presentation, illustrated by historical stories, with which we can identify and which have the power to move or call us into a new attitude as readers, as listeners, as citizens, as dwellers ourselves. He makes us more cognizant and appreciative of the profundity of our incarnate dwelling in a sensuous and tactile world deep with meaning.

### §8.--ON THE PHENOMENON OF THE CHANGING HEART AND THE METAPHORICAL NATURE OF PSYCHOLOGICAL LIFE: R. Romanyshyn

R. Romanyshyn challenges us to recognize and acknowledge the "cultural dream" we share and unquestioningly accept which is called "the science of psychology," and to recover and reclaim the full human meaning of "psychological life." Modern psychology conceived of as a natural science which tries to anchor its findings ultimately on the immutable natural laws of physiology, is the result of our historically choosing a way of viewing, understanding, and languaging human life based on empirical facts and observable data which claims objectivity. It is generated by the application of the scientific-hypothesis-testing method of doing experimental research. However, as Romanyshyn convincingly narrates and argues in his original book: **Psychological Life: From Science to Metaphor** (1982), our natural scientific psychology is just one way of seeing and storying our human psychological life, and a deficient and distorting one at that because it is not even aware of its own self-delimiting presuppositions and historical relativity.

Psychology as a natural science is itself a "specific historical appearance of psychological life, and in its psychological life appears through a physics of nature and a physiology of the body" (van den Berg, in Romanyshyn, 1982, pp. XII-XIII). We all have come to see our psychological life through the eyes of the natural scientific empirical-factual approach which is removed from our immediate and subjective experience of the life-world. Natural scientific psychology has come to dominate our modern understanding of the nature of psychological life. Both phenomenology and psychoanalysis are reactions against the objectivistic bias of natural science psychology because of its forgetfulness of the true "psychological life of the soul" which always experiences itself as involved in an ongoing story. Romanyshyn can be said to believe in the primacy of the story or of narrative in our psychological self-and world-understanding. "Psychological understanding proceeds by way of story, a point of view which Hillman advocates in a persuasive fashion. Story, not fact, defines human psychological life and in this sense psychological experience as story is to be distinguished from a factual account and experience (which is not psychological)." (p. 86) "Everyone thinks of his or her life and all lives as something that can in every sense of the word be told as a story." (Merleau-Ponty, 1964, p. 75)

Romanyshyn (1984) considers both phenomenology and psychoanalysis as disciplines of remembering:

> Phenomenology and psychoanalysis are each in their own way responses to this historical appearance of human psychological life as the (objectivistic) science of psychology. In so far as psychology's claim to be a science has meant that the soul has been dichotomized between body and mind, phenomenology and psychoanalysis share a critical rejection of this dichotomy. (p. 4)

> Phenomenology as a return from distance to proximity is a science of remembering, a praxis of uncovering out of forgetfulness the world as it is experienced. And in this respect we might add that phenomenology is a psychoanalysis of the bodily experienced world. It does for this world what psychoanalysis does for the person: it remembers what is otherwise forgotten. (p. 6)

Romanyshyn thus refers to his approach as **phenomenological depth-psychology** which:

> Seeks to uncover the landscapes within which the world events unfold as stories enacted by soul. . . . (p. 19)

Through phenomenology and psychoanalysis we can approach the
world as a landscape where soul enacts its stories. (p. 15)
    I call what I am doing a phenomenological depth-psychology whose
focus of attention is the historical-cultural world humanity has
built for itself (personal communication).

Romanyshyn wants to undertake a work of recovery, or remembering, and
of restoration to regain the full and lost meaning of human psychological
life. He portrays his approach as an enterprise of "metaphorizing," of
"de-literalizing the real," of presenting psychological life as a story
that matters to a psychological figure, the actor, who is actively engaged
in bodily confronting his or her landscape and in making sense of the
situation by figuring and storying experience, by "fictionalizing the
factual." The "craft of psychological studies" consists in the work of
remembering and recovering the meanings that have been lost. "The psychological craft consists in bearing witness for what lies forgotten beneath
the literalizing attitudes of daily and scientific life" (1982, p. 174).
The work and attitude of the psychologist is understood by Romanyshyn to
be that of a witness: "A witness whose work embodies the unheard of
stories of our age in the sense of that which an age most desires to
forget" (p. 174).
    Romanyshyn's hermeneutic work is thus directed at re-telling the
story of some of the key issues in psychology: our relationship to things,
to others, to our body, and in doing so to demonstrate that human psychological life is at base a metaphorical reality, a reality of reflection,
of finding oneself involved in stories as figures in a tale or drama, the
meaning of which changes with each biographical and historical vantage
point. "Psychological life as a reality of reflection is a recovery of how
the psychological dimension of human life matters by re-figuring the world
of fact as story and of the person as a figure in a tale" (p. 20). We
cannot escape this relativism of changing visions which we ourselves
create by our discoveries. They yield styles of vision and ways of experiencing life. Romanyshyn's approach is one of historical reflection or
"historical psychology." He is indebted to van den Berg's "Metabletics:
the science of changes" (1971) which focuses on concrete events in the
history of our human experience. Metabletics or historical psychology is a
hermeneutic enterprise which refigures our understanding of ourselves and
our view of and relationship to the world. Such changes, e.g. the appearance of the notion of childhood and of the dividedness of the soul

(1974) crop up at a certain historical time and manifest in all the diverse disciplines of the sciences and the arts and in our practical forms of life. Van den Berg has given many provocative examples of these historical interdisciplinary investigations to document the "changing nature of man" and the different worlds we inhabit. Romanyshyn is inspired by this historical approach and takes his starting point from some of van den Berg's themes.

Harvey's discovery in 1628 of **the human heart as a pump** is one of those fertile and world-changing occurrences and insights which Romanyshyn develops in his reflection on the psychological world of the human body. I will use this "effort to recover the psychological story of the cultural events of the heart as a pump" which constitutes Chapter 4 of Romanyshyn's book as an illustration of his methodological approach to the study of life-world experience.

Romanyshyn (1982) begins his attempt to recover the heart as a psychological reality by investigating our everyday language use of the word heart. How does heart appear in our discourse as a way of speaking, as a "figure of speech," i.e. as a metaphorical reality? In everyday language use: "Every language use bears witness to the wandering character of the human heart. My heart, for example, may rise up in my throat or sink to my stomach. My heart can be in my mouth or I can wear it on my sleeve. This heart about which my language speaks appears, therefore, to be a vagrant heart, a heart which is not fixed in a literal way" (p. 102). In this language use the heart is a metaphor. It discloses meaning and understanding. It matters in the conduct of my life, in the multiple contexts of self- and world-storying.

Next in the path of his investigation, in his methodology, Romanyshyn turns to the etymology of the word heart, to sample the many worlds of experience in which the human heart is reflected.

> Heart springs from the Indo-European root **kerd** which in Latin becomes cord and in English appears in such familiar words as cordial, concord, discord, record, and courage. In addition the word heart also echoes in our word belief through the Latin term credere which is connected to another Indo-European root for heart, **kerddhe.** (American Heritage Dictionary). Already, therefore, we hear how the experiences of harmony and disharmony, cordiality or courtesy, memory, courage and belief are originally matters of the human heart. (p. 103)

From the etymological reflections Romanyshyn relates the experience of the heart to memory as well as to celebrations as remembering and to the domain of manners which he illustrates through a story. In summary he states: "We have seen how the human heart is a reality of reflection. The worlds of harmony, discord and manners, for example, are reflections of the human heart. They are matters which are at the heart of daily life and which concern the everyday- heart of human life" (p. 106). Compared to the factual reality of the heart as a blood pump, which is our dominant contemporary vision, these usages of heart are "mere" figures of speech, illusions. But they matter to us as ways of figuring the rich depth of human experiences and therefore they merit our attention and acceptance as human psychological realities.

How did the vision of the human heart as a pump, come into our life and begin to dominate our understanding? It was Harvey who in 1628 published his research findings into the circulation of the blood and the role of the heart as a pump. Romanyshyn distinguishes between the courageous heart of Harvey, encouraged and supported in his daring new vision by the faith and belief of his friends to publish his findings which went contrary to all tradition and cherished belief of the time, and the actual discovery that the heart acts like a pump regulating the blood-flow of the interior body. The human heart and its movement is at this moment in history, for the first time ever, in human awareness, understood to be like the motion of a machine. The consequences of this re-visioning of the human heart into a mechanics are enormous: Harvey sees the pumping heart as a "divided heart," and as a "democratic heart" in that all hearts, as physiological pumps, are equal in their function.

Romanyshyn now turns to the political events of the era of Harvey's discovery. Harvey dedicated his book to his sovereign: Charles I of England saying: "the king is the heart of the kingdom." But, as Romanyshyn points out: "Harvey's attempt to unify the blood, divides the heart. Charles' attempt to unify the kingdom divides its heart" (p. 118). The English civil war breaks out. In 1649 Charles I was beheaded. "A pumping heart can beat only in a democratic world, in a world which is blind to differences (p. 121).

Summarizing his findings so far and at the same time reflecting on the nature of his hermeneutical methodology Romanyshyn says:

What does the divided heart of the seventeenth century mean? It means that human life has changed in such a way that what was formerly a matter of visible differences to be lived with in the world and among people has now become an interior matter of the heart. This shift in psychological life is revealed through the mutual **reflections** of the scientific and political events of the time. The gathering of these reflections is a way of **deepening** the significance of these events as a **story** of human experience. It is a way of recovering the psychological dimension of these events. (p. 119)

Another consequence of Harvey's new vision was the notion of the "empty heart," the heart-muscle squeezing blood out into the arteries in its moment of full vigor, thus emptying itself. This stands in contrast to the experiential notion of the "full heart," the "expansive heart" which we believe to be the center of our vital life. The opposite of what we believe, is true. "The systole and not the diastole is the basic motion of the heart, and emptiness, not fullness, characterizes its primary state" (p. 123). What are we to believe? In the late seventeenth century, simultaneous with Harvey's discovery we are no longer certain of what we are to believe. "This mutual occurrence is no accident. The empty heart belongs to a psychological age which doubts its most unquestioned beliefs" (p. 123). The expanding and contracting heart is not just a matter of blood. Expansion and contraction, expansiveness in the outside world of discoveries and contraction in the empty heart of loneliness become dialectically interlinked describing a way of seeing and a way of living.

Romanyshyn now turns to the realm of architecture, with pictorial illustrations, and especially to the concurrently emerging form of the Baroque style with its energetic forms resembling pulsating organisms. "Baroque elation hides an uneasiness of the human heart. It hides an implicit loss of faith, a disillusionment with human concerns (p. 124). "Baroque pessimism" reveals a struggle between reason and faith, a struggle between the "exuberance of flesh and the asceticism of spirit."

The despair of the empty heart also manifests in the literature of the age, as in Cervantes and Donne in which our place in the world is put into question, in which we come to define our place by ourselves, in ourselves as our thinking, as in Descartes. In 1654 von Guernicke creates the first vacuum-sphere which two teams of horses cannot pull apart. A triumph of the power of emptiness as a mechanical principle.

In 1673 another experience of the heart opens up: the visions of Margaret May Alacoque initiates the worship of the Sacred Heart of Christ, re-establishing a vision of the heart which speaks with the fullness of life. A counterpuntal movement to the empty heart of 1628, which is drained of blood and belief: "In the seventeenth century the **fullness** of the heart begins to matter when the **emptiness** of the human heart becomes a theme" (p. 129). Romanyshyn, in these various re-storying reflections on the theme of the heart in different domains of human life during a given era does not wish to establish any causal connection of a deterministic nature between the different events. Rather, he considers these relations to be indirect and psychological.

> They are **reflections** of each other which indicate on the one hand that human psychological existence appears through the things which we do, through the churches we build, the sciences of the heavens and the earth we create, the literature we write, and the ways in which we worship our God. On the other hand, these relations indicate the changing character of our psychological life. In the seventeenth century a new psychological existence emerges. The pumping heart is a reflection of that psychological life which is our own life in the modern world. (p. 130)

In this brief presentation of Romanyshyn's approach and method of doing hermeneutical-phenomenological work we cannot do justice to the high level of scholarship and detailed knowledge of the literature and research from various disciplines that is shown in this book. The reader must consult Romanyshyn's highly original text itself, to appreciate its interdisciplinary scope, its historical penetration, and its depth of understanding. It appears to be a difficult approach to teach because it is based on a vast stock of knowledge and level of erudition which takes a life-time of devotion to acquire. The person, who Robert Romanyshyn is, is very much also the method, the way of seeing and the way of reporting which he does. It is a profoundly idiosyncratic way of doing hermeneutical-phenomenology.

But we can try to articulate the main generalizable characteristics of Romanyshyn's approach and method: He wants to recover **human psychological life** as a reality of meaningful personal meaning-making activity, of story-making. In doing so he wants to create a new, historically based phenomenological-depth psychology. He says of this enterprise: "It leads us into a domain of living where story rather than fact or idea informs experience, and where the imaginal understanding of the human heart supercedes the empirical understanding of the observing eye, and the logical understanding of the human mind" (p. XVI). Romanyshyn stories the "appearance" of the human heart in these various domains of human life and places them in juxtaposition with each other so that we may be able to see one reality through another and thus to deepen their appearance and our understanding. It is, as he himself says, a "work of mirroring."

> A text in physiology was brought face to face, for example, with the political events of the age, and in this mutual facing each event was deepened, refigured, and de-realized through the other. A physiological fact, the division of the heart, was seen through the political divisions of the age, and in this fashion that face was de-literalized. It was not the factual status which mattered. . . but the story which appeared when that fact was imaged in this other way, **as if** it were a political event, which mattered. The fact became a way of telling a story, an image through which another meaning appeared. (p. 138)

Mirroring work is hermeneutical work, par excellence. We read one story or profile of reality against another related profile and thus engage in a disciplined dialogue between different ways of speaking and storying. The shared existential concern around which this storying occurs is enriched in meaning, we deepen our understanding of it. Such interpretative dialogue, such a spiralling hermeneutic opens up and differentiates the field of investigation and thus makes possible a deepened understanding and appreciation of the complexity and the essentially elusive, suggestible, narrative and metaphorical nature of human psychological life.

> Psychological life and psychological understanding are, therefore, no more matters of fiction than they are matters of fact. In the form of a story they cut through this dichotomy. The consequence of course is that the mode of understanding psychological life is neither empirical nor rational . . . no, the mode of psychological understanding seems closer to the reader's approach to the story. A reader understands a story and the story matters precisely to the extent that it portrays a believable world into which one can enter and within which one can dwell. (p. 87)

## §9.--HERMENEUTIC STUDY:  READING HUMAN EXISTENCE

We have presented a variety of ways of doing **analysis of life-world experience** - studying the lived and experienced personal life process. All of these existential-phenomenological researches are based on the conviction that spontaneous human living can be articulated and rendered explicit and communicated - either in retrospect or as speak-aloud account - by means of language, as story, as narrative description. This approach is thus dependent on **language** to express and gather the partially mute living experience of personal-existential involvement. We can articulate only what we are aware of. This makes it difficult to access pre-conscious and unconscious dimensions of experience which do not easily find their way into factual, narrative representation in retrospective verbal accounts. We have to acknowledge the limits of life-recordings as life-texts. Always, more is lived than is told. And yet the wisdom of speech and writing allows us to express more than we say, also. The manifest text can be read into in terms of its hidden meanings, its inner dimensions. The listener or reader picks up what was implied, what was hidden, what was disguised or unknown in the intention of the author. Thus, all study of human activities and productions, from action to texts, to art, to religious symbols and rituals, has to be essentially a **hermeneutic study.** We are involved in an interpretative enterprise in which all participants have to read the situation in order to respond. Hermeneutic study is self-disclosure and self-commitment, personal witnessing and contributing to the shared world of meanings as well as the disclosure and articulation of meaning of world-situations, of people's actions and intentions.

Hermeneutic study thus is the explicit, historical, ongoing accumulation of perspectives and knowledge on already known issues, the building of a multi-dimensional house of language in which the issue dwells and has its changeable being. Each researcher's contribution is his or her hermeneutical gift to society's deliberations adding some light to the still prevailing darkness of pre-conscious participation which is ultimately rooted in the tribal drums of ethnic flesh and kin and the mythos of a culture.

We construct the house of culture and meaning as our human dwelling place in and through language. Doing analysis of life-world experience, doing empirical hermeneutical research of whatever form implies raising the enacted and perceived event into awareness through linguistic/artistic rendering, first in terms of the existential **concreteness** of story and

then, later, on another level of discourse, in abstract, universal conceptual terms. The same experienced event is rendered several times by means
of language on distinct but interrelated and interdependent levels of
discourse. We experience meaning-enrichment and deepen our understanding
by this work in languaging human experiaction.

# CONCLUDING REFLECTIONS

## AND

## IMPLICATIONS FOR THERAPY

### §1.-THE SPECTRUM OF HUMAN SCIENCE METHODS

All psychological research methods are interested in gaining reliable access to human phenomena, to establish valid descriptions of human action which can be consensually validated, and to ascertain valid relationships, rules, laws, structures, and patterns that bring increased order into our understanding of and participation in human affairs.

The first great division in the spectrum of human science methods in psychology lies in the opposition between **natural science** approaches and the **human science** approach as formulated by Strasser (1963) and Giorgi (1970). This opposition hinges on several dimensions:

| **Causal Explanation** | versus | **Intentional Analysis** |
|---|---|---|
| Quantitative Analysis | " | Qualitative Analysis |
| Statistical Results | " | Meaning Structures |
| Hypothesis Testing | " | Meaning Elucidation |
| Observer Orientation | " | Actor Reporting |
| Focus on Behavior | " | Focus on Personal Experience |
| Representative Samples | " | Paradigm Case Descriptions |

Both the natural and the human science approaches begin with a research focus, a professional interest in a human phenomenon suggested by the body of professional literature or a real life issue that calls attention to itself. For the natural science approach this topic has to be expressed in the form of a testable hypothesis of how this behavior is caused by antecedent subject-, other- or situational/environmental variables from an observer perspective. Emphasis is placed on the measurements of the relevant variables, on research instruments, research-design, quantification and statistical analyses and comparisons establishing correlational tendencies beyond chance in the behavior of anonymous representative samples of groups. The results are generalized to human behavior as such. The aim of the natural scientific approach in psychology is to predict and control human behavior. It is thus the striving for a "knowledge of control" (Scheler, 1961). Psychology becomes a tool for behavior change.

In the human science approach we take the **actor perspective** (Schutz, 1962, Von Eckartsberg, 1971) and we are concerned with human experience in situations. The human science researcher places the emphasis on the point of view of the experiencing subject (the actor), on the stream of experi-action, on what happens in the experience of the participants in the situation. The researcher chooses the study-situation according to his professional interest and relevance structures (Schutz, 1970), and he enlists the cooperation of the "subject" as a co-researcher: Would you be willing to describe your experience for us in as detailed and vivid a manner as possible? This can be done retrospectively as a written or spoken description or it can, under certain circumstances, be done in a "speak-aloud" manner when someone verbalizes and/or videotapes the ongoing stream of experiaction into a tape recorder which can then be transcribed. (Von Eckartsberg, 1975; Wertz, 1983; Aanstoos, 1983). In either case we obtain accounts, protocols, or "life-texts" which can then be studied and analyzed in the various ways described in this book yielding situated, general, and process-structures of human experience.

Human science psychology generates knowledge of the essential meanings, the "what-ness" of human experience, i.e. what consciousness, perception, affect, memory, projecting, imagining, etc. and their specific situated manifestations really are. In Scheler's terms it aims at meta-physical-philosophical knowledge, "knowledge of essences."

There is an important variant in the human science approach which we might identify as the **case-study** which is the preferred mode of the clinicians (Binswanger, 1958; May, 1958; Boss, 1963), who have written exquisite pathographies, and of Sartre's Existential Psychoanalysis approach. Sartre has published several existential psycho-historical biographies (1950, 1964a, 1964b). This person-centered way of study is more holistic and dialectical, "progressive-regressive" in its intention because it wants to identify and articulate the overall movement, style, and "existential project" and psycho-logic of an individual's life in its historico-political context. Because of the immensity of life-data that are available or which can be generated about one person the case-study is a very difficult, holistic, hermeneutic enterprise which concerns itself with questions of fundamental choices, of style, of way of life, i.e. with complex holistic constructs.

Clinical work is a natural and valuable source of data for the factual study of persons but literature and drama, although fictional, also offer a profusion of life-texts for hermeneutic study. Impact and believability become the criteria of validity in fictional data. Literary criticism as a professional discipline and body of research already exists for this domain. It offers the advantage of many studies focusing on the same works or data, i.e. life-text. Each critical interpreter takes up the same material but reads it from a particular vantage point enriching the communication field of the "textual ensemble" (Von Eckartsberg, 1979b). The humanities which mediate the tradition, the artistic and spiritual heritage to us as originary works and as hermeneutic commentaries provide us, the readers and "consumers" of this knowledge, with important opportunities for personal growth and deepening.

The literary- and art-critics as professionals do human-science work within the canons of their hermeneutical discipline. They are interested in deciphering and interpreting the essential human meanings expressed in a work. In this way they aim at the same goal as the human science psychologist, although the relevancy structures and topics of interest and the historical context of interpretation of the two professions differ. Both aim at the production of "knowledge of essences," the fruits of hermeneutic studies: **cognitive meaning-enrichment.**

Radnitzki (1968) in his monumental study of contemporary schools of meta-science has found a twofold fundamental difference in approaches to psychology which he calls: **Logical Empiricism** connected primarily with the **natural science** approach which employs the empirical scientific method of observation and hypothesis testing and which is the dominant way of the Anglo-American speech community (i.e. Behaviorism) in the study of psychological phenomena, and the **Hermeneutic Dialectical Approach,** connected with the **human sciences** originating in and embracing most of Continental European thinking. During the last two decades a curious reversal is taking place. Anglo-Saxon psychology has become more humanistic and existential-phenomenological while Continental psychology has become fascinated with the rigor of the empirical scientific approach and the quantitative-measurement orientation.

The decisive difference between these two schools of meta-science lies in the dominant **research guiding interest.** For the natural scientific approach the ideal is causal **explanation** of occuring behavior enabling us to **predict and control** such behavior and giving rise to an ideology and praxis of behavioral engineering through the mediation of a group of experts, whereas the hermeneutic-dialectic human science approach works under the guiding ideal of **empathic understanding**, of explication of meaning, and of personal emancipation (Habermas, 1966), gaining personal freedom from hypostatized forces of conceptual understanding - ultimately freedom from theory itself - and from institutional control - freedom from political domination. Emancipation is liberation through the understanding of one's true situation what is often called: "consciousness-raising" through self-help groups, without expert-control. The natural science approach works through power manipulation while the human science approach works through insight and appeal, and through the demonstration of internal contradictions and hidden agendas.

There is a further differentiation within the hermeneutic-dialectical approach. The **hermeneutic interest** is directed primarily into the domain of language and tradition. There is an interest in the mediation of tradition through texts and art, making all historical ways of life available to us now, for improving our self-understanding. There is also a **critical-emancipatory interest** which is concerned with the development of the human sciences in a way that they become relevant for moral and social practice, and the basis for political action aimed at institutional and legal reform. The domain of critical-emancipatory work is governance and steering of conduct and "position-taking with respect to values and aims," the involvement in the ethical domain of personal and social existence. This approach thus seriously challenges the claim of value-neutrality for scientific work. Values are involved from the very beginning and their implicit role has to be clarified and criticized.

The Marxist critical-dialectical emphasis points out that the facts of social reality are the product of hidden contradictions and tensions of a hidden dialectical dynamics, and that an analysis of any situation has to delineate the status quo in terms of its historical and socio-political constitution which may be victimizing and oppressing its participants - negative dialectics. It must also include an assessment of the inherent but arrested possibilities and latent potentials for personal and social emancipation - the negation of the negative or a **constructive dialectic** - arriving at a prescription for action. This involves both a personal-political program for the individual and a social-political action plan for the interest- or value-constituency, the "existential ensemble" which is implicated and feels put upon. Critical-dialectical thinking in the tradition of the Frankfurt school - the work of Horkheimer, Adorno, Marcuse and Habermas keeps dominating the social science thinking of central Europe and South America (Freire, 1970) but seems to have not made much of a public impact on the American intellectual scene.

The other major difference between the two major approaches is the emphasis on **behavior** and the public, observable responses on the part of the natural-science oriented psychologist - the **observer perspective** - as contrasted with the emphasis on **experience, consciousness, and personal meaning,** what we call the **actor perspective** in the phenomenological and hermeneutic tradition. The differences between these two perspectives in this regard is rooted in the implicit view of human nature, conceived either as a causally determined psycho-biological organism subject to natural-law type controls, amenable to technical-managerial manipulation, or to the conception of man as an intentionally oriented, meaning-giving, value-choosing, culture-creating and partially self-determining being.

Existential-Phenomenologists clearly stand in the tradition of hermeneutics in that they understand humans to be essentially meaning-making and culture-building and they focus their reflective and empirical research on the meaning-constituting-acts of man, accessible as acts of consciousness and ascertainable only from the actor perspective of the participants in the situation as a lifetext to be interpreted in a meaning-amplifying manner so that the experienced event comes to stand revealed to us in its full context and cradled in its multiple horizons of significance and streams of feeling and emotion.

Habermas considers psychoanalysis to be the prototypical emancipatory science, because the knowledge generated by the client is used to benefit and heal the clients rather than feed some productive research interests, and thus special interest groups. This places **therapy** toward the hermeneutic and emancipatory pole of the spectrum.

Knowledge in this emancipatory context which anchors one side of the spectrum of human science methods, in the service of personal and social liberation means "existential knowing," the art of living, becoming an "artist of life" (Lebenskunstler). It is a different kind of knowing: Knowledge which helps, heals, and redeems: **"knowledge of salvation"** as Scheler (1961) has argued. It is a step beyond the intellectual "knowledge of essences" and two steps beyond the manipulatory order of "knowledge of control" and behavioral engineering administered by an institutionalized expert elite. Knowledge of salvation is knowledge of consent, of personal responsibility and voluntary co-existential involvement in the shared task of culture-building. Knowledge of salvation leads beyond analysis to the integration of life-world experience.

## § 2.--STORIES AND META-STORIES

Stories constitute the foundation of human everyday meaning-making. As Schapp (1976) states this: "We are entangled in stories." Without explicit training we are capable of giving an account of human experience and action in the form of stories, as **narratives**.

Stories allow us to identify with the experiaction and to become aware, to recognize and make contact with dimensions of one's own life experience. Let us call this the **existential impact** that a story makes. But we are also interested in raising this experience of meaning into an explicit articulation, into a formulation that we can express and share with others. Our reflective and philosophical nature calls us to articulate the essential meanings also as **ideas and concepts.**

We always do both: We consider structure, concept, meaning-configuration - the fruits of reflection - and we appreciate the existential drama of a meaningfully connected concatenation of events - the fruits of personal participation. What holds these two together and what makes their distinction possible, according to Ricoeur (1979) is our awareness of **plot**, the integrated perception of the meaning of all events in their interdependency. As Ricoeur states:

> The notions of historical **event**, as a temporal concept, and plot, as a narrative concept, are mutually definable. To be historical an event must be more than a singular occurrence, a unique happening. It receives its definition from its contribution to the development of a plot. Reciprocally, a plot is a way of connecting event and story. A story is **made out of** events, to the extent that plot makes events **into** a story.

> This notion of events made **into** story through the plot immediately suggests that a story is not bound to a merely chronological order of events. All narratives combine in various proportions, two dimensions - one chronological and the other non-chronological.

The first may be called the **episodic dimension.** This dimension characterizes the story as made out of events. The second is the **configu-**
**rational dimension** to which the plot construes significant wholes out
of scattered events. . . the notion of configurational act, which he
interprets as a "grasping together." I understand this act to be the
act of the plot as eliciting a pattern from a succession. (p. 24)

Ricoeur uses the notion of plot to integrate the two essential dimensions of storying: that of human **temporality,** i.e. our experiencing of
time in human affairs, and that of **narrativity,** i.e. our human tendency to
create meaning by "storying" a sequence of meaningful situated events
enacted by a cast of characters.

What is involved in the creation of a story has been described by
teachers in journalism as "the five w's and the h." "In gathering information about a news event, the reporter seeks answers to the WHO, WHAT,
WHERE, WHEN, WHY, and HOW of whatever happened. Of these, the first four
are basic to virtually any account" (MacDougall, 1972, p. 42) We can
understand stories, therefore, as providing answers and information to
basic and essential implicit human questions which, in their interplay,
create the meaning of: **What Happened?**

The factual content of any story is revealed by these basic questions
which we call **fundamental existentials.** They constitute the "signature of
an event" (von Eckartsberg, 1978, 1979). But we as listeners or readers
are not always satisfied with the account. We want to know more, to read
deeper into the meaning of the story, we want to understand the facts
differently, use a different interpretation. We want to reveal the "true
story," the story behind or within the given story: the **meta-story** or **sub-**
**text.** As listeners and readers we may re-story the meanings presented in
the story. Reading human existence - hermeneutic study - often involves
the creation of stories about stories and these differences center on different choices of the implicit why and how.

We attribute motives and reasons to our own and other's actions.
These attributions of causality reflect and express our own preferred view
of the world of our understanding of human nature: our philosophical
and/or religious anthropology. We bring a pre-understanding to any situation whether we are aware of this or not. We use this pre-comprehension in
constructing our stories and interpretations of events. We can summarize
this state of affairs in terms of the following schemes:

## The Story of an Event

| The Questions | The Meanings they Yield |
|---|---|
| Who in relationship to whom? | The Actors: the Cast of Characters |
| Is Involved in What? | The Action |
| When? | The Time of the Action |
| Where | The Scene of the Action |
| Why? | The Motive for the Action |
| How? | The Manner and Means of the Action |

In spontaneous story-telling we answer these implicit questions so that the listener or reader understands what happened. The account makes use of **proper names** - of persons, of groups, of times, of places - to express the existential uniqueness of the events. But the story-teller also defines the **why**, of the motives of the action in the way he or she constructs the plausibility of the plot and the **how**, the manner or means for the action. In answering why and how the story-teller interprets what happened in terms of meaningful human action: plot. The facts are interpreted in a certan light, from a certain framework of comprehension.

Professional readings, the reading of scientific psychology, whether conceived of as a natural or a human science - employ explicit meta-stories called theories or paradigms, constructed according to scientific criteria. As professional psychologists we want to explain or interpret the meaning of the actions narrated by the story in terms of a theoretically integrated account.

The various recognized theories in psychology are such meta-stories. They provide specific answers to the foundational questions of philosophical anthropology: What is the essential nature of human being (Who is man?) Why do humans act the way they do? (Why do we act?)

These two questions constitute a **personality** - and associated **motivational theory.** They give a specific answer to the basic question of **personality-structure** and **personality-dynamics.** I call these two hermeneutical questions: **Interpretationals.** They constitute our theoretical psychological view, our paradigm, in terms of which our understanding is articulated. Psychology, as a discipline is essentially **poly-paradigmatic** (von Eckartsberg, 1983). This means that multiple views regarding the essential nature of human being always coexist as schools of thought. Each theory is based on a different philosophical anthropology.

## The Interpretation (Meta-Story) of an Event

| The Questions | The Meanings They Yield |
|---|---|
| What is the implicit nature of human being? | A specific theory of personality structure |
| Why? What is the implied motivation? | A specific theory of personality dynamics |

Psychological theories are meta-stories which deepen and clarify mundane everyday life stories. As psychologists we become committed to and believe in a certain theoretical point of view although we cannot justify our adherence in a purely rational fashion. (von Eckartsberg, 1983) Commitment to a paradigm is made on a trans-rational level and resembles religious belief, i.e. the acceptance of a religious revelatory story as true on grounds of faith, not of reason. A felt affinity or kinship with the vision, based on one's biographical experience is involved.

Each theory or meta-story sheds additional light on the story presented but from a limited perspective. There does not seem to be a universal vantage-point which could contain and integrate all the meanings into an objective and universally accepted truth. We are condemned to remain in a field of open dialogue in which different views and voices regarding the "real" meaning of a narrated event compete for believers. It is a situation of "democratic pluralism." We live in an inescapable relativistic hermeneutic situation with regard to the reading of human existence. This situation has also been referred to as the "criticist frame," i.e. the attitude that we trust language, that we give ourselves over to the dia-

logal principle of the discussion of different points of view in the hope
and faith that we can arrive at an intersubjective agreement or integration at some future time or, at least, that we come to a recognition and
acknowledgement of our differences, as legitimate options, given the
premises.

## §3.--LIVING IN STORIES

Existential-phenomenologists in spite of their presuppositionless, inductive, descriptive-reflective approach make the description, the story, the
fable into a **cognitive object.** This book presents a whole spectrum of ways
of doing this kind of research, conceptualizing human experience. In the
analysis of life-world experience we create cognitive objects. We take up
the story again, in a cognitive way, as a scientific and hermeneutic task,
in order to create a meta-story of scientific validity.

What makes this possible and what thus constitutes the ground for the
possibility of intellectualizing is **the story** itself as a spontaneous
human meaning-creation of the lived life, the existential event in the
world of occurrences which it narrates. Stories are the meaning-making
foundation of our everyday shared social life. We know of others and even
of ourselves primarily through the stories of our shared living, as members of "existential ensembles" of "existential casts of characters."

In this way stories "work on us," and all of society "works" on the
communciation and sharing of stories. Stories tell of deeds and of quests
and transgressions of named individuals with whom we identify or from
which we dissociate ourselves. We hear of a person or a group's story and
it addresses us, it moves us. It can call us out, personally, and give us
meaning, values and direction as well as inspiration. Like the parables
and life of Jesus or Buddha, or even the parable of the fox and the crow,
stories can make an existential and moral impact on us and they bind us
together into communion, into the shared and cherished or cursed posses-
sion of a shared event, memory, and destiny.

In everyday life, stories can satisfy our curiosity about others but
they can also serve as occasions for an existential turn-about, a letting
oneself be moved and changed by the story and experiencing it fully,
existentially, as a normative experience and reference point, as a call
for authenticity, a call of conscience based on our intuitive ability to

sense and commit ourselves to what is right and good and beautiful and true and just.

In the words of Rosenstock-Huessy (1970) stories can generate **metanoia,** a new beginning for one's life, a letting oneself become animated and inspired again, a turning away from dead things toward a new life.

Nicholl (1975) speaks of **scientia cordis,** the science of the heart, the science which discloses how people are moved in their hearts to become great souls, to grow and mature, to become more fully and authentically human, to show courage. This seems to be the way in which stories "work" and live in our everyday life. They are the normative life-texts, the tales of the deeds of exemplary persons whom we acknowledge as heroes and saints and value-embodying martyrs of our tradition. As Nicholl (1975) states:

> This, therefore, is the primary thing to notice about the **scientia cordis,** it is science. And the next thing to note is that in no sense is it a branch of psychology. Psychology, like all positive sciences, attempts to analyze the object of its study, as if it were a fixed, given thing whose future is in principle totally predictable provided the scientist can exhaustively analyze all its parts. But the heart is the seat of aspiration, of prayer; and even an agnostic such as Iris Murdoch, for instance, is glad to acknowledge that human beings who pray live in an added dimension beyond the reach of those who do not pray. It is more exact to say not that they live in an added dimension but that they plunge into a dimension which alters every single thing about them. Their whole being is transformed by aspiration and cannot be analyzed and predicted because the aspiration, the prayer, is an affirmation that renewal is possible, that there is genuine newness in the world, that not everything can be reduced to what was given in the past. (p. 8)

Regarding "method," the way of going about it, Nicholl states:

> The characteristic medium for stating the **scientia cordis** is not the principle or law characteristic of the positive sciences; the essential point about the principle or law formula is that it leaves the situation unchanged, and it leaves both the person formulating the law and the one hearing the law in a state of detachment: there

is nothing that anyone ought to do as a result of the formulation; everyone can still say, "so what?" By contrast, both the person stating the science of the heart and the person to whom he is stating it have to be moved by it, since it is concerned with human beings in aspiration and prayer; and unless they are quickened in their aspirations then the statement has proved empty. Hence the characteristic medium of the **scientia cordis** is neither a principle nor a law but a story, a story that will move the heart. . . . And this is what we find amongst all the authorities of this science, that they do their teaching by stories that will touch the hearts of their listeners. (p. 10)

When we understand the power of stories in these terms: calling us into self-transformation, into a change of heart, into metanoia, we experience not so much their narrative nature and content but their **imperative character**, their demand character, their call for action rather than their cognitive meaning. Cognitive interest expresses the attitude of the scientist, the disinterested observer. Existential participation and the opening oneself to the moral imperative and lesson contained in the story springs from the attitude of personal responsibility and active value-engagement.

It is in this way that the great stories of our lives and of our tradition and culture, of the great personages we meet personally through their stories, act effectively in our existence and give us direction, example, value, orientation, hope and inspiration, a sense of the normative and even of the Absolute.

We can argue further that the foundation of communal life is created by our involvement in a particular shared language which bestows on us a shared world-view and basic convictions. Bruteau (1979) has coined the term: **Conviction community** to speak of the fundamental intersubjective nature of our consciousness.

It is the community which, through its common conviction system endows its members with the organs of their human personhood: language, habits of thought, rules of behavior, arts, political systems, cosmology and religion. The result. . . is a social animal who, as a cultural product, stands for the divine creative power society claims for itself. . . . All subjects are connected with a centre...our most basic convictions those ideas which really have the power to move us. (p. 104)

We establish a sense of belongingness and community by feeling and knowing ourselves bound together in a common fate and shared history and biography. The story-component is everywhere to be found as laying a shared linguistic foundation creating identity and community feeling.

> Community is constituted by the key events which it remembers and in which its members participate. It frames these memories in myths and customs, which we understand as revealing to us the cosmic order and our place in it. The collective memories guide our behavior. . . and bring us into accord with our group. (p. 109)

Our previous discussion of theories as meta-stories, paradigms and schools of thought can also be understood in terms of living in a shared story of explanation.

We live in stories, in the mythical stories of our origin as a people, in the utopian stories of our aspirations, prophecies and destinies, and in the narratives of our corporate-historical and individual-biographical struggles which trace the pathways of our collective and personal identity. As Bruteau (1979) states:

> The belief system of a community performs certain definite functions for that community and for the individuals who live in it. It is the binding energy that holds the community together and makes it be a community, in order that human persons may develop their consciousness within its context. The psychic grid is the integrating power of a society, providing its world-view, authorizing its social order, sanctioning its behavior, enabling the members, severally and corporately, to cope with conflicts within and without and in general defending the self-consciousness of the group and of the individual persons as members of the community. A community's conviction system is its castle, a walled city to protect it against alternative interpretations of the great and unknown reality in the midst of which it must somehow live. (p. 197)

When approached in this spirit, stories reveal their self-transformative and relationship- and culture-building power. In understanding the role of stories in this way, as a manner of figuring reality, we transcend our cognitive interests and address the issue of existential involvement, value-commitments, and belonging to a conviction community. "Through its recitation, a story is incorporated into a community which it gathers together."

As Romanyshyn (1982) has argued, all psychological life appears to us in the guise of stories. We appear to ourselves as figures in a story and so do the other people in our lives as members of an "existential cast of characters." The totality of all our stories is our life-story, our biography. The whole life of humankind appears to us in the form of stories, of news-stories, of history, of personages and their deeds, of myths and religious revelations. These stories are sacred to us. They have a hold on us, we identify with them, and we embody them as members and participants actively engaged in shaping our personal and collective life-course.

The work of Dunne: **Time and Myth** (1973) shows how we embrace the meanings of the most important Western myths as stories of divine-human interaction and thereby help us to deepen the meanings and to find joyous acceptance of our unique life-course and life-story in the context of the all-embracing story of humankind. Dunne (1967, 1972) has articulated a method he calls "passing over," which describes how in encountering other people, ways of life, and religions through their stories we can grow in appreciation of our starting point and existential situation and come to an integration of our own life-world experience.

## §4.--STORIES AND PSYCHOTHERAPY

In the spectrum of human science methods we next reach the region of **psychotherapy** and **human** **potential training,** where the knowledge which the professionals generate comes from the client and is returned to the client in the form of insight and existential learning, and in the offering of life-transformative options and choices. Knowledge is created in the therapist-client interaction through dialogue in a special professional situation. This knowledge and insight is articulated so that it enhances the quality of life of the client. The intent here is to help set the client free for becoming a unique and responsible person and a co-creative culture- and relationship-builder with others. The intent of psychotherapy and human potential training is to create for the client **existential meaning enrichment** and **personal empowerment**, the ability to take charge of one's existential situation.

In psychotherapy we are interested in helping people to help themselves. We are concerned with the incarnation of knowledge. The client's presenting story gives us a preliminary orientation regarding his or her life-situation. But the initial story is only a means of access into the oceans of feeling and emotions which lie behind the words. As therapists and clients we work by storying the emotional plot-line that lies behind the words of the story. We uncover the meta-story of the client's life-problematic which we might call the **intra-story**. This refers to the configuration of the personal emotional drama, the flow of feelings and passions in their variety - guilt, anger, hate, resentment, yearning for recognition, envy, jealousy, malice, etc. - and in their interplay.

The **emotional factor** of the story has to be unraveled and made speakable through the therapist-client dialogue. What clients don't want to have true has to become acknowledged by them, overcoming resistance and self-deception. Therapy is a dialogal struggle for life-formative storying, for finding the story-formulation of our personal existence with which we can identify wholeheartedly, for which we can stand up, and which gives us a solid and trusted basis for creative and responsible action.

There is also an important **time-factor** in therapeutic storying. Therapist and client may not be in synch in their respective understanding of the deeper emotional meanings of the story. The therapist may grasp the essential emotional intra-plot of the client immediately, at first hearing. But the client may not be able to perceive this reading, even if it is clearly verbalized. It may require many hearings. It takes often a long time for a client to allow him or herself to really hear and touch and acknowledge the deep feeling flow beneath the manifest story, "to go beyond the words," as we say. This time factor may help account for the peculiar spiralling character and repetitive nature of the working-through of problems in psychotherapy when dealing with problems on an emotional level, hidden from cognitive apprehension or, when confronted with intellectualizations dissociated from affect, when there is insight but no feeling or acceptance.

The work of psychotherapy which is a work of both acceptance and of challenge, proceeds by storying and re-storying one's life-involvements, of fitting and thus getting in touch with the dynamic flow of one's personal emotional involvements and entanglements that project or divert and retard us on our life-course. Our preconsicous and precognitive emotional life-flow demands our attention and appreciative acknowledgement in order to be able to flow in life-affirming, benevolent, and relationship nurturing channels, in the way of loving acceptance of one's being in the world with others. There is much resistance to understanding and accepting one's true emotional flow of existential involvement and to understand its meaning and implications in personal terms, in terms of one's own life-story. Therapy helps clients to realize and acknowledge the problematic stories they are stuck in, to free themselves from unlivable stories and to open themselves to new stories, to find a way into more livable stories. The repetitive hate-, failure-, guilt- and-horror stories of their existence have to be given a voice and a genuine hearing so that the story of person's suffering gets told. Gradually this creates room for the emergence of more livable stories, stories of hope and intimacy, of trust, of loving, of discovery, of care which weave a new context of affirmation and acceptance through the person's life-story, opening up new vistas and possibilities for adventures. In therapeutic dialogue we re-story ourselves together in the direction of our most authentic biography, our existential inscription in life.

### §5.--WRITING MARATHON THERAPY

Freud's psycho-dynamics is the paradigm case of a psychotherapeutic depth-psychological approach that uses storying and re-storying as its method. We all know the psychoanalytic plot. Freud created his revolution in psychology by inventing the **free association technique.** He formulated it as the fundamental technical rule of psychoanalytic work:

> The patient being required to put himself in the position of an attentive and dispassionate self-observer. . . to make a duty of the most complete honesty while on the other hand not to hold back any idea from communication, even if 1) he feels that it is too disagreeable or if 2) he judges that it is nonsensical or 3) too unimportant or 4) irrelevant to what is being looked for. (Freud, 1900, p. 125)

The psychodynamic emotional plot becomes revealed through this procedure, gradually. Slowly, over years of almost daily work in psychoanalytic sessions a storied and felt continuity is established between the symptom and its genesis. Freud lets the client tell his or her own story of the origin of the symptom and, finally, to cast it into the coherent story-line of Freudian psychosexual development, the "mea culpa" of an incestual and aggressive striving and imagination. It is an unflinching but also unflattering portrait of our essential psychological being. Are there other scenarios? I feel more kin to Jung's individuation story, to Maslow's scenario of self-actualization, to Frankl's plot of "will to meaning," and to Sartre's characterization of human fate as "existential project." I believe that we are, as person's, an existential epic in ongoing creation, a unique meaningful life-story in the making.

In discovering and articulating his psychoanalytic technique Freud seems to have been inspired by an essay entitled: **The Art of Becoming an Original Writer in Three Days.** This was written by Ludwig Borne in 1823 and is known to have made an impact on Freud as a 14 year old boy when he had been given this work as a present (Frey-Rohn, 1974). Borne had given the following instructions:

And here follows the practical application that was promised. Take a few sheets of paper and for three days on end write down, without fabrication or hypocrisy, everything that comes into your head. Write down what you think of yourself, of your wife, of the Turkish war, of Goethe, of Fonk's trial, of the Last Judgment, of your superiors - and when three days have passed you will be quite out of your senses with astonishment at the new and unheard-of thoughts you have had. This is the art of becoming an original writer in three days. (Borne, 1823, 1880)

Going back to this original technique, Elsa von Eckartsberg (1981) and I have been using the **marathon principle** expressed by Borne in the context of psychotherapy and counseling. We have come to call the procedure: **Writing-Marathon Therapy.**

We let our clients engage in the prolonged process of "writing them-selves out" on paper in as direct and honest a manner as possible for as long a period as the person is capable of sustaining - ideally for three days as Borne recommends - but for a minimum of 4 hours. The instructions are simple and direct.

We have developed various ways of working with the text thus generated in helping our clients to regain a more intimate and accepting contact with their own psychological feeling-dynamic and its concomitant problems and self-defeating obstructions. Doing this work, clients enhance their articulation and storying-capacity and reconnect with the vital sources of their being. This strengthens their power to be affirmative and creative in their concrete life situations.

The **writing marathon process** accellerates the work of self-disclosure when compared with psychoanalytic free-association. Self-guiding in the choice of topics presented and giving themselves over to the inherent dynamic of their existential process, clients articulate their being. They reveal almost immmediately the problematic areas of their existential concerns and psychological problems, in the emergent repetitive thematics, in the ambivalent complexity of their relationships, and the multiplicity and contradictoriness of their feelings, in their mumblings and stammering, their verbal gestures. It is a process of self-manifestation and self-diagnosis. The pressure of time and the influence of the prolonged involvement seem to loosen the logical structures of sense-making and even of story-telling, thus allowing submerged and primary meaning processes to emerge. Changes in states of consciousness seem to occur. The writing in these changed states is more revelatory of the underlying and hidden currents of a person's existential process. Metaphors and symbols abound. The most pressing problems of the person's existence are storied. At first, mostly negative stories abound, stories of hate and resentment, of disappointment, of envy, of fear, of weakness, of pain. Gradually in the course of the process, the person writes him- or herself free from these unlivable stories. Space is created for stories of longing, of hope, and of affirmation to come into focus. The curse of negative, repetitive, and compulsive self-storying is slowly and reluctantly lifted and redemptive qualities appear in the re-storyings. We liken the marathon process to a drilling through one's existential incrustation to re-connect us with the passionate magma of our ontological foundation and destiny.

The work of the writing marathon is done in the context of a depth-oriented psychotherapeutic situation. Clients are prepared for the session. They are monitored during the time of writing and guided through blockages and difficulties. The client creates an existential life document, which is an important, tangible, and re-readable representation of the person's psychological and existential situation. It represents a kind of psychogram, an existential print-out at a certain moment in one's life. This primary **marathon life-text** can then be therapeutically developed, in dialogue and directed in ways that foster insight and integration. The client becomes more interested and more hopeful about his or her prospects in living.

Doing the writing marathon makes one become spontaneously more reflective, thoughtful, and meditative about the psychological process that constitutes our life. We discover ourselves as journeying on pathways through the landscapes of our own consciousness, and those of the world as given to our consciousness, as traveling in a **psychocosm** (von Eckartsberg, R., 1981, von Eckartsberg, E., 1981) whose regions are mappable in terms of past, present and future, and in terms of levels or landscapes of consciousness. Our life unfolds as an interplay of all regions in the enactment of our concrete, embodied, and situated existence. The mapping of a person's life-world-involvement is one strategy in working with the **writing-marathon process.**

The work of writing marathon therapy consists in discerning, affirming or changing the ongoing structure and dynamic of one's own life-drama, one's own existential epic in creation, and to be freed to devote one's full attention, creativity, care and effort to the actualization of this project and one's destiny.

We have had very good results using this approach on a person-to-person level as well as in a group context. There is no fixed or inescapable plot that has to emerge, as most theorists assert. The unique biographical problematic arises out of the unique person-others-world interconnection. It is articulated, identified, questioned, felt and evaluated with regard to its creative potential enabling us to move more freely and resolutely into our unique calling.

# BIBLIOGRAPHY

Aanstoos, C. (Ed.) **Exploring the lived** world: Readings in phenomenological **psychology.** Carrolton, Georgia: West Georgia College, 1984.

Aanstoos, C. A phenomenological study of thinking. In Giorgi, A., Barton, A., Maes, C. (Eds.) **Duquesne studies in phenomenological psychology** (Vol. IV) Pittsburgh: Duquesne University Press, 1983.

Barker, R. **The stream of behavior.** New York: Appleton-Century-Crofts, 1963.

Barton, A. **Three worlds of therapy.** Palo Alto: National Press Books, 1974.

Becker, E. **The revolution in psychiatry.** New York: The Free Press, 1964.

Berger, P. and Luckmann, Th. **The social construction of reality.** Garden City: Doubleday and Company, Inc., 1966.

Berger, P. **The sacred canopy.** Garden City: Doubleday and Company, Inc. 1967.

Berger, P., Berger, B. and Kellner, H. **The homeless mind.** New York: Vintage Books, 1973.

Bilotta, V. Sexual Experience as an access to the spiritual life. **Studies in Formative Spirituality,** Vol. II, #1, Feb. 1981, 113-23.

Binswanger, L. The case of Ellen West. In May, R., Angel, E., Ellenberger, H. (Eds.) **Existence.** New York: Basic Books, Inc., Publishers, 1958.

Borne, L. **The art of** becoming an original **writer in three days, (Die Kunst, in drei Tagen ein Originalschriftsteller zu werden,** In: Gesammelte Schriften (Bd. I), Leipzig: Max Hesses Verlag, 1880).

Boss, M. **Psychoanalysis and daseinsanalysis.** New York: Basic Books, 1963.

Brown, R. **Social psychology.** New York: The Free Press, 1965.

Bruteau, B. **The psychic grid.** Wheaton: The Theosophical Publishing House, 1979.

Buckley, F. Toward a phenomenology of at-homeness. In Giorgi, A., Fischer, W., von Eckartsberg, R. (Eds.) **Duquesne studies in phenomenological psychology.** (Vol. I) Pittsburgh: Duquesne University Press, 1971.

Churchill, S. Forming clinical impressions. In Aanstoos, Ch. (Ed.) **Exploring the lived world: Readings in phenomenological psychology.** Carrolton: West Georgia College, 1984.

Coonan, T. Phenomenological psychological reflections on the mission of art. In: Giorgi, A., Knowles, R., Smith, D. (Eds.) **Duquesne studies in phenomenological psychology** (Vol. III) Pittsburgh: Duquesne University Press, 1979.

Colaizzi, P. **Reflection and research in psychology.** Dubuque: Kendall Hunt Publishing Co., 1973.

Colaizzi, P. Psychological research as the phenomenologist views it. In R. Valle & M. King (Eds.) **Existential-phenomenological alternatives for psychology.** New York: Oxford University Press, 1978a.

Colazzi, P. Learning and existence. in R. Valle & M. King (Eds.) **Existential-phenomenological alternatives for psychology.** New York, Oxford University Press, 1978b.

Crites, S. The narrative quality of experience. Academy of Religion, 1971, 39 (3), 291-311.

Czikszentmihalyi, M. Attention and the holistic approach to behavior. In: Pope, K. and Singer, J. Eds. **The stream of consciousness.** New York: Plenum Press, 1978.

de Rivera, J. **A structural theory of the emotions,** Psychological Issues Monograph 40. N. Y.: International Universities Press 1977.

de Rivera, J. (Ed.) **Conceptual encounter.** Washington: University Press of America, 1981.

Desan, W. The marxism of J.-P. Sartre. New York: Doubleday & Co., 1965.

Dunne, J. A search for God in time and memory. New York: The Macmillan Company, 1967.

Dunne, J. The way of all the earth. New York: MacMillan Publishing Co., 1972.

Ellenberger, H. A clinical introduction to psychiatric phenomenology. In: May, R., Angel, E., Ellenberger, H. (Eds.), Existence. New York: Basic Books, 1958.

Fessler, R. Phenomenology and the talking cure: Research on psychotherapy. In Giorgi, A., Barton, A., Maes, C. (Eds.) Duquesne studies in phenomenological psychology. (Vol. IV) Pittsburgh: Duquesne Unviersity Press, 1983.

Fischer, C. Toward the structure of privacy: Implications for psychological assessment. In Giorgi, A., von Eckartsberg, R. (Eds.) Duquesne studies in phenomenological psychology (Vol. I). Pittsburgh: Duquesne University Press, 1971.

Fischer, C. and Wertz, F. Empirical phenomenological analysis of being criminally victimized. In: Giorgi, A., Knowles, R., Smith, D. (Eds.) Duquesne studies in phenomenological psychology. Vol. III. Pittsburgh: Duquesne University Press, 1979.

Fischer, C. and Fischer, W. Phenomenological-existential psychotherapy. In: Hersen, M., Kazdin, A., Bellack, A. (Eds.) The clincial psychology handbook. New York: Pergamon Press, 1983.

Fischer, W. Theories of anxiety. New York: Harper and Row, 1970.

Fischer, W. Faces of anxiety. Journal of Phenomenological Psychology, Vol. 1, #I. 1970, 31-49.

Fischer, W. On the phenomenological mode of researching "being anxious." Journal of Phenomenological Psychology, Vol. 4, #2, 1974, 405-423.

Freire, P. Pedagogy of the oppressed. New York: Seabury Press, 1970.

Freud, S. **The interpretation of dreams.** Standard Edition, 1900.

Frey-Rohn, L. **From Freud to Jung.** New York: Dell Publishing Co., 1974.

Frings, M. **Max Scheler.** Pittsburgh: Duquesne University Press, 1965.

Gadamer, H. **Truth and method.** New York: Crossroads Publishing Co., 1975.

Giorgi, A. Phenomenology and experimental psychology, I. **Review of Existential Psychology and Psychiatry,** Vol. 5, #3, 1965, 228-238.

Giorgi, A. Phenomenology and experimental psychology, II. **Review of Existential Psychology and Psychiatry,** Vol. 6, #1, 1966, 37-50.

Giorgi, A. The experience of the subject as a source of data in a psychological experiment. **Review of Existential Psychology and Psychiatry,** Vol. 7, #3, 1967.

Giorgi, A. Toward phenomenologically based research in psychology. **Journal of Phenomenological Psychology,** Vol. I, #1 1970a.

Giorgi, A. **Psychology as a human science: A phenomenologically based approach.** New York: Harper and Row Publishers, 1970b.

Giorgi, A., Fischer, W. von Eckartsberg, R. (Eds.) **Duquesne Studies in Phenomenological Psychology** (Vol. I) Pittsburgh: Duquesne University Press, 1971.

Giorgi, A. An application of phenomenological method in psychology. In Giorgi, A., Fischer, W., von Eckartsberg, R. (Eds.) **Duquesne Studies in phenomenological psychology** (Vol. II). Pittsburgh: Duquesne University Press, 1975a.

Giorgi, A. Convergence and divergence of qualitative methods in psychology. In Giorgi, A., Fischer, C., Murray, E. (Eds.) **Duquesne Studies in phenomenological psychology** (Vol. II). Pittsburgh: Duquesne University Press, 1975b.

Giorgi, A. Knowles, R., Smith, D. (Eds.) **Duquesne studies in phenomenological psychology** (Vol. III) Pittsburgh: Duquesne University Press,
1979.

Giorgi, A. On the relationship among the psychologist's fallacy, psycho-
logism, and the phenomenological reduction. **Journal of Phenomenological** Psychology, Vol. 12, #1, 1981, 75-86.

Giorgi, A. **Phenomenology and psychological research.** Pittsburgh: Duquesne
University Press, 1985.

Giorgi, A., Barton, A., Maes, C. (Eds.) **Duquesne studies in phenomenological psychology** (Vol. IV) Pittsburgh: Duquesne University Press,
1983.

Greiner, D. A foundational theoretical approach toward a comprehensive
psychology of human existence. Dissertation. Ann Arbor: University
microfilms, 1964.

Gurwitsch, A. **The field of consciousness.** Pittsburgh: Duquesne University
Press, 1964.

Habermas, J. Knowledge and Interest, **Inquiry,** 1966, 9, 285-300.

Halling, S. Eugene O'Neill's understanding of forgiveness. In Giorgi, A.,
Knowles, R., Smith, D. (Eds.) **Duquesne studies in phenomenological
psychology** (Vol. III). Pittsburgh: Duquesne University Press, 1979.

Hall, C. and Lindzey, G. **Theories of personality.** New York: John Wiley &
Sons, 1978.

Heidegger, M. **Being and time.** New York: Harper & Row, 1962 (1927)

Heidegger, M. **Poetry,** language, **and thought.** New York: Harper & Row, 1971.

Heider, F. **The psychology of interpersonal relations.** New York: John Wiley
& Sons, 1958.

Holzner, B. **Reality construction in society.** Cambridge, Mass.: Schenkman
Publishing Co., 1968.

Husserl, E. **Ideas.** New York: Collier, 1962.

Husserl, E. **The crisis of European sciences and transcendental phenomeno-logy.** Evanston: Northwestern University Press, 1970.

Ihde, D. **Hermeneutic** phenomenology: **The** philosophy of Ricoeur. Evanston: Northwestern University Press, 1971.

Jager, B. Theorizing, journeying, dwelling. In Giorgi, A., Fischer, C., Murray, E. (Eds.) **Duquesne studies in phenomenological psychology** (Vol. II) Pittsburgh: Duquesne University Press, 1975.

Jager, B. Dionysos and the world of passion. In Giorgi, A., Knowles, R., Smith, D. (Eds.) **Duquesne studies in phenomenological psychology** (Vol. III) Pittsburgh: Duquesne University Press, 1979.

Keen, E. **A primer in phenomenological psychology.** New York: Holt, Rinehart & Winston, 1975.

Kierkegaard, S. **Concluding unscientific postscript.** Princeton: Princeton University Press, 1968 (1846).

Klinger, E. Modes of normal consciousness flow. In: Pope, K. and Singer, J. (Eds.) **The Stream of Consciousness.** New York: Plenum Press, 1978.

Knowles, R. Suggestions for an existential-phenomenological understanding of Erickson's concept of basic trust. **Journal of phenomenological psychology,** Vol. 7, 1977, 183-194.

Knowles, R. **Human development and human possibility: Erikson in the light of Heidegger.** Lanham, MD. University Press of America, 1985.

Kraft, W. **Normal modes of madness.** New York: Alba House, 1978.

Kuhn, Th. **The structure of scientific revolutions.** Chicago: University of Chicago Press, 1962.

Kracklauer, Ch. **The drug problem problem.** Unpublished Doctoral Dissertation, Pittsburgh: Duquesne University, 1974.

Kruger, D. An introduction to phenomenological psychology. Pittsburgh: Duquesne University Press, 1981.

Leary, T. The diagnosis of behavior and the diagnosis of experience. In: A Mahrer (Ed.) New approaches to personality classification. N. Y.: Columbia University Press, 1970.

Lyons, J. and Barrel, J., People: An introduction to psychology. New York: Harper and Row, 1979.

Maes, Ch. Listening, silence and obedience. Studies in Formative Spirituality, Vol. V #2 May 1984, 211-217.

May, R. Angel, E. & Ellenberger, H. Existence. New York: Basic Books, 1958.

McClelland, D. The achievement motive New York: Appleton-Century-Crofts, 1953.

MacDougall, C. Interpretive Reporting. N. Y.: Macmillan, 1972.

Merleau-Ponty, M. The phenomenology of perception. London: Routledge & Kegan Paul, 1962.

Merleau-Ponty, M. Indirect language and the voices of silence. In: Signs. Evanston: Northwestern University Press, 1964.

Merleau-Ponty, M. The visible and the invisible. Evanston: Northwestern University Press, 1968.

Minkowski, E. Lived Time. Evanston: Northwestern University Press, 1970.

Murray, E. The phenomenon of metaphor: Some theoretical considerations. In Giorgi et al. Duquesne studies in phenomenological psycho      logy (Vol. II) Pittsburgh: Duquesne University Press, 1975.

Murray, E. Be-ing. . .Think-ing. . . Thank-ing. . . In Giorgi, A., Barton, A., Maes, C. (Eds.) Duquesne studies in phenomenological psychology. (Vol. IV) Pittsburgh: Duquesne Universty Press, 1983.

Murray, E. **Imaging our life.** Pittsburgh: Duquesne University Press, (in press).

Natanson, M. **The journeying self.** Reading: Addison-Wesley Publishers, 1970.

Nicholl, D. **Scientia Cordis.** Santa Cruz, Ca.: William James Press, 1975.

Palmer, R. **Hermeneutics.** Evanston: Northwestern University Press, 1969.

Polkinghorne, D. **Methodology for the human sciences.** Albany: State University of New York Press, 1983.

Pollio, H. **Behavior and Existence.** Monterey: Brooks-Cole, 1982.

Radnitzki, G. **Contemporary schools of metascience.** New York, Humanities Press, 1970.

Richer, P. A phenomenological investigation of the perception of geometric illusions. **Journal of Phenomenological Psychology,** Vol. 8, #2, 1978, 123-135.

Richer, P. The concept of subjectivity and objectivity in Gestalt psychology. **Journal of phenomenological psychology.** Vol. 10, #1, 1979, 33-55.

Richer, P. Alterations in the reality character of perception and the concept of sensation. In Giorgi, A., Knowles, R., Smith, D. (Eds.) **Duquesne studies in phenomenological psychology** (Vol. III). Pittsburgh, Duquesne University Press, 1979.

Ricoeur, P. **Freedom and Nature.** Evanston: Northwestern University Press, 1966.

Ricoeur, P. The model of the text. **Social Research,** 38. 1971, 529-562.

Ricoeur, P. The human experience of time and narrative. **Research in Phenomenology,** 9, 1979, 17-34.

Romanyshyn, R. **Psychological life: From science to metaphor.** Austin: University of Texas Press, 1982.

Romanyshyn, R. Life-world as depth of soul: phenomenology and psychoanalysis. Invited Address: 3rd Annual Human Science Research Conference. West Georgia College, May 1984.

Rosenstock-Huessy, E. **Speech and reality.** Norwich: Argo Books, 1970.

Rosenberg, S. **The film experience.** Unpublished doctoral dissertation. The Humanistic Psychology Institute, San Francisco, 1979.

Sartre, J.-P. **Baudelaire.** New York: New Directions Publishing Co. 1950.

Sartre, J.-P. **Being and nothingness.** New York: Philosophical Library, 1953.

Sartre, J.-P. **Saint Genet.** London: W. H. Allen & Co., 1964.

Sartre, J.-P. **Search for a method.** New York: Vintage Books, 1968.

Sartre, J.-P. **The words.** New York: George Braziller, 1968.

Schapp, W. **In Geschichten verstrickt.** Wiesbaden: Heymann, 1976.

Scheler, M. **The nature of sympathy.** London: Routledge & Kegan Paul, 1954a.

Scheler, M. **Ressentiment.** New York: The Free Press of Glenco, 1954b.

Scheler, M. **Man's place in nature.** Boston: Beacon Press, 1961.

Schutz, A. **Collected papers Vol.** I The Hague: Nijhoff, 1962.

Schutz, A. **Collected papers Vol.** II The Hague: Nijhoff, 1964.

Schutz, A. **Collected papers Vol.** III The Hague: Nihoff, 1966.

Schutz, A. **Reflections on the problem of relevance.** New Haven: Yale University Press, 1970.

Smith, D. Freud's metapsychology. In Giorgi, A., Fischer, C., Murray, E. (Eds.) **Duquesne studies in phenomenological psychology,** (Vol. II) Pittsburgh: Duquesne University Press, 1975.

Smith, D. Phenomenological psychotherapy: A why and a how. In Giorgi, A., Knowles, R., Smith, D. (Eds.) Duquesne studies in phenomenological **psychology.** (Vol. III) Pittsburgh: Duquesne University Press, 1979.

Smith, D. The history of the graduate program in existential-phenomenological psychology at Duquesne University. In Giorgi, A., Barton, A., Maes, C. (Eds.) **Duquesne studies** in phenomenological psychology (Vol. IV) 1983.

Spiegelberg, H. **The phenomenologial movement,** (Vols. I & II) The Hague: Martinus Nijhoff, 1960.

Spiegelberg, H. **Phenomenology in psychology and psychiatry.** Evanston: Northwestern University Press, 1963.

Strasser, S. **Phenomenology and the human sciences.** Pittsburgh: Duquesne University Press, 1963.

Tillich, P. **Theology of culture.** New York: Oxford University Press, 1959.

Titelman, P. Some implications of Ricoeur's conception of hermeneutics for phenomenological psychology. In Giorgi, A., Knowles, R., Smith, D. (Eds.) **Duquesne studies in phenomenological psychology** (Vol. III) Pittsburgh: Duquesne University Press, 1979.

Valle, R. & King, M. **Existential-phenomenological alternatives for psychology.** New York: Oxford University Press, 1978.

Valle, R. & von Eckartsberg, R. **The metaphors of consciousness.** New York: Plenum Press, 1981.

van den Berg, J. H. **The changing nature of man** N.Y.: Dell Publishing Co., 1961.

van den Berg, J. H. Phenomenology and metabletics **Humanitas** Vol. VII #3, 1971, 279-290.

# BIBLIOGRAPHY 225

van den Berg, J. H. **Divided existence and complex society,** Pittsburgh: Duquesne University Press, 1974.

von Eckartsberg, Elsa. God conscious and the "poetry of madness." in R. Valle & R. von Eckartsberg (Eds) **The metaphors of consciousness,** New York, Plenum Press, 1981.

von Eckartsberg, R. On experiential methodology. In: Giorgi, A., Fischer, W., von Eckartsberg, R. (Eds.) **Duquesne studies in phenomenological psychology.** (Vol. I) Pittsburgh: Duquesne University Press, 1971.

von Eckartsberg, R. Experiential psychology: A descriptive protocol and reflection. **Journal of phenomenologial psychology,** 1972, 2, 161-173.

von Eckartsberg, R. The eco-psychology of motivational theory and research. In: Giorgi, et al. **Duquesne studies in phenomenological psychology.** (Vol. II) Pittsburgh: Duquesne University Press, 1975.

von Eckartsberg, R. Person perception revisited. In R. Valle & M. King (Eds.) **Existential phenomenological alternatives in psychology.** New York: Oxford University Press, 1978.

von Eckartsberg, R. The eco-psychology of personal culture-building: an existential-hermeneutic approach. In: Giorgi, A., Knowles, R. and Smith, D. (Eds.) **Duquesne studies in phenomenological psychology Vol. III.** Pittsburgh: Duquesne University Press, 1979.

von Eckartsberg, R. Maps of the mind: the cartography of consciousness. In: Valle, R. & von Eckartsberg, R. (Eds.) **The metaphors of consciousness.** New York: Plenum Press, 1981.

von Eckartsberg, R. Validity and the transpersonal ground of psychological theorizing. In Giorgi, A., Barton, A., Maes, C. (Eds.) **Duquesne studies in phenomenological psychology Vol IV,** Pittsburgh: Duquesne University Press, 1983.

von Eckartsberg, R. Existential-phenomenological knowledge building. In Susskind, E. & Klein, D. (Eds.) **Community research.** New York: Praeger, 1985.

van Kaam, A. The experience of really feeling understood by a person. Unpublished doctoral dissertation, Western Reserve University, 1958.

van Kaam, A. **Existential foundations of psychology.** Pittsburgh: Duquesne University Press, 1966.

Wertz, F. From everyday to psychological description. **Journal of Pheno-menological Psychology.** Vol. 14. #2. 1983, 197-241.

Wertz, F. Procedures in phenomenological research and the question of validity. In Anstoos, C. (Ed) **Exploring the lived world: readings in phenomenological psychology.** Carrolton: West Georgia College, 1984.

# INDEX OF NAMES

# INDEX OF TOPICS

Psychotherapy 30, 148-153, 169, 200, 209-211
Psychotherapy, existential 54

Reconciliation 106-118
Reduction 34, 35, 37, 98
Reflective attitude 19
Reflection 30, 46, 106, 124-125, 142-148, 151, 192
Reflection, empirical phenomenological 43, 44, 50
Reflection, individual phenomenological 43, 44, 50, 63, 100, 103, 171
Research, existential-phenomenological 22, 24, 30, 42, 46, 56, 63, 119
Research, qualitative 20, 41, 99
Research, quantitative 20
Researcher 58-59, 150
Research-guiding interest 198
Research genre 30
Research-partner 159, 162

Scientia cordis 206-207
Situation analysis 131
Social reality 9, 139
Space 119, 128-129
Speak-aloud protocol 139
Story 31, 56, 117, 187-188, 201-204, 205-209, 209-211
Story, intra- 210
Story, meta- 202, 204
Structure 21, 28, 57, 59, 62, 78, 121, 131
Structure, fundamental 43, 44, 46, 50, 51, 63
Structure, general 21, 27, 28, 53, 59, 64-78, 80, 85, 92-97, 115, 116

Structure, situated 28, 59, 64-78, 80, 85, 92-96
Style 62, 64-77
Subjects 29, 32, 39, 120, 154, 163
Synchronic 105

Texts 23, 134-135, 137-138, 170
Theme 61, 63-77
Theoretical attitude 170, 181-185
Thought 17, 161, 181
Time 119, 127-128, 202
Typification 10

Validation 160
Values 10, 11

Way of life 197
Writing marathon 211-214